S0-BIK-861

*Philosophical Interpretations*

# Philosophical Interpretations

## Robert J. Fogelin

New York     Oxford

OXFORD UNIVERSITY PRESS

1992

# Oxford University Press

Oxford   New York   Toronto
Delhi   Bombay   Calcutta   Madras   Karachi
Petaling Jaya   Singapore   Hong Kong   Tokyo
Nairobi   Dar es Salaam   Cape Town
Melbourne   Auckland

and associated companies in
Berlin   Ibadan

## Copyright © 1992 by Robert J. Fogelin

Published by Oxford University Press, Inc.
200 Madison Avenue, New York, NY 10016

Oxford is a registered trademark of Oxford University Press

All rights reserved. No part of this publication may be reproduced,
stored in a retrieval system, or transmitted, in any form or by any means,
electronic, mechanical, photocopying, recording or otherwise,
without the prior permission of the publisher.

Library of Congress Cataloging-in-Publication Data
Fogelin, Robert J.
Philosophical interpretations / Robert J. Fogelin.
p. cm.   Includes bibliographical references and index.
ISBN 0-19-507162-X
1. Hermeneutics.   2. Philosophy.   I. Title.
BD241.F63   1992   190—dc20      91-16826

1 3 5 7 9 8 6 4 2

Printed in the United States of America
on acid-free paper

*for*
FCF

# Preface

Since the essays that make up this volume were written over a period of twenty-two years and at various venues, I will not try to acknowledge my debt to all those who have made important contributions to them. Of the fifteen essays, two are previously unpublished. "Hume's Worries about Personal Identity" was presented at an NEH Institute on Hume held at Dartmouth College in the summer of 1990. I profited from the vigorous criticisms that were leveled against it. Walter Sinnott-Armstrong made a number of very useful suggestions concerning the introductory essay on philosophical interpretation.

This project is due to the encouragement of Florence Fogelin and Walter Sinnott-Armstrong, and to the support of Oxford University Press—its editors and its urbane, erudite, anonymous referee.

*Hanover, N.H.*                                                    R. J. F.
*April 1991*

# Contents

*Introduction,* 3

1. Three Platonic Analogies, 12
2. A Reading of Aquinas's Five Ways, 26
3. Hume and Berkeley on the Proofs of Infinite Divisibility, 45
4. Hume and the Missing Shade of Blue, 70
5. Hume's Worries about Personal Identity, 81
6. What Hume Actually Said about Miracles, 95
7. Kant and Hume on Simultaneity of Causes and Effects, 102
8. The Tendency of Hume's Skepticism, 114
9. Richard Price on Promising: A Limited Defense, 132
10. a. Hamilton's Quantification of the Predicate, 149
    b. Hamilton's Theory of Quantifying the Predicate —
       a Correction, 166
11. Wittgenstein on Identity, 169
12. Negative Elementary Propositions, 186
13. Wittgenstein and Intuitionism, 196
14. Wittgenstein and Classical Scepticism, 214
15. Thinking and Doing, 232

*Index,* 251

*Philosophical Interpretations*

# Introduction

The essays that make up this volume — with only a few exceptions — offer readings of philosophical texts that depart, sometimes radically, from standard readings. Yet the principles of interpretation that underlie these essays are not themselves radical. Nothing is deconstructed. Nowhere have I argued that a philosopher's words should not be taken at face value. My principle of interpretation is just the reverse of this: granting the possibility of inadvertent slips, misleading modes of expression, and the like, I hold that there is a very strong *presumption* in favor of the claims that philosophers meant to say precisely what they did say and that what they did say means precisely what it seems to mean.

In a sense, then, these essays are governed by a principle of charitable interpretation that might be called the *semantic* principle of charity. Our assumption, unless there is strong reason to the contrary, is that the philosopher as writer and we as readers are semantically competent. This principle should not be confused with another principle that might be called the *alethic* principle of charity. It has been maintained that to interpret a system of beliefs, we must assume that most of the beliefs that comprise this system are *true*, where what *we* take to be true governs what is considered true. For all I know, this may be correct when the task at hand is to translate the utterances of a people whose language is wholly cut off from our own — the so-called problem of radical translation. It seems reasonable to assume that there are certain core beliefs concerning rudimentary dealings with the world that all human beings share. The assumption that most of these core beliefs, at least, are true provides an entré for the linguist engaged in radical translation. But the situation is fundamentally different when con-

3

fronted with a philosophical text: the interpretation of a philosophical position does not demand a parallel assumption that most of its core philosophical doctrines are true. It is possible, for example, to understand the core doctrines of Leibniz's *Monadology*, Kant's *Transcendental Aesthetic*, or Wittgenstein's *Tractatus* without supposing that any of the core doctrines are true. With only rare exceptions, the meanings of most of a philosopher's words get fixed before the philosopher starts doing philosophy. Philosophical discourse is remote from the core practical discourse that supplies the entry point for radical translation. For this reason it is possible to suppose that a philosopher is speaking sense while at the same time holding that most of what that philosopher says in expounding the central tenets of her position is false. Therefore, to understand a philosopher, we need not assume that the claims made are *mostly true by our standards*. Making this assumption embodies the fallacy of presentism: i.e., the dogma that the best interpretation of a philosophical text is the one that makes it square best with what we (whoever this is) now believe to be true.[1]

Beyond this, the correct interpretation of a philosophical text can even be compatible with the judgment that most of what the philosopher says is, *in a certain way*, senseless. To adapt an example from Wittgenstein, what are we to make of the question: "What time is it at the center of the earth?"[2] It would certainly be odd (wrong) to say that we do not understand this question, for, after all, we do. Furthermore, it is because we understand it that we realize, perhaps after some reflection, that it admits of no answer. Conventions exist that fix times for Peoria and Waga Waga, but no convention exists, as far as I know, for fixing the time at the earth's center. If someone were to ask this question, we might say, speaking in an ordinary way, that it makes no sense to ask it.

In a parallel fashion, we might hold that assertions with no determinate truth values are, again *in a certain way*, senseless. Here senseless does not mean gibberish. Sometimes it takes a very subtle understanding of what a philosopher is saying to see that what is being said is in fact senseless in something like the way in which the question about the time at the center of the earth is senseless. It may look as if a philosopher is making a substantive claim that reality is disposed in one way rather than another, and in virtue of this the assertion has determinate truth value (whether known or not). But with a full understanding of what is being said, we may come to realize that this is not so.

Thus, to the earlier claim that it is possible to understand a philosophical position without assuming that most of the propositions that comprise it are true, I will now add that it is possible to understand a philosophical position without supposing that the assertions possess a determinate truth value. Of course, we might *object* to a philosophical position if its propositions have this status and go on to say that it is senseless to *put forward* such propositions, just as it is senseless to *ask* questions that admit of no answer. We might even say that such propositions are *themselves* senseless (lacking in cognitive significance, are pseudopropositions, or something like that). But decisions on this matter are independent of the intelligibility of what a philosopher has said. It seems to me, for example, that the fundamental propositions of Leibniz's *Monadology* have no determinate truth values. I suspect that the same is true of the basic propositions of many global philosophical positions. So if it is said to be senseless to put forward a proposition lacking a determinate truth status, and if we go on to call any proposition so put forward senseless, then, perhaps, certain philosophical propositions are senseless. But to be senseless in this way is not the same thing as being unintelligible. Indeed, to repeat the point, to see that a proposition is senseless in this particular way can demand a very subtle grasp of its meaning.[3]

Finally, even consistency need not be an overriding consideration in choosing between competing interpretations. All things being equal, an interpretation that represents a position as consistent is preferable to one that does not. At times, however, inconsistency and other logical misdemeanors are simply part of a philosophical position, and understanding the position involves recognizing this. We should, of course, be chary of attributing simple logical blunders to obviously competent philosophers — though, if the truth be told, simple blunders are far from absent in the writings of great philosophers. More deeply, speculative philosophers are often driven by competing insights that they cannot fully bring into coherent balance — here, Kant comes to mind — or they are attempting to develop radically new ideas within a received framework that is not fully compatible with them — Hume, I think, labored under this difficulty. Indeed, it seems to be a mark of great philosophers that their insights strain and sometimes overstep the resources of their own official positions.[4] Inconsistencies that arise from tensions of this kind are *part* of the philosophical position, and understanding such a position involves understanding the interplay of forces that gives rise to such deep inconsistency.

But if we abandon the *mostly true by our lights* as the overriding principle of philosophical interpretation, and give up the idea that we must at least understand what *would* make a position true if it *were* true, and even allow that sometimes an interpretation can correctly reveal a position as logically inconsistent, what principles can govern our interpretation of a philosophical text? I think that the fundamental assumption in interpreting a philosophical text is that it is motivated by particular philosophical concerns, perplexities, or problems. Thus, to understand the *point* of a philosophical remark or philosophical argument, we have to understand the role that this remark or argument plays in responding to these concerns, perplexities, or problems.

This interpretative principle can take two forms — or be given two contrasting emphases. The first I will call the principle of *local interpretation*. To understand the point of a philosophical remark or philosophical argument, we must ask what that remark or argument is intended to do in just the context in which it appears. Precisely how does it move the enterprise along? Now I do not think that many will disagree with this principle. I think that people will agree but then insist on the importance of placing the particular remark (together with the context that immediately surrounds it) in the broader context of the total philosophical position in which it appears. Beyond this, some will insist on the importance of placing the philosophical position itself in the broader context of the philosophical culture in which it came into existence. This is a holistic principle of interpretation: I will label it the principle of *global interpretation*.

It seems to me that the principles of local interpretation and global interpretation are both essential for understanding a philosophical text. It strikes me as platitudinous to say so. Yet both principles are violated often enough. The tendency to attribute some favored contemporary view to a past philosopher often leads to violations of the global principle of interpretation. It is possible, for example, to find isolated passages that suggest that Hume was a commonsense realist. But this attribution loses plausibility as soon as we examine it from the perspective of Hume's total philosophical position within the intellectual environment in which it arose.

Most bad interpretation — certainly most grotesquely bad interpretation — arises from violations of the principle of global interpretation, usually from a misguided application of the alethic principle of charity. Though they are more subtle and more difficult to detect, violations of the principle of local interpretation also occur. Interpreting a particular portion of a text in the light of the overarching themes of the system in which it appears is, in general, exactly the right way to proceed. It is a mark of scholarly attainment to be able to do this well. But there are dangers with this holistic or global approach to interpretation. One is that the philosophical position becomes homogenized and the philosopher emerges as saying pretty much the same thing over and over again. I cite an example of this tendency toward homogenization below. Another danger is that the tensions and incompatible motifs that form part of most historically important philosophical positions become suppressed. Plato is reduced to a Platonist, Descartes to a Cartesian, and so on. For example, in the service of reading Hume as a thorough-going naturalist, commentators often ignore the large tracts of skeptical argumentation found in Hume's writings. When such passages cannot be ignored, it is sometimes claimed that they do not mean what they transparently seem to mean. It has even been suggested that for Hume the word "sceptical" simply meant "scientific," an interpretation refuted by even a casual reading of the text.[5] As a last resort, contrary texts are sometimes dismissed as ironic — an almost certain sign of interpretive chicanery. The principle of local interpretation places checks on these tendencies to homogenize and to suppress texts by demanding close attention to what is actually said in the logical or dialectical development of the position. In this way it forces us to acknowledge complexity and diversity.

But a check runs in the other direction as well. Most arguments, even those carefully spelled out, rely on background premises or principles, and these background premises and principles often have considerable force in shaping the explicitly stated argument. It is often an important part of interpreting a text to fill in these missing premises. But what a philosopher in some previous period finds too obvious to say may not be obvious to us now, and this opens the possibility for radical misunderstanding. Here again a misguided use of the alethic principle of charity can cause problems. The suppressed premises we supply must be those that the philosopher under consideration would take to be true, and they may or may not square with what we take to be true. To avoid such misattributions, the close analysis of a philosopher's explicitly stated arguments must be guided by principles of global interpretation. Proper interpretation involves a complex interplay between global interpretation and local interpretation.

This volume contains three instances in which an application of the principle of local interpretation yields novel — and I am sure controversial — results. On the standard reading, Plato's Divided Line and Allegory of the Cave are taken to present pretty much the same ideas, though the Allegory of the Cave is more picturesque. I take this to be an example of the homogenizing tendency of global interpretation. Over against the standard interpretation, I hold that Plato uses the Divided Line to make a set of points quite different from those he makes in presenting the Allegory of the Cave.[6] Roughly, the Divided Line offers a mathematical analogy explaining the nature of *mathematical* thought; the Allegory of the Cave offers a complex analogy relating levels of being to stages of thought. The standard reading treats both analogies as relating levels of being to stages of thought. On that reading, Plato's story is twice told.

I think that the standard reading is wrong, but I do not think that it can be shown to be wrong using the principle of global interpretation. The doctrines used in the standard interpretation of the Divided Line are, in fact, central Platonic doctrines. I have no quarrel on that point. My claim is that the immediate context of the *Republic* where the Divided Line appears shows that Plato was there worried about the character of mathematical reasoning and offered a mathematical analogy to explain it. I therefore offer a radically different interpretation of its significance, but one that invokes the same global commitments used in the standard interpretation. Thus, my disagreement with the standard reading turns on an application of the principle of local interpretation, not on an application of the principle of global interpretation.

The most radical — and I am sure the most problematic — application of the principle of local interpretation occurs in my treatment of Aquinas's Five Ways (Essay 2). There I offer an alternative to the standard view that the Five Ways present a series of schematic *a posteriori* demonstrations of God's existence based on Aristotelian scientific principles. In place of this reading, I suggest that the Five Ways offer a response to the challenge of science. In particular, they are offered to counter the objection that immediately precedes the appearance of the Five Ways in the text:

> [I]f a few causes fully account for some effect, one does not seek more. Now it seems that everything we observe in this world can be fully accounted for by other causes, without assuming a God. Thus natural effects are explained by natural causes, and contrived effects [i.e., purposeful acts] by human reasoning and will. There is therefore no need to suppose that God exists.

Reading the text as a response to this objection is not without difficulties, and I acknowledge them. But difficulties arise on all readings of the Five Ways. It seems to me that my reading squares with the immediate text and in no way runs counter to Aquinas's global commitments. I think that it does this at least as well as the standard reading.

The most narrowly focused example of the use of the principle of local interpretation appears in Essay 5, "What Hume Actually Said about Miracles." There, through a close analysis of two consecutive paragraphs in the *Enquiry Concerning the Principles of Human Understanding*, I argue that Hume, contrary to what commentators have repeatedly said, did put forward an *a priori* argument intended to establish that there must always be sufficient *empirical* evidence available to show that miracles cannot *exist*. Hume also argued that even if a miracle could exist, no testimony could *establish* its existence. Commentators have found this second argument, but missed the first.

Most of the essays in this volume illustrate a commitment to the importance of local context, but the volume contains a number of global-context essays as well. In Essay 4 I argue that Hume's notoriously casual way of dealing with the problem of the missing shade of blue was perfectly justified. I argue that there is nothing embarrassing about this counterexample once we see it in the context of Hume's overall program of offering *causal* accounts, not analyses, of mental phenomena. Essay 7 offers a synoptic view of Hume's skeptical commitments. Essay 13 relates Wittgenstein's later philosophy to Pyrrhonism.

In three of these essays I offer a defense of positions that have received very little support and sometimes very little attention, largely, I think, because their subtlety and insight have not been appreciated. In Essay 3 I argue that Berkeley's attack on the traditional proofs of infinite divisibility was, in fact, correct. Furthermore, in presenting this attack he showed a deep understanding of both finitist and constructivist notions in mathematics. In Essay 8 I argue that Richard Price's attempt to reduce our obligation to keep a promise to our obligation to tell the truth, if not exactly correct, is at least worth taking seriously. In Essay 9 I argue that Hamilton's theory of quantifying over the predicate—which is known almost exclusively, if known at all, through its unsympathetic critics from De Morgan to Geach—is, in fact, formally correct and provides an elegant way for evaluating the validity of syllogisms. It also contains a modest extension of the traditional theory of the syllogism.

Two of these essays are attempts to elucidate difficult notions that appear in Wittgenstein's philosophy of logic and mathematics. Essay 10 examines Wittgenstein's profoundly original, though obscure, comments on identity. Essay 12 examines his remarks about the nature of mathematical proof.

Only one essay, Essay 11, is critical of the philosopher under consideration. In that essay I argue that, had Wittgenstein thought matters through, he would have come to the surprising and theoretically simplifying conclusion that negative elementary propositions are possible. Certainly an arcane point, but one that sheds light on the tensions between Wittgenstein's commitment to a picture theory of propositional meaning and his commitment to a truth-functional account of complex propositions.

It must be admitted that one essay, Essay 14, has little to do with the interpretation and evaluation of a philosophical text. It begins with some brief interpretive remarks about Aristotle's account of the practical syllogism, but then goes off quite on its own. If it were offered as an explicit interpretation of Aristotle's views on the practical syllogism, then it would certainly commit the sin of presentism. The most I claim is that it is written in the spirit of Aristotle.

## NOTES

1. What I say here runs counter to at least the general tenor of Donald Davidson's essay, "A Coherence Theory of Truth and Knowledge," *Truth and Interpretation*, Ed. Ernest Lepore (Oxford: Blackwell, 1986). In this essay (and in others) Davidson seems committed to what I have called the *alethic* principle of charity.

2. Wittgenstein's example concerns what time it is on the sun. (*Philosophical Investigations*, # 350.)

3. Although I cannot remember who it was, I recall that someone made precisely this point against the logical positivists' use of the verifiability principle to show the meaninglessness of certain sentences. The application of this principle presupposes a very nice understanding of the meaning of the sentence that the principle declares meaningless.

4. I think that this struggle with incoherence is one thing that separates first-rate philosophers from talented second-rate philosophers: for example, Thomas Reid, who argued with marvelous clarity and precision, from David Hume, who often did not. Hume's writings—especially in the *Treatise*—are attempts to articulate a vision that gets formed and changes as it develops. In contrast, Reid's simply lays out a position and defends it.

5. I admit, of course, that sometimes we can misunderstand a philosophical text because we misunderstand what a philosopher's words mean. For example, in Hume's *Dialogues Concerning Natural Religion*, Philo is described as a *careless* skeptic, which to modern ears suggests that Philo is being criticized for the looseness of his argumentation. This impression is removed when we learn that in the eighteenth century the word "careless" could mean "free of care." Technical terms and neologisms can also cause difficult interpretative problems since their connection with common language is sometimes obscure. It seems to me, however, that *major* questions of philosophical interpretation rarely turn on purely lexical issues of this kind.

6. Actually, the content of the Divided Line is embedded as one segment in the Allegory of the Cave—the stage just outside the cave where things are seen only as reflections—a point that I might have made more clearly in the essay.

# 1

# Three Platonic Analogies

At the center of the *Republic*, Plato displays central features of his position in a series of striking analogies: the Form of the Good as compared with the Sun, the Divided Line, and the Allegory of the Cave. This portion of the text has stirred debates at two levels: the first concerns the import of each of these analogies; the second concerns the interrelationships between them. Without making large claims for originality at any particular point, I shall suggest a unified interpretation that may settle some of these debates.

If we turn to the text we first discover that the theory of Forms is virtually assumed with only the barest argument by way of explanation or justification.

> Socrates. Let me remind you of the distinction we drew earlier and have often drawn on other occasions, between the multiplicity of things that we call good or beautiful or whatever it may be and, on the other hand, Goodness itself or Beauty itself and so on. Corresponding to each of these sets of things, we postulate a single Form or real essence, as we call it.
>
> Glaucon. Yes, that is so.
>
> Socrates. Further, the many things, we say, can be seen, but are not objects of rational thought; whereas the Forms are objects of thought, but invisible.
>
> Glaucon. Yes certainly.[1]

"Three Platonic Analogies," *Philosophical Review*, Vol. LXXX, No. 3 (July 1971). Reprinted by permission of the publisher.

Now if this much of the theory of Forms is already in hand, we might wonder what the succession of analogies is intended to illuminate. The answer must be not the theory of Forms at large but certain special features within this previously understood framework.

In the first analogy, *The Form of the Good as the Sun*, Plato invites us to make the following comparison:

[T]he Sun, then, [is] that offspring which the Good has created in the visible world, to stand there in the same relation to vision and visible things as that which the Good itself bears in the intelligible world to intelligence and to intelligible objects.

For Plato, the Sun performs a double service in vision: it not only illuminates the object of vision, but it also activates the organ of sense. Before pursuing the analogy in any further detail, we can notice at once that the Sun is assigned a *privileged* position relative to the eye and the objects seen: it is more than just one visible object in the midst of others. The analogy first tells us that the Form of the Good enjoys a similar *privileged* position relative to intelligence and intelligible objects.

Plato quite obviously wants to reveal more than this through the use of the analogy, but as we press further we encounter difficulties. Plato tells us that "the Sun is not vision, but it is the cause of vision and is seen by the vision it causes." The last clause involves the claim that the Sun, although more than one object of vision among others, *is at least an object of vision in its own right*. The Sun is something that we see. Yet when Plato speaks about the Form of the Good, his remark is not obviously analogous.

It is the cause of knowledge and truth; and so, while you may think of it as an object of knowledge, you will do well to regard it as something beyond truth and knowledge and, precious as these both are, of still higher worth.

There is both a weak and a strong reading of the clause "while you may think of it as an object of knowledge." On the weak reading it amounts to this: whereas it is perfectly correct to treat Goodness as an object of knowledge, we must also keep in mind its special status midst other objects of knowledge. This weak reading certainly plays down the idea that Goodness is "beyond truth and knowledge" but does maintain the parallel with the Sun as an object of vision. On the other side, there is reason to believe that Plato intends something much stronger: although you might (rather superficially) treat the Form of the Good as an object of knowledge, you ought instead to view it as something quite transcending knowledge. The strong reading seems to go beyond the original analogy, for whereas the Sun is an object of vision, Goodness is not (really) an object of knowledge.

The continuation of the above passage gives some slight support to the weak reading:

> And just as in our analogy light and vision were to be thought like the Sun, but not identical with it, so here both knowledge and truth are to be regarded as like the Good, but to identify either with the Good is wrong. The Good must hold yet a higher place of honor.

This gives some support to the weak reading, for here Plato is making a modest point that stays within the bounds of the original analogy: just as the Sun is not to be *identified* with light and vision, the Good must not be *identified* with knowledge and truth. Yet this says nothing about the question that concerns us: whether the Form of the Good is itself an object of knowledge (which maintains the analogy) or is not an object of knowledge (which seemingly goes beyond the analogy).

Plato's final remark seems to tilt the balance in the direction of the strong reading. Having assigned an *epistemological* priority to the Form of the Good, Plato develops the analogy in order to assign it an *ontological* priority as well.

> You will agree that the Sun not only makes the things we see visible, but it also brings them into existence and gives them growth and nourishment; yet he is not the same thing as existence. And so with the objects of knowledge: these derive from the Good not only their

power of being known, but their very being and reality; and Goodness is not the same thing as being, but even beyond being, surpass-
ing it in dignity and power.

Although this passage is not entirely unambiguous—it may even
trade upon ambiguity—the main point seems to be this: those
things that come into existence and pass away depend for their
existence upon the Sun, yet the Sun itself does not possess this
generated sort of existence. Similarly, the Forms owe their existence (as well as knowability) to the Form of the Good, but this
sort of existence does not pertain to the Form of the Good. At
their own level the Forms possess a dependent kind of existence,
but this sort of existence does not belong to the Form of the Good.
If we say that Being is the mode of existence pertaining to the
Forms, we must further say that the Form of the Good is something that lies "even beyond being."

The smooth interpretation of this analogy is snagged at only one
point. Plato plainly states that the Sun is an object of vision, yet,
on a plausible reading that maintains an ontological–epistemological
parity, we want to say that the Form of the Good lies beyond the
objects of knowledge just as it lies beyond Being. Perhaps we can
work out this last matter by attending to the pattern of the ontological analogy. In saying that the Form of the Good lies even beyond
Being, Plato is not declaring it a mere nothing. If, somewhat arbitrarily, we use the notion of *existence* as our widest ontological category, we can then spell out the ontological analogy this way:

> The Sun exists, but enjoys a higher status of existence than those
> generated objects that depend upon it for their mode of existence.

Similarly, but at a higher level:

> The Form of the Good exists, but enjoys a higher status of existence
> than those dependent objects that rely upon it for their mode of
> existence.

Here we cannot speak of the Forms as generated objects for they
do not come into being and pass away, but still they are dependent
objects.

Somewhat more arbitrarily we can use the notion of being *cognized* as the widest epistemological notion. (Nothing turns upon the choice of this particular word.) Then the parallel epistemological analogy will take the following form:

> The Sun is an object of vision, but even so, it is seen in a different and higher way than those objects that depend upon it to be seen.

Then again at a higher level:

> The Good is an object of cognition, but it is recognized at a different and higher level than the Forms which are cognized in virtue of it.

If we define *knowledge* as cognition of the Forms, it then follows that the Good is even beyond knowledge.

To establish this interpretation we must find some reason for supposing that the Sun itself is seen in some different and higher way than those objects which are seen in virtue of it. Cornford offers a terse account of Plato's theory of vision as it appears in the *Timaeus*:

> Plato's theory of vision involves three kinds of fire or light: (1) daylight, a body of pure fire diffused in the air by the Sun; (2) the visual current or "vision," a pure fire similar to daylight, contained in the eye-ball and capable of issuing out in a stream directed toward the object seen; (3) the color of the external object, "a flame streaming off from every body, having particles proportioned to those of the visual current, so as to yield sensation" when the two streams meet and coalesce.

If we take this account seriously, and also suppose that Plato had something like it in mind when he produced his comparison between the Sun and the Form of the Good, we can produce a uniform and strong reading of the analogy. Our vision of the sun is distinguished from our vision of other objects both in its purity and directness. When we see the sun, the pure light sent out from the eye enters into a direct (that is, unmediated) relationship with the pure light sent out from the sun. We now complete the analogy by asserting that the same kind of higher relationship exists between the Form of the Good and the mind.

Our conclusion, then, is that the main thrust — and almost the exclusive thrust — of this first analogy is to adumbrate both the ontological transcendence and the epistemological transcendence of the Form of the Good *relative to the other Forms.*

The basic metaphor of the *Divided Line* is that of *an image to its object.* Its mathematical format reflects the main — and almost exclusive — point of this analogy: it is intended to elucidate the character of mathematical thinking.

The development of this analogy begins with an allusion to the previous analogy:

> Consider, then, that there are these two powers I speak of, the Good reigning over the domain of all that is intelligible, the Sun over the visible world.

Plato represents these two domains by "a line divided into unequal parts, one to represent the visible order, the other the intelligible." Here, in order to capture the idea of the Good reigning *over* one domain and the Sun reigning *over* the other, we seem forced to draw the line horizontally:

|              |              |
| :----------: | :----------: |
|  *The Good*  |   *The Sun*  |

Nothing, however, forces us to decide which of these unequal lengths should be made longer beyond a feeling that it is more suitable to assign a greater length to the region of greater dignity. As the analogy unfolds, we shall see, however, that nothing crucial depends upon this decision concerning lengths.

We are next told to "divide each part again in the same proportion, symbolizing degrees of comparative clearness or obscurity." The line now looks like this:

|  *(D)*  |  *(C)*  |  *(B)*  |  *(A)*  |
| :-----: | :-----: | :-----: | :-----: |

It is important to underscore the idea that it is a certain *proportionality* that represents "degrees of comparative clearness or obscurity." As we shall see later, insisting upon this point rules out one alternative interpretation of the Divided Line.

> Then (*A*) one of the two sections in the visible world will stand for images. By images I mean first shadows, and then reflections in water or in close grained, polished surfaces, and everything of that kind, if you understand.

> Let the second section (*B*) stand for the actual things of which the first are likenesses, the living creatures about us and all the works of nature or of human hands.

Having filled in this region of the Divided Line, Plato immediately notices the following proportionality:

> Will you also take the proportion in which the visible world has been divided as corresponding to degrees of reality and truth, so that the likeness shall stand to the original in the same ratio as the sphere of appearances and beliefs to the sphere of knowledge?

The interesting thing here is that Plato notices this proportionality and then says little about it. Indeed, it is only when we come to the Allegory of the Cave that the center of attention is focused upon the relationship between the Intelligible Order as a whole and the Visual Order as a whole.

The key passage for understanding the Divided Line occurs when Plato describes the (*C–D*) division, once more invoking an image-object metaphor:

> (*C*) the mind uses as images those actual things which themselves had images in the visible world; and it is compelled to pursue its inquiry by starting from assumptions and travelling, not up to principle, but down to a conclusion. In the second (*D*) the mind moves in the other direction, from an assumption up to a principle which is not hypothetical; and it makes no use of the images employed in the other section, but only of Forms, and conducts its inquiry solely by their means.

Plato immediately tells us that the (*C*) region concerns mathematical reflection.

We can first concentrate upon the striking suggestion that the mathematician uses "*as images* those actual things which themselves had images in the visible world." That is, the mathematician deals with visible things — that is what he has before his mind — with the distinguishing difference that he employs these visible things in quite a special way. He uses them as images of something higher. More concretely, the mathematician deals with *diagrams*, for a diagram precisely fits the description of a visible thing that is used as an image or representation.

> [T]hey are not reasoning, for instance, about this particular square and diagonal which they have drawn, but about *the* Square and *the* Diagonal; and so in all cases. The diagrams they draw and the models they make are actual things, which may have their shadows or images in water; but they serve in their turn as images, while the student is seeking to behold these realities which only thought can apprehend.

Here, at least, Plato's intention seems absolutely unambiguous: he has simply doubled the object–image metaphor in order to bring out the following analogical proportionality:

*Diagrams* : *Mathematical Forms* :: *Images* : *Visible Objects*

If at this point we inquire into the character of the "mathematical objects" located at the (*C*) region of the Divided Line, we will have to say that they are diagrams of squares, circles, and so forth. The alternative idea that *the* Square or *the* Diagonal is located in this region makes no sense whatsoever of the text.

It should also be clear what Plato has in mind when he says that the mathematician is "compelled to pursue [his] inquiry by making assumptions and travelling, not up to principle, but down to conclusion." Plato is pointing to the fact that the mathematician, given the nature of his method, must always proceed from assumptions that are not themselves justified by proof.

> You know, of course, how students of subjects like geometry and arithmetic begin by postulating odd and even numbers, or the various figures and the three kinds of angles, and other such data in each subject. These data they take as known; and, having adopted them as assumptions, they do not feel called upon to give any account of them to themselves or to anyone else, but treat them as self-evident. Then, starting from these assumptions, they go on until

they arrive, by a series of consistent steps, at all the conclusions they set out to investigate.

Dialectic, which is stationed at the (*D*) region of the Divided Line, does not take such assumptions as self-evident, but instead treats them as "hypotheses in the literal sense, things 'laid down' like a flight of steps up which it may mount all the way to something that is not hypothetical, the first principle of all. . . . "

I can summarize this discussion by presenting the Divided Line in the following way. Using the root metaphor of image and object first introduced for the right-hand regions of the Divided Line, the metaphor is first extended in this fashion:

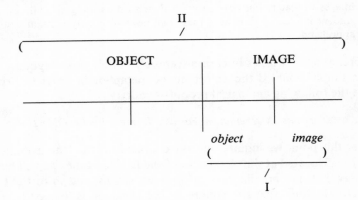

Then finally in this fashion:

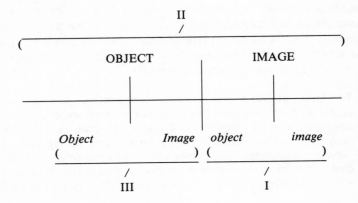

It is this third object–image metaphor — which concerns the status of mathematical reasoning — that constitutes the predominant theme of the text. The second object–image metaphor, though explicitly noticed here, becomes the center of attention only in the Allegory of the Cave.

This interpretation stands opposed to another that places the Form of the Good at the very top of the line and then measures degrees of "comparative clearness and obscurity" in terms of *distance* from the Form of the Good. But Plato does not place the Form of the Good on the Line at all — not even at the very top — for this would depart from his first analogy that enunciated the transcendence of the Form of the Good. In keeping with this idea of transcendence, the Form of the Good is said to *"reign over* the domain of all that is intelligible" and thus the Form of the Good stands in no linear relationships to the objects represented by various segments of the Line. Given this, the metaphor of distance is out of place: the Divided Line is not a linear metaphor of distance from something highest; instead, it is a linear metaphor of the proportionality of comparative degrees of clearness and obscurity.

The Allegory of the Cave is a "parable to illustrate the degrees in which our nature may be enlightened or unenlightened." Since the allegory is rather long in telling, I shall assume that its main features are well known.

Certain central features of the two previous metaphors are carried over into this allegory, and the task here is to see how this works out in detail. To begin with, the comparison between the Form of the Good and the Sun is reintroduced, but since the Sun is actually used as a stand-in for the Form of the Good, the Sun must itself be assigned a surrogate. This, of course, is the fire within the cave.

> Every feature of the parable, my dear Glaucon, is meant to fit our earlier analysis. The prison dwelling corresponds to the region revealed through the sense of sight, and the fire-light within it to the power of the Sun.

Given this principle of demotion, visible objects are treated as semblances of visible objects (that is, statues) and images of visible objects become images of these semblances of visible objects.

The most striking feature of the Allegory of the Cave is, however, the manner in which it takes over the image–object metaphor from the Divided Line. This is the central characteristic of the situation within the cave, but the metaphor is repeated (as in the Divided Line) outside the cave. When the prisoner is first dragged from the cave he is blinded, but eventually is able to "make out shadows and then images of men and things reflected in water." With the Divided Line, the central image–object metaphor had the following form:

*Diagrams* : *Mathematical Objects* :: *Images* : *Visible Objects*

In the Allegory of the Cave, where everything is moved down one ontological step, this comes out:

*Images* : *Visible Objects* :: *Images of Semblances of Objects*
: *Semblances of Objects*

Now, if we keep the image–object metaphor clearly before our minds, we can see how the regions of the Divided Line are mapped into the levels in the Allegory of the Cave.

| *The Divided Line* | | *The Cave* |
|---|---|---|
| D | Forms | Visible Objects |
| C | Representations of Forms | Images of Visible Objects |
| B | Visible Objects | Semblances of Visible Objects (Statues) |
| A | Images of Visible Objects | Images of Semblances of Visible Objects |

To return to the main point, the Allegory of the Cave is a "parable to illustrate the degrees in which our nature may be enlightened or unenlightened." What we have seen thus far is that this voyage of enlightenment involves a twofold transition from image to object: first within the cave and then outside of it. But, of course, the dominant thrust of the Allegory of the Cave is to contrast life within the cave with life outside of it.[2] The cave is described as a prison and anyone who had become free of it

would far sooner "be on earth as a hired servant in the house of a landless man" or endure anything rather than go back into his old beliefs and live in the old way.

The prisoner dwelt in the world of semblances. In his original state he merely confronts semblances of semblances, and even after his first degree of illumination, he is still only dealing with semblances (statues). This brings us to the final application of Plato's central image–object metaphor. The statues whose images are cast upon the wall of the cave are themselves only images of things that exist outside of the cave. Indeed, the *entire* setting of the cave is but a semblance of the structure of the outside world. We thus return to the proportionality mentioned briefly in the discussion of the Divided Line:

*The Intelligible World* : *The World of Appearance* :: *Visible Objects*
: *Images and Shadows*

Even though this is a simple analogy, it is possible to get it wrong. In particular, we might view the ascent of the soul as a progressive stripping away of levels of semblance. This will not work out in detail. Within the cave there is a transition from a semblance to its object and this process repeats itself outside of the cave. Yet the movement from the perception of visible objects to mathematical thinking is not itself from a semblance to its object. Visible objects are not semblances of diagrams.

Thus the following diagram characterizes neither the structure of the Divided Line nor the voyage of enlightenment in the Allegory of the Cave:

*Forms*
*Semblances of Forms*

---

*Semblances of Semblances of Forms*
*Semblances of Semblances of Semblances of Forms*

We have already seen that the Divided Line has quite a different structure:

| *Forms* | *Semblances of (Mathematical) Forms* | *Visible Objects* | *Semblances of Visible Objects* |
|---|---|---|---|
| | | | |

To this basic analogy, the Allegory of the Cave develops another that has remained in waiting from the discussion of the Divided Line: the World of Appearance (*including its semblance relationships*) is a semblance of the Intelligible World (*including its semblance relationships*).

In closing, we can notice one further feature of the Divided Line and then examine it in relationship to the Allegory of the Cave. As a purely mathematical consequence of the proportions laid down in the Divided Line, segment (*C*) is identical in length with segment (*B*). This might be viewed as an accidental feature of the analogy or even as an analogical inconsistency.[3] In fact, it is neither. Given the proportionality

$$D : C :: B : A$$

together with the fact that (*C*) is equal to (*B*), we can derive yet another proportionality:

$$D : B :: B : A$$

Under the semblance metaphor this comes out as the claim that Forms stand to visible objects as visible objects stand to their images. This, of course, is precisely correct relative to the structure of the Allegory of the Cave. The statues in the cave (which are the counterparts of visual objects on the Line) are mere semblances of the visible objects outside the cave (which are the counterparts of the Forms on the Line).

The identity in length between (*B*) and (*C*) generates yet another proportionality:

$$D : C :: C : A$$

In other words, Forms are to their representations as their representations are to images of visual objects. This certainly sounds curious until we recall that mathematical diagrams are themselves visible objects, only employed in a certain way. Thus, as visible objects, they have images in the same manner as any other visible object. At this point Plato's words return to us with a ring of unmistakable genius:

[T]he mind uses as images those actual things which themselves had images in the visible world.

This is precisely the relationship formulated in the above proportionality.[4]

I must confess that I do not see how the Allegory of the Cave exemplifies this last proportionality with any clarity, for by sharply separating the domain within the cave from the domain outside it there seems no way to represent the idea that *one and the same thing* can both have an image and be used as an image. Here (perhaps!) the unity of these analogies breaks down. But the best analogies break down sooner or later, and every other analogy I know breaks down sooner than this.

## NOTES

1. All citations are to the Cornford translation of *The Republic of Plato* (Oxford, 1941), pp. 217–235. I take it that there is no need to identify these familiar passages more closely.

2. There is no need here to discuss the metaphor of blindness, which concerns both the ascent from the cave and the descent back into it. This metaphor is at once striking, apposite, and hardly in need of interpretation.

3. It is certainly an analogical inconsistency on the distance interpretation of the Divided Line.

4. The proportionality $D : B :: C : A$ admits of a similar treatment.

# 2

# A Reading of Aquinas's Five Ways

As they appear in the *Summa Theologica*, Thomas Aquinas's so-called Five Ways are bracketed by two objections and two replies to these objections. In commenting on the Five Ways, many twentieth-century writers on Aquinas, including Kenny,[1] Copleston,[2] and Gilson,[3] make no reference to these objections and the replies to them. This is surely odd, for throughout the *Summa Theologica* objections and replies provide the framework within which Aquinas unfolds his ideas, and they thus provide basic keys for interpreting the text. With this in mind, and in contrast with the writers just mentioned, I propose to examine Aquinas's Five Ways as answers to the objections that precede them and as grounds for the replies that follow them. As we shall see, this approach is not without difficulties, but, in any case, it yields a reading of the Five Ways that is different, indeed radically different, from the interpretations that have now become standard.

The first objection that Aquinas raises concerns the problem of evil. He asks how the existence of an infinitely good (*bonum infinitum*) being is compatible with the presence of evil in the world. The problem, as Aquinas initially states it, is how such an infinitely good being could, so to speak, *leave room* for bad things. He puts it this way:

> For if, of two mutually exclusive things, one were to exist without limit, the other would cease to exist. But by the word 'God' is implied

"A Reading of Aquinas's Five Ways," *American Philosophical Quarterly*, Vol. 27, No. 4 (August 1990). Reprinted by permission of the publisher.

some limitless good (*bonum infinitum*). If God then existed, nobody
would ever encounter evil. But evil is encountered in the world. God
therefore does not exist. (Ia, 2, 3)[4]

Read uncharitably as an argument concerning infinite *magnitudes*, the reasoning would, of course, be fallacious. The existence
of infinitely many even numbers, for example, is compatible with
the existence of infinitely many odd ones, even though being even
is incompatible with being odd. Or again, the existence of an infinite region of luminosity ending at South Bend is compatible with
the existence of an infinite expanse of darkness beginning there.
But surely Aquinas had in mind infinite goodness combined with
the other traditional attributes of God, and he is asking how an
infinitely good being could *allow* the existence of evil. Indeed,
when we turn to his response to the objection, we see that Aquinas
attempts to answer precisely this question.

> As Augustine says, *Since God is supremely good, he would not
> permit any evil at all in his works, unless he were sufficiently al-
> mighty and good to bring good even from evil.* It is therefore a
> mark of the limitless goodness of God that he permits evils to exist,
> and draws from them good. (Ia, 2, 3)

Now my suggestion that we interpret the Five Ways in the light
of the objections and responses that enclose them gains little support from this first objection and the response to it. Although some
of Aquinas's proofs bear on this objection (in particular, the fourth
and fifth proofs), I do not think that any of them addresses it
directly. Even so, this objection and the one to follow share a
common feature: They are both challenges to the existence of a
traditional Christian God. The first objection provides a reason
for saying that God *does not* exist. The second objection, as we
shall see, draws the weaker conclusion that *there is no need to
suppose* that a God exists. In his response to the first objection,
Aquinas clearly attempts to vindicate antecedently accepted Christian doctrine in the face of a specific challenge. The leading idea of
this essay is that the Five Ways are intended to supply a vindication
of Christian doctrine specifically in response to the challenge presented in the second objection.

Objection 2 reads as follows:

[I]f a few causes fully account for some effect, one does not seek more. Now it seems that everything we observe in this world can be fully accounted for by other causes, without assuming a God. Thus natural effects are explained by natural causes, and contrived effects by human reasoning and will. There is therefore no need to suppose that God exists. (Ia, 2, 3)

For the understanding of the natural world, God, this objection tells us, is, as Laplace was supposed to have said to Napoleon, an unnecessary hypothesis.

The form of this objection specifies the form that Aquinas's response must take. He will have to show:

1. Nature is not fully explicable in terms of *natural* causes.

and

2. The purpose found in the universe cannot be fully explained by an appeal to *human* reason and *human* will.

With these threats removed, Aquinas will have vindicated the traditional Christian belief in God the creator and sustainer of the world specifically against the charge that this belief is unnecessary for understanding the world. This, I suggest, is precisely what the Five Ways are intended to show. Despite the general language ("There are five ways to prove [*probari*] that God exists"), the point of these *proofs* might better be expressed in these words: *There are five ways of showing that appeals to natural principles and appeals to human reason and human will do not wholly explain* **natural** *phenomena. Thus for a complete explication of natural phenomena, these natural principles must be supplemented by an appeal beyond the natural realm.*

Let me say at once that some textual evidence creates a presumption against this reading. At Ia, 2, 2, the article immediately preceding the presentation of the Five Ways, Aquinas speaks explicitly of "demonstrating from effects that God exists," and says quite explicitly:

God's effects . . . can serve to demonstrate that God exists, even though they cannot help us to know him comprehensively for what he is.

On the other side, in the presentation of the Five Ways, Aquinas nowhere refers to his arguments as demonstrations, instead, he speaks of them as proofs. Now to prove something can mean to put it to the test and it is in this sense that I think that Aquinas is attempting to prove the existence of God. But I do not want too much to turn on the difference between a demonstration and a proof, for the question at issue is what form Aquinas's arguments actually take. Accepting the immediate context of the objections and replies as controlling, I shall argue, despite earlier suggestions at Ia, 2, 2 to the contrary, that Aquinas is not offering demonstrations of the existence of God based on natural principles,[5] but is, instead, arguing that a recognition of the explanatory *inadequacies* of natural principles forces us to go beyond them.[6]

## The Fifth Way

The pattern of reasoning I am attributing to Aquinas emerges clearly in the Fifth Way, where Aquinas explicitly responds to the claim that human reason and human will can be taken as the causes of all purposeful acts. There he tells us:

> An orderedness of actions to an end is observed in all bodies obeying natural laws, even when they lack awareness. For their behaviour hardly ever varies, and will practically always turn out well; which shows that they truly tend to a goal, and do not merely hit it by accident. (Ia, 2, 3)

Provided that we are willing to join Aquinas in ascribing final causes to the activities of physical objects, we are thus presented with a vast number of examples of purposive events that cannot be attributed to the operations of human reason and will.

This much, however, does not show that something *beyond* nature is needed to account for the purposiveness in the world. We might think of final causes as themselves natural principles needing no external support; that is, the objector could argue that a *natural* teleology is adequate to explain all the purposive events found in the world, and, therefore, with respect to these purposive events, the hypothesis of a divine cause is unnecessary. Against this claim, Aquinas responds with breathtaking brevity:

> Nothing however that lacks awareness tends to a goal, except under the direction of someone with awareness and with understanding; the arrow, for example, requires an archer. Everything in nature, therefore, is directed to its goal by someone with understanding, and this we call 'God.' (Ia, 2, 3)

As a response to a natural teleology this is, of course, baldly question-begging. We might better say that Aquinas is gesturing toward an argument rather than giving one. Yet the pattern of the reasoning is clear: Aquinas is arguing that appeals to merely human teleology or to merely natural teleology are inadequate for the explanation of what we observe in nature, and therefore these principles demand for their completion an appeal to God.

Furthermore, read as a freestanding demonstration of the existence of God, the argument is just awful. Even if we grant that purposiveness in the world cannot be explained by appeals to natural teleology or human teleology, and further grant that it must be explained by an appeal to a supernatural intelligence, it still does not follow that we must postulate the existence of anything like a traditional Christian deity to account for it. To get *that* result, a detailed, full-blown argument from design is needed that eliminates alternative hypotheses to the postulation of a being possessing the unity, perfection, providence, etc. of the traditional Christian God. Since Aquinas provides no such argument, the Fifth Way, read as a teleological proof of God's existence, is simply a failure. Yet if we read it as an attempt to vindicate the claim of God's existence (to *prove* it in this sense) against the counterclaims of natural science, the rhetorical situation changes in an important way. The dialectical development unfolds as follows:

1. We begin with the presumption that the world is the product of a Christian God's creation.
2. The natural scientist tells us that the world can be fully explained on natural principles; therefore, this presumption is idle and can be set aside, at least when we are doing natural science.
3. It is then argued that the world (here with respect to its teleological

features) cannot be fully explained by natural principles, therefore, the presumption in 1 is restored.

Read in this manner, the Fifth Way is not a sketchy, incomplete (bad) argument from design intended to establish the existence of a deity with certain determinate features. On the contrary, a belief in the existence of a deity with certain determinate features is antecedently given, and the Fifth Way is an attempt to defend the belief in such a being against a specific challenge.

## The Fourth Way

Continuing in reverse order, Aquinas's Fourth Way concerns "gradations found in things."

> Some things are found to be more good, more true, more noble, and so on, and other things less. But such comparative terms describe varying degrees of approximation to a superlative; for example, things are hotter and hotter the nearer they approach what is hottest. Something therefore is the truest and best and most noble of things, and hence the most fully in being; for Aristotle says that the truest things are the things most fully in being. Now *when many things possess some property in common, the one most fully possessing it causes it in the others* . . . There is something therefore which causes in all other things their being, their goodness, and whatever other perfection they have. And this we call God. (Ia, 2, 3)

As a first approximation, the argument seems to run as follows:

1. We observe in nature that some things are better, truer, or more noble than others.
2. But such ascriptions presuppose a top member of each scale (the superlative), which serves as the standard by which such gradations are established.

Therefore

3. The best, truest, most noble things must exist.

Of course, stated this way, the argument has no tendency to prove the existence of a deity. With respect to beauty, for example, some corporeal entity, perhaps Helen, might occupy the top rung. Something more is needed to force us beyond the natural order. As Kenny puts it:

> It is at this point that St. Thomas needs to appeal implicitly to Plato to fill the gap; for on Plato's view, to be more or less F precisely is to participate more or less fully in the Idea of F which is the most F thing, the one and only thing which is fully F. (81)

What form should this appeal to Plato take? Here it is tempting to go back to Plato's writings and examine his (various) reasons for introducing forms, and then ask how the doctrine of forms, so introduced, can be serviceable for Aquinas's purposes. Taken this way, the Fourth Way will swim or, more likely, sink relative to the plausibility of Plato's theory of forms. This approach leads to a deep and complicated inquiry, since many of Aquinas's Aristotelian commitments place him in opposition to these Platonic doctrines.[7] But perhaps Aquinas's appeal to Platonism has a more general form, and goes something like this: there can be no natural explanation of the ranking of natural things, for all such rankings presuppose the existence of an antecedent standard that gives each of these natural objects a place in the ranking. So even if Helen was, *de facto*, the most beautiful woman, we recognize that even she might have been more beautiful—with a face that could, let us say, launch 1500 ships—and thus her place at the top of the natural order can be grasped only against the background of an ideal ordering. What is needed here is an argument showing that no natural object can, *in principle*, stand at the top of a hierarchy of values, thus determining it. Aquinas presents no such argument, but Aristotle waves a hand in this direction in his early, Platonic-sounding (largely lost) dialogue *On Philosophy*. I shall quote the surviving argument in full:

> Where there is a better, there is a best; now among existing things one is better than another; therefore there is a best which must be divine.[8]

Admittedly, this is rather enthymematic, for no justification is given for the claim that the best "must be divine." In any case, my suggestion is that in the Fourth Way, Aquinas, like Aristotle, is arguing that certain things found in the natural order (in this case, rankings according to value) cannot be explained on natural principles alone. Contrary to Objection 2, this is another respect in which nature cannot take care of itself; thus the *prior* presumption in favor of a transcendent source of value is preserved.

## The Three Cosmological Ways

If we take the denial of the possibility of an infinite regress as the signature of a cosmological argument, then Aquinas's first three Ways count as cosmological arguments. The first concerns *motion*, the second *efficient causality*, and the third *necessity and contingency*. In each case the arguments are presented against the background of Aquinas's own complex, sometimes obscure, metaphysical position. For these reasons, these arguments do not have the accessibility suggested by their standard appearance in introductory philosophy anthologies.

Since the argument in the Third Way refers back to the argument in the Second, I shall reverse my reverse order and examine the Second Way before the Third.

## The Second Way

Sharply edited, the Second Way reads as follows:

> The second way is based on the nature of [efficient] causation.[9] In the observable world causes are found to be ordered in series; we never observe, nor ever could, something causing itself, for this would mean it preceded itself, and this is not possible. Such a series of causes must however stop somewhere. . . . [Extensive Deletion] One is therefore forced to suppose some first cause, to which everyone gives the name 'God.' (Ia, 2, 3)

In presenting the Second Way, I have here deleted the argument intended to show that an infinite regress of efficient causes is impossible, i.e., I have left out the core argument of the Second Way.

I have done this to bring the *point* of the argument into prominence. What the passage seems to say is that the impossibility of
an infinite regress of efficient causes demands that sometime *back*
in this series of efficient causes, a first (uncaused) efficient cause
must exist. Such a reading is actually forced on us by the second
sentence in the passage, which clearly indicates that *all* efficient
causes in the observable world are temporally prior to their effects.[10] Borrowing the term from Copleston, I will say that treating
efficient causation in this way yields the *horizontal* interpretation
of the Second Way (123).

However natural (and I think forced) this horizontal reading of
the text may seem, it is now generally rejected in favor of a *vertical*
reading. Copleston describes the difference between these two interpretations in these words:

> [W]hen Aquinas talks about an 'order' of efficient causes he is not
> thinking of a series stretching back into the past, but of a hierarchy
> of causes, in which a subordinate member is here and now dependent
> on the causal activity of a higher member. (122)

Thus:

> We have to imagine, not a lineal or horizontal series, so to speak,
> but a vertical hierarchy, in which a lower member depends here and
> now on the present causal activity of the member above it. (123)

A similar vertical interpretation of the Second Way is found in
works of Kenny, Gilson, Garrigou-Lagrange, and others.

Since it is contrary to the simplest reading of the text, why should
the vertical interpretation of the Second Way be preferred to the
horizontal interpretation? The main reason that commentators reject the horizontal interpretation is that it seems to conflict with
other texts in Aquinas's writings. Copleston describes the situation
this way:

> [T]hough as a Christian theologian [Aquinas] was convinced that
> the world was not created from eternity he stoutly maintained that
> philosophers had never succeeded in showing that creation from
> eternity is impossible. . . . That is to say, no philosopher had ever

succeeded in showing the impossibility of a series of events without a first assignable member. (57)[11]

Although Copleston cites no passage to support this claim, his wording on page 122 of his *Aquinas* suggests that he almost certainly has in mind the following difficult passage cited explicitly by Kenny:

> It is not impossible to go on for ever *per accidens* in a series of efficient causes . . . as a smith may act by using many different hammers, *per accidens*, if one after the other is broken. For it is not essential for any particular hammer to act after the action of another, and it is likewise not essential for any particular man, *qua* begetter, to be begotten by another man; for he begets *qua* man, and not *qua* son of another man. . . . Hence it is not impossible to go on for ever in the series of men begetting men; but such a thing would be impossible if the generation of one man depended on another and on an element, and on the sun, and so on to infinity. (Ia, 46, 2, 7)[12]

Commenting on this passage, Kenny tells us:

> The series of causes in the Second Way . . . does not stretch backwards in time, but stretches into the heavens simultaneously. It is this series which must come to an end with God. (42)

Before commenting on Ia, 46, 2, 7 directly, it is important to be clear about the argumentative situation. Both Copleston and Kenny seem to be reasoning in the following way:

1. In the Second Way, Aquinas is attempting to demonstrate the existence of God.
2. A key move in the argument is that a certain kind of natural infinite regress is impossible.
3. But Aquinas (elsewhere) acknowledges that no philosopher has ever succeeded in showing the impossibility of a series of events without a first assignable *temporal* member.

Therefore:

4. Aquinas was not arguing that the series of *temporally antecedent* efficient causes must terminate in a first cause, but, instead, he was

arguing that the system of *simultaneous* efficient causes must terminate in a first cause.

What does Ia, 46, 2, 7 actually say? First, it does not speak *directly* about a contrast between temporally prior and simultaneous efficient causation. At most, it cites examples that suggest this contrast. I say *at most* it suggests this, for although the series of begetters (and the series of hammers) does stretch back into the past, thus supplying a clear example of temporal antecedence, the allusion to "an element and the sun" does not carry an obvious reference to simultaneity. More to the point, the central theme of the passage is not about temporal antecedence as opposed to simultaneity, but about something else: a contrast between efficient causes *per se* and efficient causes *per accidens*. This is not evident in Kenny's citation of the passage, for he has simply deleted all references to efficient causes *per se*. Here is the entire passage with the material Kenny has deleted given in bold print.

> **An infinite series of efficient causes essentially subordinate to one another is impossible, that is causes that are *per se* required for the effect, as when a stone is moved by a stick, a stick by a hand, and so forth: such a series cannot be prolonged indefinitely.** [But] it is not impossible to go on forever *per accidens* in a series of efficient causes, **as when they are all ranged under causal heading and how many there are is quite incidental,** as a smith may act by using many different hammers, *per accidens*, if one after the other is broken. For it is not essential for any particular hammer to act after the action of another, and it is likewise not essential for any particular man, *qua* begetter, to be begotten by another man; for he begets *qua* man, and not *qua* son of another man. **For all men in begetting hold the same rank in the order of efficient causes, namely that of being a particular parent.** Hence it is not impossible to go on forever in the series of men begetting men; but such a thing would be impossible if the generation of one man depended on another and on an element, and on the sun, and so on to infinity.[13]

As far as I can see, this passage makes no reference to, and has no implications for, a contrast between simultaneous (vertical) efficient causation and temporally prior (horizontal) efficient causation. The passage concerns the contrast between causes *per se* and causes *per accidens*. I shall try to give a relatively simple explanation of this distinction.

Using Aquinas's examples as our guide, we might explain the distinction between causes *per se* and causes *per accidens* in the following way: sometimes we pick out (refer to, name) a cause by using language that indicates *how* it acts as a cause. That is, sometimes in indicating a cause we use descriptive terms that are nomologically relevant. If asked who caused a disturbance, I might reply that the man waving a political sign caused the disturbance, thereby indicating (but not directly saying) how he caused it. Here (without obvious qualifications needed) I shall say that I have identified the cause *per se*. I might also merely pick out the cause in a nomologically irrelevant way by saying, perhaps, that the man wearing the gray shirt caused the disturbance. Here the cause has been identified, but only *per accidens*.[14]

Reading Aquinas this way makes him into a proto-Davidson; but he could be in worse company.[15] Anyway, the reading makes good sense of Aquinas's examples. It is not in virtue of being begotten that a father can beget a child, even though if he had not been begotten, he would not be available as a begetter. As a member of the series of begetters and begotten, he is only *per accidens* the cause of the child. Viewed in this nomologically arbitrary way, an infinite regress is not repugnant to reason.[16] The situation is different with efficient causality *per se* where we are concerned with *dependence* between the cause and effect. It is offensive to reason (many, including Aquinas, think) to have a chain of dependence that lacks an ultimate mooring. We might call this the *brute cosmological instinct*. Looked at this way, there is nothing offensive to reason in a chain of causes *per accidens* going back (one damn thing before another) infinitely far. It is offensive to reason for a series of causes *per se*, a series of dependencies, to do this, since it leaves the brute ontological instinct unsatisfied.

To go back to the Second Way, Ia, 46, 2, 7 so interpreted provides a guide for elucidating the core argument of the Second Way—the passage I had previously deleted. It reads as follows:

> Such a series of causes must however stop somewhere; for in it an earlier member causes an intermediate and the intermediate a last

(whether the intermediate be one or many). Now if you eliminate a cause you also eliminate its effects, so that you cannot have a last cause, nor an intermediate one, unless you have a first. Given therefore no stop in the series of causes, and hence no first cause, there would be no intermediate causes either, and no last effect, and this would be an open mistake. (Ia, 2, 3)[17]

On my reading, Ia, 46, 2, 7 would limit this argument to efficient causation *per se*, and that, I think, is the right way to see the relationship between the core argument of the Second Way and the discussion of efficient causality in Ia, 46, 2, 7. The suggestion that Ia, 46, 2, 7 concerns a contrast between simultaneous and temporally prior efficient causality is textually unfounded, and thus its use to impose a vertical interpretation on the Second Way is wholly arbitrary.

If textual considerations do not favor a vertical reading of the Second Way over the horizontal reading, are there philosophical reasons involving the principle of charity that favor the vertical reading? I cannot see that there are. Read either way, the argument depends on the claim that an infinite chain of dependence is repugnant to reason. For my own part, I cannot see why an infinite chain of efficient causes that stretches into the heavens simultaneously should be more repugnant to reason than an infinite chain of efficient causes stretching infinitely far back in time. Part of the difficulty in making this comparison is that it is hard to see what commentators have in mind when they speak of a hierarchy of simultaneous efficient causes. They are certainly not forthcoming with detailed illustrations. Perhaps the following example adapted from Kant will serve our purposes. A ball resting on a cushion is said to be the simultaneous cause of the hollow it makes in that cushion. Now let us replace the ball with another cushion that will make at least some depression in the cushion below it. On top of that cushion we place another, then another, and so on *ad infinitum*.

Of course, there are *physical* reasons why such an unending stack of pushed-downward–downward-pushing pillows is impossible, but there does not seem to be any reason to suppose that the bottom cushion could not be pushed down on unless there exists a topmost pillow that is *not* itself pushed downward. Admittedly, there may be independent reasons for rejecting the possibility of an *actual* infinity of stacked pillows, but these may apply equally well against both the horizontal and vertical infinite regresses. As far as I can tell, then, there are no reasons derived from the principle of charity that should lead us to replace the supposedly naive horizontal reading of the Second Way with the more sophisticated vertical reading.

Now my general thesis that the Five Ways present *vindications* rather than *demonstrations* of God's existence is, strictly speaking, independent of a horizontal rather than a vertical reading of the Second Way. Yet they are connected in the following important way. Read as an attempted demonstration of God's existence and interpreted horizontally, the Second Way may seem to demonstrate (or try to demonstrate) that at some time in the past the world was created by God. This would be embarrassing, for Aquinas is unequivocal in asserting "that the world has not always existed cannot be demonstratively proved but is held by faith alone" (Ia, 46, Reply). But this embarrassment disappears if we give up the idea that the Five Ways in general, and the Second Way in particular, are intended to demonstrate God's existence using premises derived from the natural sciences. Conversely, if we interpret the Second Way as a vindication of traditional religious belief in the face of a threat from (supposedly adequate) natural explanations in terms of efficient causes, then it surely concerns horizontal (i.e., temporally prior) causes, since this is where the threat comes from. For, of course, the view that the world has always existed and is wholly determined by temporally antecedent efficient causes is flatly *in*compatible with the Christian doctrine of creation. Thus Aquinas, who is generally committed to the compatibility of faith and reason, must reject all arguments intended to establish the eternality of anything save God.[18]

## The First Way

Whereas the Second Way concerns efficient causes, the First concerns motion — in the very broad sense in which the Aristotelian tradition uses this concept. A key feature of this argument is the following principle:

> [To] cause change is to bring into being what was previously only about to be, and this can only be done by something that already is.

That is, only something *actual* can cause the *potentially* F to become *actually* F. Aquinas illustrates this principle with the following example:

> Thus fire, which is actually hot, causes wood, which is able to be hot, to become actually hot, and in this way causes change in the wood. (Ia, 2, 3)

This example has led a number of commentators to read the principle as saying, in Kenny's words, that "only what is actually F will make something else become F."[19] But this is not what Aquinas says. He simply says that for something to pass from being potentially F to being actually F this must be caused by something else that is actual. *He does not say that the cause must actually be F.* Furthermore, this cannot be what Aquinas means. God, the ultimate cause of all change is, according to Aquinas, unchangeable.[20] God, then, is not only an unmoved mover in the sense of a mover that is not itself moved, but also an unmoving mover.

Having gotten this straight, we are back on familiar ground. Those who hold that "natural effects are explained by natural causes" can account for change only by citing an endless ungrounded sequence of moved movers. To avoid this affront to our brute cosmological instincts (which some people have), we must transcend the natural order and acknowledge the existence of an unchanging being that is the first cause of change and is not itself changed by anything.

## The Third Way

The Third Way concerns contingency and necessity. I do not fully understand what Aquinas means by these notions, but I am quite sure that we will misread him if we give them a contemporary (modal logician's) interpretation. The difference between Aquinas's use of these notions and a contemporary interpretation comes out in the following crucial passage:

> Some of the things we come across can be but need not be, for we find them springing up and dying away, thus sometimes in being and sometimes not. Now everything cannot be like this, for a thing that need not be, once was not; and if everything need not be, once upon a time there was nothing. (Ia, 2, 3)

This passage seems to involve a simple scope fallacy that goes something like this: If for every contingent being there is some time at which it does not exist, then there is some time at which no contingent being exists. Now I am sure that commentators have found ways of giving this argument a charitable reconstruction, but I do not want to talk about that. For the present purposes, it is more important to notice that for Aquinas — unlike the contemporary modal logician — the contingent (the nonnecessary) has temporal limitation built into its nature. Termination is an essential feature of contingent beings.[21]

With these thoughts in mind, we can return to those who think that all "natural effects can be explained by natural causes." If we assume that natural things possess only contingent existence and find some way of rendering plausible the argument that if everything were contingent then, at some time in the past, nothing would have existed, we can reach Aquinas's conclusion with (relatively) little difficulty:

> But if that were true [i.e., that once upon a time there was nothing] there would be nothing even now, because something that does not exist can only be brought into being by something already existing. . . . Not everything therefore is the sort of thing that need not be; there has got to be something that must be, etc.[22]

Good or bad, it is at least clear what this argument is intended to show. It is not presented as an *a posteriori* demonstration of God's existence based on natural principles. To the contrary, it is an effort to show that the very existence of a natural contingent world is inexplicable on the basis of natural principles alone.

The central thesis of Kenny's *The Five Ways* is that "it is much more difficult than at first appears to separate [the Five Ways] from their background in medieval cosmology," and for that reason, "any contemporary cosmological argument would have to be much more different from the arguments of Aquinas than scholastic modernizations customarily are" (3–4). To simplify, Kenny argues — and his book is an attempt to establish the point in detail — that the science of Aquinas's day is so radically different in its underlying concepts from the science of our day that it is impossible to transpose those arguments into the idiom of modern science.

It should be clear that if my reading of the Five Ways is correct, then Kenny's criticisms are out of focus. On the present reading, medieval principles of cosmology do not appear as *premises* in proposed demonstrations of God's existence. Thus they do not stand in need of replacement. Furthermore, we can imagine those engaged in what Kenny calls "scholastic modernizations" of the Five Ways attempting to produce arguments against the pretensions of modern science precisely in the style that Aquinas used with respect to the science of his day. As Kant saw, the longings that produce cosmological reasoning have their source in the felt dissatisfaction with any natural explanation of the world. The science of our day is better science than that of Aquinas's, but to a person driven by the ideals of reason, with its demands for unconditioned completeness, both sciences will seem unsatisfactory — and for the very same reasons.

# NOTES

1. A. Kenny, *The Five Ways* (London: Routledge & Kegan Paul, 1969).

2. See F. C. Copleston, *Aquinas* (Harmondsworth: Penguin Books, 1955), pp. 14–30.

3. See É. Gilson, *The Philosophy of St. Thomas Aquinas*, translated by Edward Bullough (Cambridge: W. Heffer & Sons, 1924), pp. 36–75.

4. Unless otherwise indicated, all citations are to the *Summa Theologica* (London: Blackfriars, 1964).

5. It is this reading that gives Kenny's basic criticism its point.

6. Following the tradition, we may, if we like, speak of these arguments as being *a posteriori* in at least two ways: they all depend on observed facts and in a broad sense of "cause," they all involve inferences back from effects to causes. My claim is that they are not, however, *a posteriori*

in the sense of being empirical arguments. They are not exercises in natural theology. At least that is what I will attempt to show.

7. See Kenny, pp. 71–95.

8. Fr. 1476 b22–24.

9. The Latin reads "causæ efficientis." Perhaps the translator did not translate the word "efficientis" because it is clear from the context that efficient causes are at issue.

10. How God functions as an efficient cause is another matter. We will come back to this.

11. A similar claim is made by É. Gilson, pp. 56–58.

12. The translation, including deletions, is Kenny's, pp. 41–42.

13. The passages printed in bold were deleted by Kenny and restored from the Blackfriars translation. The remaining passages preserve Kenny's translation.

14. It should go without saying that if the man waving the political sign caused the disturbance, though not by waving a political sign, then it would still be *true*, though perhaps misleading, to say that he, referred to as the waver of a political sign, caused the riot. We can also imagine contexts in which wearing a gray shirt could provoke a riot (the hated Gray Shirts).

15. I am not, of course, suggesting a deep similarity between Aquinas and Davidson. Aquinas was not, for example, an anomalous monist. On the other hand, some of the occasionalist Moslem theologians whom Aquinas attacks held views that seem Davidsonian in at least the following, admittedly remote, respect. Where Davidson denies the existence of psychological laws, these occasionalists denied the existence of natural laws or natural causes, reasoning that since God causes everything, "fire would not heat, but God would cause heat at the presence of fire." For Aquinas's response to this view, see, for example, *Summa Contra Gentiles*, III, 64–70. Aquinas is thus involved in a twofold task. On the one side, he is attempting to protect religious belief from the presumptions of natural science. That, if I am right, is the point of the so-called Five Ways. On the other side, he wishes to grant the natural sciences a domain of autonomy, provided, of course, that its practitioners do not pridefully reject religion in its favor.

16. Similarly, it is not in virtue of being one hammer in a series of hammers that a particular hammer is efficacious; thus an infinite regress here is, again, not an affront to reason.

17. This argument hardly seems persuasive, since a parallel line of reasoning would yield the result that there must be a first *left-hand* member of the series: . . . , $-3, -2, -1$.

18. At Ia, 46, 1, Aquinas explicitly attacks arguments intended to show

that creatures have always existed. Here he rather desperately tries to get Aristotle on his side even in the face of apparently explicit texts to the contrary, e.g., *Physics* VIII, 1 and 2.

19. Kenny, p. 21.

20. This is stated explicitly in Aquinas's *Reply to the second objection* where he speaks of God as "an original cause which is unchangeable and necessary *per se.*"

21. For most contingent beings there is both a time when they have not yet come into existence and a time at which they will no longer exist. The only exceptions are those contingent beings whose existence commenced at the moment of creation, since, according to Aquinas, time did not exist before creation. (See Ia, 46, 3.) So, strictly speaking, Aquinas is wrong in saying that anything "that need not be, once was not." Since, however, these exceptions presuppose the existence of God, admitting them does not weaken Aquinas's argument.

22. Citing the reasoning in the Second Way, Aquinas goes on to argue that an infinite regress of necessary beings is impossible.

# 3

# Hume and Berkeley on the Proofs of Infinite Divisibility

The philosophers of the seventeenth and eighteenth centuries were perplexed by and fascinated with the notion of infinite divisibility. On the one side, there seemed to be proofs, some of them geometrical demonstrations sound as one could imagine, showing, for example, that a line must be infinitely divisible. On the other side, the notion that a finite line could be made up of infinitely many parts struck some as being either unintelligible or absurd. Some philosophers were quick to put this apparent conflict to use. For Bayle the perplexities surrounding infinite divisibility evened the skeptical balance by providing arguments against the pretensions of *reason* on a par with the Cartesian assault on the *senses*.[1] Arnauld and Nicole enlisted the perplexities of infinite divisibility in the service of the mysteries of the Catholic faith, declaring that these proofs force us to confess "that there are some things which exist although we are not able to comprehend them"; then adding, "hence it is well for a man to weary himself with these subtilities, [*sic*.] in order to check his presumption, and to take away from him the boldness which would lead him to oppose his feeble intelligence to the truths which the Church proposes to him, under the pretext that he cannot understand them. . . . "[2]

Of course, *philosophical* arguments for and against infinite divis-

"Hume and Berkeley on the Proofs of Infinite Divisibility," *Philosophical Review*, Vol. XCVII, No. 1 (January 1988). Reprinted by permission of the publisher.

ibility go back to the ancient world and in various places I shall discuss them in some detail, but I am chiefly concerned with the proposed *mathematical* proofs of infinite divisibility and the responses to them, specifically in the writings of Hume and Berkeley. In fact, most of their arguments are ineffective in refuting the mathematical proofs of infinite divisibility, sometimes because they contain errors of reasoning and sometimes because they rely on philosophical commitments that are themselves dubious. In the end, however, we shall see that Berkeley did raise subtle and, I believe, original objections to these demonstrations that are independent of the problematic features of his general philosophical position, and of considerable interest in their own right.

## The Mathematical Proofs of Infinite Divisibility

Since mathematical proofs of infinite divisibility were well known to writers of the seventeenth and eighteenth centuries, they often alluded to them in a general way without spelling them out in detail. For this reason, it will be helpful to give a brief description of some of these proofs. One collection of them is found in *The Port-Royal Logic*, and it seems reasonable that writers interested in this topic would be familiar with this famous work. Another set of proofs of infinite divisibility is found in Isaac Barrow's *Lectiones Mathematicae*. Berkeley cites these lectures numerous times in his *Philosophical Commentaries*, and Bayle and Hume were familiar with them as well. In what follows, I shall primarily use the demonstrations found in *The Port-Royal Logic*, since they are elegantly stated and, presumably, widely known. I have taken one additional demonstration from Barrow's lectures because it is forceful, and because Berkeley responds to it in detail.

These mathematical demonstrations of infinite divisibility fall into two categories. The first employs arguments in the *reductio ad absurdum* form, that is, given the assumption that extension is *finitely* divisible, certain absurdities are supposed to follow, and it is therefore concluded that extension must be infinitely divisible.[3] For example, by a famous proof we know that the diagonal of a square is incommensurate with its sides, but if both the diagonal and the sides were composed of "a certain number of indivisible parts, one of these indivisible parts would be the common measure of these two lines, and, consequently, these two lines cannot be composed of a certain number of indivisible parts."[4] More elaborately:

> It is demonstrated, again, . . . that it is *impossible for a square number to be double of another square number*, while, however, it is very possible that an extended square may be double another extended square. Now, if these extended squares were composed of a certain number of ultimate parts, the large square would contain double the parts of the small one, and both being squares, there would be a square number double another square number, which is impossible.[5]

The second kind of mathematical argument in behalf of infinite divisibility employs constructions. *The Port-Royal Logic* contains one such argument which is intended to show that the infinite *extendability* of a line, which is countenanced in classical geometry, implies its infinite divisibility as well. The authors of *The Port-Royal Logic* ask us to imagine a ship sailing off on an infinitely broad flat sea. As the ship gets further away, its apparent size becomes smaller through, of course, infinitely many possible degrees, each corresponding to a possible division of a line.[6]

In another proof, this one found in Barrow's *Lectures*, a construction is used as the basis for a *reductio ad absurdum*:

> [I]f the Circumference of a Circle be supposed to consist of any Number of Points to every one of which *Radii* are drawn from the Center, it is very evident, that the Circumferences of more concentric Circles will consist of the same number of Points with the former, and consequently are equal to it, which is most absurd: Or otherwise these *Radii* do touch, meet, or intersect one another in some Place else than the Center.[7]

Finally, a more direct argument using a construction depends upon the claim that infinitely many angles can be drawn approximating the angle of intersection of a tangent to a circle.[8]

Arguments in response to these demonstrations move at two levels: (1) some ignore the details of these proofs and are content to point out supposed absurdities involved in the notion of infinite divisibility, whereas (2) others attack the presented demonstrations themselves. In this essay I shall be primarily concerned with the second sort of response, but since it is often combined with more general philosophical arguments of the first kind, it will be helpful to note some of the general forms these arguments took. I shall only mention those that resurface in the writings of Berkeley and Hume.

## The Philosophical Arguments

Since antiquity, philosophers have presented arguments, some at a very high level of sophistication, for and against the possibility of infinite divisibility in various domains.[9] The seminal arguments in behalf of the infinite divisibility of magnitudes are found in Aristotle.[10] A favorite argument on the other side — Bayle, Berkeley, and Hume all rang changes on it[11] — is attributed to Epicurus by Lucretius:

> Moreover, if there be not a least thing, all the tiniest bodies will be composed of infinite parts, since indeed the half will always have a half, nor will anything set a limit. *What difference then will there be between the sum of things and the least things? There will be no difference*, for however completely the whole sum be infinite, yet things that are tiniest will be composed of infinite parts just the same.[12]

That is, as the italicized portion indicates, if extension were infinitely divisible, then everything would be the same size. The underlying argument seems to be this: if two things are composed of the same number of fundamental parts of the same size, then they must be equal in size; thus if every object were composed of infinitely many fundamental parts of the same size, then everything would be the same size. The argument is, of course, off the mark, since the believers in infinite divisibility deny that a line is composed of fundamental parts — a line is divisible all the way down without a stopping place.

Epicurus also argued, and Bayle, Berkeley, and Hume again followed him, that an extension composed of infinitely many finite extensions must constitute an infinite extension.[13] This argument isn't any good either. It is true that if we take a finite extension (however small) and repeat it *ad infinitum*, we will get an infinite extension. That, however, is quite beside the point, because the proof of infinite divisibility depends upon the possibility of constructing ever smaller finite extensions, as in the sequence [1/2, 1/4, 1/8, etc.] whose sum approaches, but does not exceed, 1.

Other philosophical arguments are reminiscent of Zeno's paradoxes.[14] Hume argued, in one place, that if extension were infinitely divisible, then no point could be specified as terminating a line, and, in another, that if time were infinitely divisible, it would be impossible for a finite time to elapse.[15] Again, these arguments seem to be based upon a misunderstanding of the concept of a limit, but I shall not discuss them further in this paper; not because their correct analysis is altogether easy, but because my interests lie elsewhere. I wish to examine the ways in which Hume and Berkeley responded directly to the mathematical proofs of infinite divisibility. After all, if these proofs are good proofs, then we might (as most mathematicians have done) reason in reverse fashion that there must be something wrong with the supposed derivations of Zeno-like paradoxes from the notion of the infinite divisibility of extension.

## Hume's Counterarguments in the *Treatise*

In arguing for his own position that space (and time) are the manner in which colored and tactile extensionless minima present themselves, Hume attacks what he takes to be all possible alternatives. *Pure mathematical points*, he claims, would be nonentities. *Physical points* (that is, *extended* minima) would be *in* space and hence divisible. Finally, he argues that extension cannot be *infinitely divisible*, for reasons we shall now examine.

## The Arguments from Minimal Sensibles

Following Berkeley, and more remotely, Epicurus,[16] Hume attacks the doctrine of infinite divisibility by invoking the doctrine of minimal conceivables and sensibles. He first argues that at least our *ideas* of space and time are not infinitely divisible. If you take any object of the imagination, you will not be able to resolve it into infinitely many parts. Indeed, given an *idea* of a grain of sand, we will find that it is not even separable into twenty distinct ideas, "much less into a thousand, ten thousand, or an infinite number of ideas."[17] Hume makes a similar claim for impressions of sensation. Inspection shows that our capacity to discern distinct parts quickly reaches a limit, and we then encounter partless (and apparently extensionless) perceptual minima.[18]

So much for our *ideas* of space and time; how about space and time themselves? Are they infinitely divisible? Hume makes the transition from claims about our *ideas* of space and time to assertions about space and time *themselves* in the following remarkable passage which is a match for anything found in the writings of the rationalists.

> Wherever ideas are adequate representations of objects, the relations, contradictions and agreements of the ideas are all applicable to the objects; and this we may in general observe to be the foundation of all human knowledge. But our ideas are adequate representations of the most minute parts of extension; and thro' whatever divisions and subdivisions we may suppose these parts to be arriv'd at, they can never become inferior to some ideas, which we form. The plain consequence is, that whatever *appears* impossible and contradictory upon the comparison of ideas, must be *really* impossible and contradictory, without any further excuse or evasion.[19]

Given this principle, Hume restates one of the standard philosophical arguments against infinite divisibility as follows:

> I first take the least idea I can form of a part of extension, and being certain that there is nothing more minute than this idea. I conclude, that whatever I discover by its means must be a real quality of extension.[20]

Then, by starting with a particular finite quantity, Hume has no difficulty showing that their infinite repetition will generate an infinite quantity.

The difficulty with this argument is that the defenders of infinite divisibility do not hold that a line is composed of infinitely many finite parts of a fixed quantity; they hold that it is composed of infinitely many continuously diminishing finite quantities. Hume responds to this reply in a footnote:

> It has been objected to me, that infinite divisibility supposes only an infinite number of *proportional* not of *aliquot* parts, and that an infinite number of proportional parts does not form an infinite extension. But this distinction is entirely frivolous. Whether these parts be call'd *aliquot* or *proportional*, they cannot be inferior to those minute parts we conceive; and therefore cannot form a less extension by their conjunction.[21]

Exactly why is it impossible for the parts of a line itself to be inferior to those minute parts we conceive? Hume's answer goes back to the claim that "our ideas are adequate representations of the most minute parts of extension," and "wherever ideas are adequate representations of objects, [they] are applicable to the objects." If this is the basis of Hume's argument, as it surely is, then two things are worth noting. (1) The resuscitation of this traditional argument against infinite divisibility is unnecessary, since Hume could have argued directly that we have an adequate idea of extension as containing only finitely many minimal parts, and therefore extension itself has only finitely many minimal parts. (2) Hume certainly owes us a defense of the specific claim that we have an adequate idea of the ultimate parts of extension and also a defense of the general rationalist principle that adequate ideas of objects are *eo ipso* true of them. (If it is definitionally guaranteed that adequate ideas are true of their objects, then he owes us an account of adequacy.)

Hume's first use of the notion of perceptual minima as the basis for an argument against infinite divisibility of space and time rests upon the strong claim that our adequate ideas of extension guarantee certain things about the nature of extension itself. In this same context he offers, for the first time in his writings, a distinctive pattern of argument that he uses repeatedly throughout his philosophical career — we might call it the left tong of Hume's Fork. First he tells us:

> *That whatever the mind clearly conceives includes the idea of possible existence*, or in other words, *that nothing we imagine is absolutely impossible.*[22]

Now we know, or at least have been told, that we never imagine objects as having infinitely many parts, but rather we always imagine them as having finitely many parts. But, given the above *maxim of metaphysics*, as Hume calls it, he can argue in the following way: since we both imagine and perceive finite extensions as composed of only finitely many parts, that idea implies no contradiction; it is thus *possible* that space itself is only finitely divisible; and thus "all the arguments employ'd against the possibility of mathematical points [and in favor of infinite divisibility] are mere scholastick quibbles, and unworthy of our attention."[23]

The argument depends upon two theses: (1) we can (since, in fact, we always do) imagine extension as being composed of finitely many indivisible parts; and (2) that which is imaginable is possible and thus cannot be demonstrated to be nonexistent. I confess that I find the first principle baffling and hardly know what to say about it. I do not know how I would go about answering the question, "Does this line seem to you to be composed of finitely many or infinitely many parts?" It looks like something that will admit of a great many cuts, but will it admit of infinitely many cuts? I do not see how that question could be answered by inspection. Second, I find the argument from imaginability (or conceivability) unpersuasive, since it ignores the possibility that we might misidentify or misdescribe the objects of our conception or imagination. But I shall not pursue that issue here. In any case, if Hume's arguments were persuasive, we would know in advance that any proffered proof of infinite divisibility must be mistaken, and thus we would be under no constraint to examine these proofs before rejecting them. And that is what Hume says in calling them "mere scholastick quibbles . . . unworthy of our attention."[24] Yet Hume does attend directly to these "demonstrations," I suppose because they have the power to persuade, and this should be neutralized.

## The Nondemonstrative Character of Geometry

Hume's more direct attack upon these supposed proofs does not consist in finding errors in the derivations themselves; instead, it turns on a general claim concerning the nature of geometric reasoning:

I . . . maintain, that none of these demonstrations can have sufficient weight to establish such a principle, as this of infinite divisibility; and that because with regard to such minute objects, they are
not properly demonstrations, being built on ideas, which are not
exact, and maxims, which are not precisely true.[25]

According to Hume, we can never know, as geometers often claim
they know, that two lines are exactly equal, for whether two lines
are equal or not is a matter of observation, and when differences
are minute, errors are possible. Similar remarks hold concerning
the distinction between a right line and a curved line. At times it is
beyond doubt that a line curved rather than right, but close cases
exist where we simply cannot tell the difference. From these observations Hume concludes that

It appears . . . that the ideas which are most essential to geometry,
*viz.* those of equality and inequality, of a right line and a plain
surface, are far from being exact and determinate, according to our
common method of conceiving them.[26]

I think that Hume wished to draw two conclusions from this
claim: first, the general conclusion that geometry, despite a long
tradition to the contrary, is an empirical discipline rather than a
purely intellectual discipline; second, while admitting that geometry for the most part yields proofs that are beyond doubt, he further holds that it can lead to error when its reflections are carried
beyond the observational claims that serve as its basis. Geometry
typically yields results that are beyond doubt because it proceeds
from observations that are themselves beyond doubt. The situation
is quite different with respect to the proofs of infinite divisibility.
Here we are asked to make comparisons beyond our level of acuity,
and, in the end, we arrive at results which, far from being supported by observation, actually contradict it.

There are, of course, a number of things wrong with Hume's
argument. To begin with, in geometrical proofs, equalities are *stip-
ulated* rather than discovered by observation. In geometry, lines
are *set* equal to each other. Yet even if Hume is wrong in arguing
that geometry is an empirical discipline on the grounds that it relies
on observing the physical properties of diagrams, his *conclusion*,

that geometry is an empirical discipline, may still be correct. He could have argued, as some modern empiricists have argued,[27] that when the nonlogical terms of the propositions of geometry are given a physical interpretation, they become contingencies whose truth can only be established empirically.[28] If so, we get the result that Hume was trying to reach: the supposed *a priori* proofs of infinite divisibility do not show that *physical* space is infinitely divisible, since no purely demonstrative argument can establish the features of physical space. I shall return to this issue at the close of this essay.

## Hints in Hume's *Enquiry*

When he came to write the *Enquiry Concerning Human Understanding*, Hume seems to have changed his mind about the nondemonstrative character of geometric reasoning, for there he lists Geometry as one of the sciences derived wholly from Relations of Ideas.[29] Yet Hume's fascination with the problem of infinite divisibility is carried over to the *Enquiry*, where the discussion is curious and, in fact, not altogether forthcoming. In the body of the text he argues, in the style of Bayle, that the paradoxes generated by the proofs of infinite divisibility should undermine the pretensions of reason. We find passages of the following kind:

> Reason here seems to be thrown into a kind of amazement and suspense, which, without the suggestions of any sceptic, gives her diffidence of herself, and of the ground on which she treads. She sees a full light, which illuminates certain places; but that light borders upon the most profound darkness. And between these she is so dazzled and confounded, that she scarcely can pronounce with certainty and assurance on any one object.[30]

But this brief alliance with Bayle is broken in a curious footnote appended to the close of the discussion. It begins with these words:

> It seems to me not impossible to avoid these absurdities and contradictions, if it be admitted, that there is no such thing as abstract or general ideas, properly speaking.[31]

Hume goes on to sketch, very briefly, his critique of what he takes to be the standard theory of abstract ideas and outlines his positive account of how general terms function. He then says that on this approach:

> [I]t follows that all the ideas of quantity, upon which mathematicians reason, are nothing but particular, and such as are suggested by the senses and imagination, and consequently, cannot be infinitely divisible.[32]

He ends coyly by telling us that "it is sufficient to have dropped this hint at present, without prosecuting it any further."[33] To my knowledge, Hume does not return to this topic in his published works.[34]

In the *Treatise* Hume gives Berkeley highest marks for his critique of the received doctrine of abstract ideas, calling it "one of the greatest and most valuable discoveries that has been made of late years in the republic of letters."[35] In the passage just cited from the *Enquiry*, we again find Hume invoking Berkelean ideas concerning abstract ideas. Here, without saying so, Hume simply takes over Berkeley's extraordinarily sophisticated attack upon the standard proofs of infinite divisibility. This will become evident as we examine Berkeley's position on this matter.

## Berkeley's Critique of Infinite Divisibility

Berkeley discusses proofs for infinite divisibility in the *Principles of Human Knowledge*, (##123–132), in a set of queries (in particular, ##5–21) subjoined to the main text of *The Analyst* (a work *Addressed to an Infidel Mathematician*, in particular, Dr. Edmund Halley), and in his *Philosophical Commentaries*[36], where there is a large number of remarks bearing on infinite divisibility. We can notice first that two of Hume's main arguments against infinite divisibility appear in these passages. Like Hume, Berkeley invokes the Epicurean argument that an extension composed of infinitely many finite parts must be infinite in extension. Berkeley puts it this way: "when we say a line is infinitely divisible, we must mean a line which is infinitely great."[37]

Another of Hume's arguments, or at least its leading premise, also appears in Berkeley's writings: this is the argument from minimal perceptibles. Hume, as we saw, claimed that our *perceptions* of space and time are not infinitely divisible. Here is Berkeley:

> If . . . I cannot perceive innumerable parts in any finite extension that I consider, it is certain they are not contained in it: but it is evident, that I cannot distinguish innumerable parts in any particular line, surface, or solid, which I either perceive by sense, or figure to myself in my mind: wherefore I conclude they are not contained in it.[38]

Thus, for both Berkeley and Hume, it is a phenomenological fact that apprehended extensions are not infinitely divisible but, instead, are composed of finitely many *minimal* parts.

Given this shared premise concerning our idea of extension, Berkeley and Hume actually reason differently. Given his general position, Berkeley can conclude at once that extension *itself* is not infinitely divisible, for, as he says, "Nothing can be plainer to me than that the extensions I have in view are no other than my own ideas, and it is no less plain that I cannot resolve any one of my ideas into an infinite number of other ideas, that is, they are not infinitely divisible."[39] Since Hume maintains a distinction between extension and our idea of extension, he cannot argue in this way, and instead, must present arguments linking our ideas of extension to extension itself. We saw that he presented two: the stronger argument is intended to show that our adequate idea that extension is only finitely divisible guarantees that extension itself is only finitely divisible. The weaker argument is that there can be no demonstrative proofs of infinite divisibility, since the *possibility* of only finite divisibility is established by the fact that we imagine and perceive extension as only finitely divisible; what is imaginable or perceivable is possible; and what is possible cannot be demonstrated not to exist. The following rough chart shows these three variations on the arguments from sensible minima:

Both imagination and perception reveal minimal sensibles in extension.

| 1. Our ideas of extension are adequate (true of) extension. | 2. Our ideas of extension are possibly true of extension. | 3. Extension has no existence outside the mind. |
|---|---|---|

*Therefore*

| | | |
|---|---|---|
| Extension is not infinitely divisible. | There can be no proof that extension is infinitely divisible.[40] | Extension is not infinitely divisible. |

I confess that I find none of the arguments against infinite divisibility so-far canvassed persuasive. The supposed derivations of contradictions from the notion that a finite extension has infinitely many finite parts rest (in both Berkeley and Hume) upon a misunderstanding of limits. The arguments from minimal sensibles, even if considered phenomenologically correct, rely, in each case, on further principle that are themselves dubious. The attack on the demonstrative character of mathematics rests, at least as Hume states it, on a misunderstanding of the character of geometrical reasoning. In fact, I think that this literature contains only one interestingly strong argument against the proofs for infinite divisibility. Hume apparently missed it, or failed to appreciate it, in his first foraging trip through Berkeley's writings, but he alludes to it, without specific acknowledgment, in the *Enquiry*. We will look at it next.

## Diagrams as Signs

It is a persistent theme of Berkeley's writing that the learned, though not often the vulgar, are constantly misled by the false doctrine of abstract ideas. Abstract ideas were used, among other things, to explain the function of general terms. Roughly, singular terms were said to stand for particular ideas, whereas general terms were said to stand for abstract ideas.[41] Berkeley objected to this on the grounds that there are no abstract ideas. Every idea of a triangle must be either scalene, right or obtuse, and no idea of a triangle can be more than one of these. In sum, for Berkeley, every idea must be a coherently determinate particular. How then do general terms achieve their generality? Berkeley's answer is that terms become general, not through their objects of reference, but through their modes of reference. General terms become general by indifferently referring to a range of particulars. Here I shall not comment on Berkeley's theory of general terms at large—there are troubles with it[42]—but concentrate on his application of these ideas to proofs involving geometric diagrams.

Proofs from diagrams are puzzling. We establish something concerning a particular diagram on a piece of paper and then conclude that the same conclusion holds for all like figures. What justifies this apparently hasty generalization? The abstractionist might answer that the drawing of a particular triangle is merely a convenient stand-in for our abstract idea of a triangle. Rejecting abstract ideas, Berkeley gives a wholly different account of the generality of proofs that rely on diagrams.

> [T]he particular lines and figures included in the diagram, are supposed to stand for innumerable objects of different sizes: or in other words, the geometer considers them abstracting from their magnitude: which does not imply that he forms an abstract idea, but only that he cares not what the particular magnitude is, whether great or small, but looks on that as a thing indifferent to the demonstration.[43]

Thus it is the way in which the diagram is employed, not its reference to some special kind of object, that gives it its generality. We could also say that a diagram is not a flawed attempt to picture an abstract idea, but instead a *sign* that can be successfully used to refer to indefinitely many particulars. Berkeley puts it just this way in Query #6 in the *Analyst*:

> Whether the diagrams in geometrical demonstrations are not to be considered as signs, of all possible finite figures, of all sensible and imaginable extensions or magnitudes of the same kind?

The expected answer to this question is yes.

But those who are under the influence of the theory of abstract ideas are liable to misunderstand the manner in which diagrams are employed.[44] Indeed, the tendency toward misunderstanding seems entirely *natural*, for

> a line in the scheme, but an inch long, must be spoken of, as though it contained ten thousand parts, since it is regarded not in it self, but as it is universal: and it is universal only in its signification,

whereby it represents innumerable lines greater than it self, in which may be distinguished ten thousand parts or more, though there may not be above an inch in it.

Then the key passage:

> After this manner the properties of the lines signified are (by a very usual figure) transferred to the sign, and thence through mistake thought to appertain to it considered in its own nature.[45]

Berkeley's point here is remarkably subtle. He is not simply saying, as Wittgenstein would,[46] that a misunderstanding of the way in which a sign functions can lead us to posit curious entities, for example, the abstract ideas of the conceptualist or the abstract particulars of the Platonic realist. He is further indicating that such misunderstandings can foster absurd views about objects right before our eyes: that, for example, we can be led to think that a one-inch line drawn on a page must be composed of infinitely many (mostly indiscernible) parts.

But even if Berkeley's arguments are remarkably subtle, are they sound? There are a number of things worth saying on this score. First, unlike his other arguments intended to show the absurdity of the notion of infinite divisibility, this argument does not depend upon misunderstandings of the notion of a limit. Second, unlike the argument from minimal sensibles, it does not rely on any of the dubious features of his general subjective idealist position. *Indeed, his argument can be stated, and for the most part is stated, in a way that is independent of his general immaterialist philosophical position.* Finally, unlike his other arguments, it is not intended to show that extension is only finitely divisible. Its point is wholly negative: it is intended to show that certain so-called proofs of infinite divisibility are not really proofs at all.

But isn't Berkeley wrong about this? Aren't the proofs from *The Port-Royal Logic* that we began with as forceful as any that can be imagined? Don't these proofs rest on their own bottoms? Consider the Port-Royal proof about the ship moving away over an infinitely flat plane. Doesn't that show that a line admits of infinitely many degrees of diminution and hence must be infinitely divisible? To answer this, it is important to see that this argument is not a proof or demonstration in the sense that the standard derivation of, say, the Pythagorean Theorem is a proof or demonstration. In that case the formula for the Pythagorean Theorem is the last step in the derivation; it occurs as a line in a proof. Here, instead, we are presented with a vivid example which tempts us to view things in a certain way. The fact that, presented with this picture, we are strongly inclined to accept the conclusion that a line is infinitely divisible does not convert the reasoning into a geometrical derivation. Furthermore, if Berkeley is right, he has explained, and explained away, this temptation.[47]

## Countering the Indirect Proofs of Infinite Divisibility

We saw at the beginning that two sorts of mathematical proofs were available for the infinite divisibility of lines: some of these arguments involved geometrical constructions of the kind that we have just been examining; others involved indirect proofs that depended upon showing the absurdity involved in the supposition of only *finite* divisibility. We can begin with the first argument mentioned, that is, if lines were only finitely divisible, then, *per impossibile*, the diagonal of a square would be commensurate with its sides.[48]

To examine possible responses, let me fill out this argument in detail. If a line were composed of finitely many *equal* minimum parts, then, so the argument goes, the diagonal would have some finite number of such parts $d$, and the sides would have some finite number of such parts $s$. The ratio between them would be the rational fraction $d/s$. We know from the Pythagorean Theorem that the ratio of the diagonal of a square to its sides is the square root of 2 to 1. We also know from a famous proof that the square root of 2 is irrational, that is, it cannot be expressed as a rational fraction. Thus the doctrine of finite divisibility seems to be in conflict with at least one central theorem of classical mathematics.

As far as I know, Berkeley never discusses this argument for infinite divisibility in the writings he published, but in the *Philosophical Commentaries* he discusses it explicitly and at length. In an early entry he asks himself whether the incommensurability of the diagonal with the side is consistent with his principle. Two hundred thirty-six entries later he declares flatly:

> The Diagonal is commensurable with the Side.[49]

But if Berkeley is going to maintain this thesis, something in the classical line of reasoning sketched above must be rejected. At one point he attacks the Pythagorean Theorem, saying:

> One square cannot be double of another. Hence the Pythagoric Theorem is false.[50]

This, in fact, is a straightforward consequence of Berkeley's position, but it may help to begin with an easier case. For Berkeley, any diagram that is actually drawn must have commensurable components.

> Diagonal of particular square commensurable with its side they both containing a certain number of M: V: [that is, minimal visibles].[51]

This is a fact that will hold quite generally for all figures; for example, there must be a rational ratio between the diameter and the circumference of a circle. From this it follows that actual figures never exemplify a true square with its diagonal perfectly inscribed. If the square is perfect, then the actual diagonal must either fall short of one of the corners of the square or overshoot it. If the diagonal does not overshoot or undershoot the corners, then the square cannot be perfect. These results may seem outrageous, but they are, after all, natural consequences of the doctrine of minimal sensibles. And now we can see why the Pythagorean Theorem must be false. Just as there cannot be true squares with exactly inscribed diagonals, there cannot be squares corresponding to every possible area. For example, there could not be a square composed of 137 minimal visibles, since 137 does not have an integral square root.[52]

It is clear from a number of passages in his *Philosophical Commentaries* that Berkeley was not shy about embracing such results. There, we find him making remarks of the following kind:

> It seems that all lines can't be bisected in 2 equall parts. Mem: to examine how the Geometers prove the contrary.[53]

If a line were composed of an odd number of MV's, then it would not be possible to divide it into two equal parts. Or again:

> It seems all Circles are not similar figures there not being the same proportion betwixt all circumferences & their diameters.[54]

That is, those things that we commonly and, for Berkeley, *rightly* call circles will not all be strictly congruent because of the constructive constraints put on figures by minimal visibles. Anyway, Berkeley's fundamental argument is that these proofs that appeal to incommensurability cannot be used to prove that extension is infinitely divisible, since the possibility of constructing lines, areas, etc., of any assignable size and shape presupposes that infinite divisibility is possible and thus cannot be used to prove it.

> Mem. To Enquire most diligently Concerning the Incommensurability of Diagonal & side. whether it Does not go on the supposition of unit being divisible ad infinitum, i.e. of the extended thing spoken of being divisible ad infinitum (unit being nothing also V. Barrow Lect. Geom:). & so the infinite [divisibility] deduc'd therefrom is a petitio principii.[55]

## Physical Space vs. Pure Space

Still, isn't it just obvious that a line is infinitely divisible, for if we cut it in half, there will always be something left over to cut in half again?[56] But is that even true? With a pencilled line we finally get down to gaps between the pieces of graphite, and whatever method is used to produce the line, we will finally arrive at atomic gaps where there is nothing available to divide. And this is precisely how Berkeley can deal with Barrow's concentric circle argument for infinite divisibility.[57] Given two concentric circles, Barrow tells us, in effect, that we can put the points on the outer circle into one-to-one correlation with the points on the inner circle by drawing lines from the outer circle through the inner circle to the common center. This, he maintains, would not be possible if these circumferences contained only finitely many points. For Berkeley this is false, and just obviously false, for when we actually attempt to perform this feat, with a pencil however sharp, we discover that the lines merge together before they reach the center point.

To this, the defender of infinite divisibility will reply that it is not the *physical* lines that are here in question, but the pure widthless *mathematical* lines. Berkeley, of course, will have none of this:

> The Mathematicians think there are insensible lines, about these they harangue, these cut in a point, at all angles these are divisible ad infinitum. We Irish men can conceive no such lines.[58]

## Conclusion

I do not want to take sides on this debate, but it should be clear that those who maintain that segments of extension are infinitely divisible (whether they are exemplified or not) are thereby committing themselves to the existence of Platonic abstract particulars. Or, to take sides a bit, it is not implausible to suppose that the question whether *physical space* is infinitely divisible is an empirical question, albeit a high-level, theory-laden empirical question. If in response it is argued that *pure space*, at least, is infinitely divisible, then we are owed an explanation of the nature of pure space and a further explanation of its relation to physical space. Now the burden of embarrassment shifts from Berkeley's shoulders to those of his opponents.

My own inclination is to think the question *Is extension infinitely divisible?* has a clear sense only when it is interpreted as meaning *Is physical space infinitely divisible?* and that question in turn expands into the further question: *What kind of mathematics is needed to generate the best theory of physical reality?* So far, the answer seems to be that the real number system forms part of the system that provides the most adequate interpretation of physical reality. That, of course, carries the implication that physical space is, after all, infinitely divisible. Still, this thesis about physical space cannot be established by the kind of *a priori* arguments that Berkeley rejected. My tentative conclusion is that Berkeley may well have been wrong in denying that physical space is infinitely divisible,[59] but he was surely right in denying that this thesis can be established using the traditional proofs for infinite divisibility of the kind we have examined.[60]

## NOTES

1. See Pierre Bayle's "Zeno of Elea," in his *Historical and Critical Dictionary*, translated with an introduction and notes, by Richard Popkin (Indianapolis, Ind.: Bobbs-Merrill, 1965).

2. *The Port-Royal Logic*, translated with introduction, notes, and appendix by Thomas Spencer Baynes, B.A., 2nd ed., enlarged (Edinburgh, Scotland: Sutherland and Know, 1851), pp. 307–308.

3. Bayle rejected this argument because he held that the notion of infinite divisibility leads to absurdities of its own. That is, he held that *divisibility* itself (whether finite or infinite) leads to absurdity. *Op cit.*, p. 366.

4. *The Port-Royal Logic*, p. 306.

5. *Ibid.*, p. 306.

6. *Ibid.*, pp. 306–307.

7. Isaac Barrow, *The Usefulness of Mathematical Learning Explained and Demonstrated: BEING MATHEMATICAL LECTURES READ IN THE PUBLIC SCHOOLS AT THE UNIVERSITY OF CAMBRIDGE.* Translated by the Reverend Mr. John Kirkby (London, England: Stephen Austin, 1734), p. 154. These lectures were presented at Cambridge University in the years 1664–66. They were first published, in Latin, in 1683.

A similar argument turns on the consideration that a set of lines parallel to one side of a square will put the adjoining sides of the square in one-to-one correlation with its diagonal. This suggests, though the argument demands elaboration, that the atomist is committed to holding that the diagonal of a square is equal in length to the side of a square. Richard Sorabji has found this argument in the writings of the ninth-century Islamic philosopher Nazzam. See his *Time, Creation and the Continuum* (Ithaca, N.Y.: Cornell University Press, 1983), pp. 391–393.

8. Hume cites this argument in the *Enquiry Concerning Human Understanding*. Introduction and Analytical Index by L.A. Selby-Bigge, 3rd ed., with text revised and notes by P.H. Nidditch (Oxford, England: Oxford University Press, 1975), pp. 156–157.

9. In recent years there has been rising interest in infinity, the contin-

uum, and related topics as they were discussed in ancient and medieval times. Two works that provide an excellent entry into this field of philosophical scholarship are *Infinity and Continuity in Ancient and Medieval Thought*, edited by N. Kretzmann (Ithaca, N.Y.: Cornell University Press, 1982); and Richard Sorabji, *Time, Creation and the Continuum* (n. 7 above).

10. Aristotle's argument appears in various places, for example, *Categories* 4b22ff.; *Physics* V 3 and VI 1; *De gen. et corr.* I 2. These passages are conveniently collected in Appendix A in N. Kretzmann, ed., *Infinity and Continuity* (n. 9 above).

11. For Bayle, *op cit.*, pp. 361–364.

12. Titi Lucreti Cari, *De Rerum Natura*, edited and translated by Cyril Bailey, 3 vols. (Oxford, England: Clarendon Press, 1947) I, pp. 615–618, emphasis added.

13. Epicurus, *Letter to Herodotus*, p. 57.

14. For a superb discussion of Zeno's Paradoxes and the role they played in arguments against infinite divisibility, see Richard Sorabji, *Time, Creation and the Continuum* (n. 7 above), in particular Chapters 21 and 22.

15. The first argument is found in *A Treatise of Human Nature*, Analytical Index by L. A. Selby-Bigge, 2nd ed., with text revised and notes by P. H. Nidditch (Oxford, England: Oxford University Press, 1978), p. 44. The second argument is found in the *Enquiry*, p. 157.

16. *Letter to Herodotus*, p. 58. For a discussion of Epicurus' appeals to minimal sensibles, see Sorabji, *op cit.*, pp. 371–372.

17. *Treatise*, p. 27.

18. *Ibid.*, pp. 27–28.

19. *Ibid.*, p. 29.

20. *Ibid.*

21. *Ibid.*, 30n.

22. *Ibid.*, p. 32.

23. *Ibid.*, p. 32. Writers who have compared Epicurus and Hume on minimal extensions sometimes ignore Hume's second argument from minimal sensibles. Sorabji, for example, claims that Epicurus' appeal to minimal sensibles was "intended to show how conceptually indivisible parts are *possible*, rather than to prove that they actually exist"; adding that "this makes Epicurus' argument differ at this point from those of Berkeley and Hume. Both of these thinkers argued from a minimum extension in our ideas to the conclusion that there must be, not merely that there can be, a minimum conceivable extension in reality" (*op cit.*, p. 72). Now in his first argument Hume does appeal to the existence of minimal perceivables to establish the *existence* of minimal extensions, but in this second argument

they are invoked only to establish the *possibility* of minimal extensions. Hume then attempts to exploit the possibility of minimal extensions in a way *not* found in Epicurus, that is, to refute intended demonstrations of infinite divisibility.

Again, in the tenth chapter of his *Two Studies in the Greek Atomists* (Princeton, N.J.: Princeton University Press, 1967), David J. Furley elegantly details a wide range of similarities between the atomistic treatment of space and time found in Epicurus and in Hume. He does not, however, discuss Hume's second argument from perceptual minima and for this reason does not recognize at least one of the important differences between the treatment of indivisibles in Epicurus and Hume.

24. *Ibid.*, p. 32.

25. *Ibid.*, pp. 44–45.

26. *Ibid.*, pp. 50–51.

27. See, for example, C. G. Hempel's classic paper "Geometry and Empirical Science," *American Mathematical Monthly* 52 (1945).

28. This is not the same as saying that they are empirical truths *because* they are contingencies.

29. *Enquiry*, p. 25.

30. *Ibid.*, p. 157.

31. *Ibid.*, 158n.

32. *Ibid.*

33. *Ibid.*

34. In his correspondence, Hume mentions an apparently completed brief treatise on mathematical and physical subjects, but it was never published, and is now lost. Thus in a letter to Andrew Millar written 12 June, 1755, he speaks of a work containing "Considerations previous to Geometry and Natural Philosophy." More than sixteen years later (on 25 January, 1772) he speaks of apparently the same work in a letter to William Strahan referring to it by the title *On Metaphisical Principles of Geometry*. Both letters are found in *The Letters of David Hume*, edited by J. Y. T. Greig (Oxford, England: The Clarendon Press, 1932). Don Garrett pointed out these references to me.

35. *Treatise*, p. 17. Remarkably, there are only two references to abstract ideas or abstracting in the *Enquiry Concerning Human Understanding* (the other is on pages 154–155). An entire section is dedicated to this topic in the *Treatise*, and Hume returns to the topic in a number of places later in that work.

36. Quotations from Berkeley's writings come from *The Works of George Berkeley*, edited by A. A. Luce and T. E. Jessup, 9 vols. (London, England: Nelson, 1947–48). Citations are given to the sections of various works using the following abbreviations: *P* for *A Treatise Concerning the*

*Principles of Human Knowledge, PC* for *Philosophical Commentaries*, and *A* for *The Analyst.* I have also profited from the citations and cross-references in A. A. Luce's editio diplomatica of the *Philosophical Commentaries* (London, England: I. Nelson & Sons, 1955).

37. *P*, #128.

38. *P*, #124. Berkeley had a remarkable response to those who argued that microscopes showed that objects are composed of unobservable parts. First, he recognized a threat from that direction, saying, "They who knew not [magnifying] Glasses had not so fair a pretense for Divisibility ad infinitum" (*PC*, #237). That is, those who have not viewed things under magnifying glasses would not be misled into thinking that such magnification could be carried on indefinitely, revealing more and more minute parts, thus showing that a line, for example, is infinitely divisible. Berkeley's rejoinder is that the line seen with the naked eye is not numerically identical with the line seen under the magnifying glass (see *PC*, #249). In *A New Theory of Vision*, he puts the matter this way: "A microscope brings us as it were into a new world: it presents us with a new scene of visible objects, quite different from what we behold with the naked eye" (#LXXXV).

39. *P*, #124.

40. In this argument Berkeley does not consider the possibility that God, at least, may comprehend extension as infinitely divisible. His response, I think, would be that such a speculation should be dismissed as unintelligible. We have no idea of something being infinitely divisible, and, where an idea is wanting, thought about it is impossible.

41. Locke, who is the specific target of Berkeley's attack on abstract ideas, is not treated altogether fairly by him.

42. In particular, in its attack on abstract ideas, it relies heavily on an imagist account of concepts.

43. *P*, #126. Berkeley first makes this same point in ##15 and 16 of the Introduction.

44. See Query 7 in the *Analyst*.

45. *P*, #126. Query 17 in the *Analyst* makes the same point this way: "Whether the considering geometrical diagrams absolutely or in themselves, rather than as representatives of all assignable magnitudes or figures of the same kind, be not a principal cause of the supposing finite extension infinitely divisible; and of all the difficulties and absurdities consequent thereupon?"

46. The remarkable similarity between Berkeley's and Wittgenstein's treatments of mathematics is obvious. ##119–122 of the *Principles*, which concern arithmetic, is similarly very close to Wittgenstein.

47. Although this is not the place to go into detail, it is worth noting

that Berkeley takes essentially the same nominalistic approach to arithmetic. Here too he argues that philosophers have misunderstood the way mathematical signs, this time numerals, function.

> In *arithmetic*, . . . we regard not *things* but the *signs*, which nevertheless are not regarded for their own sake, but because they direct us how to act with relation to things, and dispose rightly of them. . . . [T]hose things which pass for abstract truths and theorems concerning numbers, are, in reality, conversant about not object distinct from particular numeral things, except only names and characters which originally came to be considered, on no other account but their being *signs*, or capable to represent aptly, whatever particular things men had need to compute. Whence it follows, that to study them for their own sake would be just as wise, and to as good a purpose, as if a man, neglecting the true use or original intention and subserviency of language, should spend his time in impertinent criticisms upon words, or reasonings and controversies purely verbal. (*P*, #122)

I think that this passage has a deep point hidden under a more superficial point. The more superficial point is that mathematicians waste their time when they attempt to establish truths of pure mathematics. The proof, for example, that there is no greatest prime may be both elegant and ingenious but will serve no useful purpose in "directing us how to act with relations to things and of disposing rightly of them." The deeper point is that arithmetic has no subject matter of its own in the sense of a system of *entities* somehow beyond particular signs and the things enumerated by these signs. Just as with geometry, the assumption that such special mathematical entities must exist is the result of misunderstanding the way in which certain mathematical signs function, a misunderstanding seconded by the faulty doctrine of abstract ideas.

48. The second indirect proof in *The Port-Royal Logic*, though different in detail, turns on the same basic consideration, that is, that the square root of 2 is irrational. If a square number, that is, a number with an integral square root, could be the double of another square number, then the following equation would hold: $x^2 = 2y^2$. Solving for $x$, we get that $x = y^* \sqrt{2}$. Since the square root of 2 is irrational, $x$ can have no integral solutions. But, and this begins the *reductio*, if extension were only finitely divisible, then every area would be composed of only finitely many minimal areas and there would, *per impossibile*, be an integral solution to this equation. (Incidentally, this argument fails because it turns on the assumption that there must be a square corresponding to every assignable area. A believer in minimal extension would deny this—a point that will become clear when we examine the simpler argument concerning the incommensurability of the diagonal of a square with its sides.)

49. *PC*, #264.

50. *Ibid.*, #500.

51. *Ibid.*, #258.

52. Actually, there is a problem here that Berkeley was aware of but does not face up to: what are the *shapes* of minimal visibles? Could they come in a variety of shapes? If they are square, for example, then squares of various sizes, but not all sizes, could be built up of them, but, of course, no true triangles or circles could be constructed.

53. *Ibid.*, #276.

54. *Ibid.*, #340.

55. *Ibid.*, #263. The text actually reads "the infinite *in*divisibility deduc'd therefrom is a petitio principii." This is obviously a slip, since the text makes no sense read that way.

56. The *Port-Royal* logicians put it this way: "there is nothing more clear than this principle, *that two non-extensions cannot form an extension*, and that an extended whole has parts. Now, taking two of these parts, which we assume to be indivisible, I ask, whether these have extension, or whether they have not? If they have, they are therefore divisible, and have many parts: if they have not, they are two negations of extension, and thus it is impossible for them to constitute an extension." (*Op cit.*, 306).

57. Berkeley cites this proof at *PC*, #315.

58. *PC*, #393.

59. In denying the existence (and intelligibility) of what philosophers call matter (or corporeal substance), Berkeley was not, of course, denying the existence of physical space. Berkeley, along with others, thought, for example, that Dublin was some distance from London.

60. My colleagues Timothy Duggan and Richard Kremer have made a great many important suggestions concerning this paper. I am also indebted to the editors of the *Philosophical Review* for their helpful suggestions.

# 4

# Hume and the Missing
# Shade of Blue

In the *Treatise* and then again (*verbatim*) in the *Enquiry*, Hume raises an objection to his thesis that every simple idea is derived from a simple impression.

> Suppose . . . a person to have enjoyed his sight thirty years, and to have become perfectly well acquainted with colours of all kinds, excepting one particular shade of blue, for instance, which it never has been his fortune to meet with. Let all the different shades of that colour, except that single one, be plac'd before him, descending gradually from the deepest to the lightest; 'tis plain, that he will perceive a blank, where that shade is wanting, and will be sensible, that there is a greater distance in that place betwixt the contiguous colours, than in any other. Now I ask, whether 'tis possible for him, from his own imagination, to supply this deficiency, and raise up to himself the idea of that particular shade, tho' it had never been conveyed to him by his senses? I believe there are few but will be of the opinion that he can; and this may serve as a proof, that the simple ideas are not always derived from the correspondent impressions; tho' the instance is so particular and singular, that 'tis scarce worth our observing, and does not merit that for it alone we should alter our general maxim. (p. 6)[1]

This passage raises two questions that are not directly answered in the text. The first, I think, has not been attended to enough:

"Hume and the Missing Shade of Blue," *Philosophy and Phenomenological Research*, Vol. XLV, No. 2 (December 1984). Reprinted by permission of the publisher.

Why is Hume confident that the imagination can supply this missing shade of blue? The second question has produced bewilderment, even indignation: Why is Hume completely undisturbed in acknowledging this counter-example to what he has called "the first principle I establish in the science of human nature"? (p. 7). I shall offer an answer to the first question that, I believe, provides a basis for answering the second.

# I

Hume offers an inductive argument in behalf of the claim that all simple ideas (in their first appearance) are derived from corresponding simple impressions. We find a constant conjunction between resembling perceptions that "is convincing proof, that one are the causes of the other" (p. 5) and since the impressions (i.e., the more lively perceptions) are uniformly prior to the corresponding ideas (i.e., the less lively perceptions), we may conclude that our impressions are the *causes* of the corresponding ideas, and not conversely. To confirm this general principle, Hume cites what he calls "a plain and convincing phenomenon," namely, "where-ever by an accident the faculties, which give rise to any impressions, are obstructed in their operations, as when one is born blind or deaf; not only the impressions are lost, but also their correspondent ideas" (p. 5). To this he adds, "Nor is this only true, where the organs of sensation are entirely destroy'd, but likewise where they have never been put in action to produce a particular impression. We cannot form to ourselves a just idea of the taste of pine-apple, without having actually tasted it" (p. 5).

Now Hume's concession concerning the missing shade of blue forces him to acknowledge that the first principle he has established does not hold universally, for under certain specifiable conditions it seems possible for a simple idea to first emerge without being caused by a corresponding simple impression. Of course, this principle might still be said to be *generally* true and, indeed, be sufficiently exceptionless to serve as a useful guide for inquiry. But, as Robert Cummins has shown,[2] we cannot let matters rest here. We are faced with the perplexing question of how *Hume's concession*, as Cummins calls it, squares with Hume's other more specific claims. First, Hume has told us that a person lacking the appropriate organ of sense must lack the relevant set of ideas, but if the imagination can, of itself, produce a single simple idea, why can it not produce a whole system of such ideas? Hume's second confirming consideration is more perplexing still. We are told that we "cannot form to ourselves a just idea of the taste of a pine-apple" unless we have first (by tasting one) received the corresponding impression of this flavor. What makes these two simple ideas so different, such that the one could be called up by the imagination whereas the other could not?

To answer these questions, we must take a fresh look at Hume's views on perception and, in particular, be careful not to impose an atomistic interpretation on his position without textual support. Now atomism can mean various things, and in certain respects Hume certainly is an atomist. But an atomist in *perceptual* theory would deny the existence of any structure below the lowest level of the perceptual ontology and thus would hold that each simple impression is a pure content standing in no systematic relationship to any other simple impression except for being qualitatively identical with it or simply qualitatively different from it. From this it would follow that only *complex* ideas could enter into *degrees* of resemblance, e.g., the complex *ABC* would resemble the complex *ABD* more than the complex *ADE* in virtue of sharing more constituents with it. Given this kind of atomism, there would be no reason to suppose that the imagination could supply the missing shade of blue, for a particular shade of blue would stand in no closer relationship to another shade of blue than it would, for example, to the taste of a pineapple.

Hume's discussion of the missing shade of blue shows that he does not accept such a theory of perception, but it is not easy to find a clear statement of his positive views on these matters. In the body of the text he speaks metaphorically about the relationship between simple and complex ideas as a relationship between wholes and parts. He says very little, however, about the relationships that might exist between various simple ideas. The one place that he addresses himself explicitly to this problem is in the Appendix to the *Treatise*, where he is concerned with the following problem: how can there be resemblances and, indeed, degrees of resemblances between simple ideas. Here is what he says:

'Tis evident, that even different simple ideas may have a similarity or resemblance to each other; nor is it necessary, that the point or circumstance of resemblance shou'd be distinct and separable from that in which they differ. *Blue* and *green* are different simple ideas, but are more resembling than *blue* and *scarlet*; tho' their perfect simplicity excludes all possibility of separation or distinction. 'Tis the same case with particular sounds, and tastes and smells. These admit of infinite resemblances upon general appearance and comparison, without having any common circumstance the same. And of this we may be certain, even from the very abstract terms *simple idea*. They comprehend all simple ideas under them. These resemble each other in their simplicity. And yet from their very nature, which excludes all composition, this circumstance, in which they resemble, is not distinguishable nor separable from the rest. 'Tis the same case with all the degrees in any quality. They are all resembling, and yet the quality, in any individual, is not distinct from the degree. (p. 637)

This passage raises issues of two different kinds. Briefly, one turns upon an apparent paradox generated by the notion of a simple idea. Simplicity is, in the language of the schoolmen, a transcendental concept, and we fall into confusion if we misunderstand the distinctive features of such concepts. In particular, it seems that every simple idea must be complex. For example, the simple idea of a particular shade of blue seemingly has at least *two* qualities — its determinate hue and its simplicity — hence it must be complex. In response, Hume just says that this "circumstance" of being simple is "not distinguishable nor separable, from the rest." He does not say why, but he seems to be alluding to what he elsewhere calls distinctions of reason.

More important for our present purposes is the remark that Hume makes about *material* similarities among simple ideas. Blue and green resemble each other, but they do so without having anything in *common* in virtue of which this resemblance holds. Furthermore, blue and green are more resembling than blue and scarlet even though there is no third thing that blue and green share more of than blue and scarlet.

Thus for all of Hume's talk about ideas being separate and loose, he views the perceptual field as exhibiting a system of internal relationships that are not further reducible to more primitive perceptual contents. Distinct simple ideas may resemble each other, and this resemblance admits of degrees. Colors, for example, can be more or less perceptually distant from each other without there being any "third ingredient" whose variation explains this distance. As we shall see in a moment, Hume's discussion of the missing shade of blue depends upon a recognition of this perceptual distance.

A further feature of Hume's understanding of perception does have an atomist quality: he holds that the color spectrum is composed of *distinct* hues. This is shown by the passage that immediately precedes the discussion of the missing shade of blue.

> I believe that it will readily be allow'd, that the several distinct ideas of colours, which enter by the eyes, or those of sounds, which are convey'd by the hearing, are really different from each other, tho' at the same time resembling. Now if this be true of the different colours, it must be no less so of the different shades of the same colour, that each of them produces a distinct idea, independent of the rest. For if this shou'd be deny'd, 'tis possible, by the continual gradation of shades, to run a colour insensibly into what is most remote from it; and if you will not allow any of the means to be different, you cannot without absurdity deny the extremes to be the same. (pp. 5–6)

The passage states that an individual color is made up of a set of distinct hues. It seems a plain implication of the passage that there will be *finitely* many hues associated with each color. I do not think that Hume would entertain the thought that the mind is capable of discerning indefinitely many different hues for each color, for this runs counter to his general commitment to minimal discernibles.

The argument Hume uses to establish this point is certainly curious. He argues that if a particular color were not a system of distinct and independent hues, then each hue would run insensibly into another and, ultimately, there would be no way of distinguishing any hue from any other. This argument turns upon the principle that not being discernibly different is a transitive relation: if $A$ is not discernibly different from $B$ and $B$ is not discernibly different from $C$, then $A$ is not discernibly different from $C$. Of course, that principle is just false. The differences between $A$ and $B$ on one hand and $B$ and $C$ on the other may fall below our threshold of discrimination, but the difference between *A* and *C* may lie above this threshold. Perhaps the reason that Hume does not see this is that he is thinking about the *ideas* of objects and not about objects themselves. In particular, he may hold that the notion of an indistinguishable difference between ideas makes no sense. There is nothing more to an idea than that which can be discerned within it. If this is Hume's position, then the notion that two ideas can be different without being discernibly different would be a contradiction in terms.

Whatever we might think of this account of perception, we are now in a better position to understand the character of the thought experiment that Hume has proposed. We are not to think of our simple ideas of colors as an unorganized set of wholly distinct entities. The various hues are internally related to one another in degrees of resemblance. Hume also takes it for granted that these internal relations form the linear ordering of a spectrum: each hue occupies a determinate location within a color space composed of distinct (and presumably finitely many) hues. One such hue can be noticeably absent. Given these surroundings, the imagination is not faced with the insuperable task of producing a brute content *ex nihilo*. To speak metaphorically, it is asked to produce a specific peg to fit a determinate hole provided for it. To speak somewhat less metaphorically, it would only have to give substance to a formally determinate apprehension.

Of course, the situation is totally different with the person blind from birth. Such a person (if Hume is right) has no access to the color field at all. Such a person would have to begin by producing an original brute datum *ex nihilo*—that is, without any guidance concerning what that datum should be like. The details of Hume's thought experiment also separate it from the taste-of-pineapple instance. Notice that Hume speaks carefully of a *just* idea of the taste of pineapple. A person might get some idea of the taste of pineapple by being told that it tastes a bit like a mixture of things he has tasted, say, apples and pine needles. Admittedly, this will not give an adequate or just idea of how a pineapple tastes, but it would be better than suggesting a mixture of chalk and benzene. (The fact that we can make even these gross comparisons shows that we have a least a rudimentary notion of a flavor field.) Now I think that Hume would willingly admit that, with sufficient previous experience with other tastes, a person might be able to form a reasonably adequate idea of the taste of pineapple through locating it within a flavor field or flavor space. The difference between the two cases is simply factual: with respect to flavors, we have had little experience corresponding to the highly structured presentation of a color spectrum.

# II

We can now turn to our second question: Given the fact that Hume has apparently found a counterexample to one of the fundamental theses of the *Treatise*, how can we account for the equanimity with which he treats it? Hume tells us that the instance "is so particular and singular, that 'tis scarce worth our observing, and does not merit that for it alone we should alter our general maxim." Prichard's response is worth repeating:

> It is really effrontery on [Hume's] part and not mere naiveness to ignore an instance so dead against a fundamental doctrine of his own. And if he had considered the idea of cause as also to be ignored as being an isolated exceptional case, he would have had no reason to write the *Treatise* at all.[3]

We can try to be more charitable. Looking ahead in the *Treatise*, we can notice the kinds of ideas that will attract Hume's attention. These will include our ideas of space and time, our ideas of causal relations and necessary connections, such philosophical ideas as substance and attributes, the plain man's idea of continued and distinct existence, our idea of personal identity, ideas of moral qualities and relations, ideas of property, etc. It is characteristic of Hume's discussion of all these topics to invite us "to turn the object on every side" to see if we can find simple ideas or complexes of simple ideas that correspond to these notions. It is also characteristic of his position to claim that no immediate candidate presents itself to play this role. What then follows is an elaborate associationalist account of how the imagination produces some counterpart idea, the nature of which is persistently misunderstood by both the plain man and the plain philosopher who have not taken the trouble to inspect the ideas associated with these notions. For example, it is altogether natural to suppose that a causal relation is a connecting link, a *nexus*, between two events. Inspection reveals no such link. Philosophers speak with ease about substances and their attributes, but examining our ideas of particular objects presents us with no content corresponding to the notion of substance. Plain men and philosophers alike suppose that moral attributes inhere in certain actions, yet when we inspect the actions, nothing is found corresponding to this notion of a moral attribute. What we do find in each case is an associated product of the imagination that is projected upon the object—a fact that is almost wholly unknown to the great mass of mankind who uniformly and almost universally are deluded on these matters.

But suppose someone were to argue, as both Thomas Reid and Richard Price did, that there are ideas whose content is not derived from sense. They are the product of an intellectual insight into *a priori* structures and their content is not sensible, but cognitive. And here Hume's critics can point to the example of the missing shade of blue (and also perhaps to distinctions of reason) as examples of such *a priori* insights.

To this Hume could reply, and I think with some force, that the instance of the missing shade of blue will not provide a model for the acquisition of these other ideas. Hume's counter example has two crucial features: (1) the idea in question is an instance of a *degree of some quality*, and (2) we have had impressions of contiguous instances of this quality. We must now inquire whether the ideas we have catalogued as central to Hume's concerns exhibit both of these features. It may be possible that such notions as substance, necessary connection, and specific moral relations do admit of degrees. Indeed, for some of these notions, though I do not think for all of them, it seems to make sense to speak of the degree to which one of these characteristics is present. Everyone speaks about obligations being more or less stringent, and philosophers, at least, have spoken about degrees of substantiality. So the first feature of Hume's counterexample does not clearly separate it from the ideas that are Hume's central concern. But the second feature of the counterexample plainly does. For example, if we have had past experience of necessary connections of varying degrees, then the imagination might, using this previous experience as its guide, supply one particular degree of necessary connection without having any antecedent impression of it. If we have had prior experience of various degrees of personal identity, then the imagination might be able to supply an idea of a particular degree of personal identity, again without ever having enjoyed an impression of that degree of personal identity. And so on. But it is Hume's contention that we have had no impressions of these kinds at all. For this reason, the *gap filling* feature of Hume's counterexample is missing.

I think that we are now in a better position to understand Hume's equanimity in dealing with the missing shade of blue. If he had so chosen he could have modified the maxim, "Every simple idea is derived from a simple impression," with the rider "except possibly for those cases where (1) we are dealing with a quality admitting of degrees, and (2) we have had suitably many impressions of other degrees of that quality." But such a modification would have a point only if the *Treatise* were to concern itself with similar phenomena, e.g., degrees of temperature or levels of pitch. Of course, the central topics of the *Treatise* are quite remote from phenomena of this kind. Since the relevant combination of circumstances will not reappear in the *Treatise*, the rider will not come into play and thus, having been recorded, may be safely set aside.

But Prichard's indignation may be a sign of a deeper worry and, with it, a deeper confusion. He speaks of the instance being "so dead against a doctrine of his [i.e., Hume's] own." Why should Prichard speak about a mere *limitation* of a principle in this way? The answer, I think, was that Prichard supposes that Hume was trying to delineate the *essential* features of the human mind and, if that was what Hume was trying to do, then a counterexample, however isolated, should really have forced him to rethink his entire position. And those who think that Hume was, perhaps without realizing it, offering an *analysis* of perceptual statements, may not join Prichard in accusing Hume of effrontery, but they will have to charge him with a profound misunderstanding concerning the status of his basic theses. But the plain fact is that Hume is presenting a causal thesis, and given his own account of causal relations, in particular, that, independent of experience, anything might be the cause of anything else, a charge of conceptual incoherence is out of place. Stroud makes the point this way:

To understand Hume's acceptance of the example one must remember that he puts forward his 'general maxim' that simple ideas are derived from simple impressions as a straightforward causal hypothesis. It is to be taken as contingent, as something that might well have been, or might even be found to be, false. But if there are exceptions it might well be possible to explain how they could occur without having to invoke any general principles that are not part of, or in line with, Hume's theory of mind.[4]

I think that this is precisely the right thing to say, but Stroud is diffident about suggesting how this exception can be explained in a way that coheres with the main features of Hume's system. Here it might help to describe the situation in general terms. Hume is committed to the following principles concerning causal relations between *perceptions*.

    I. A perception may be the cause of an exactly resembling perception. (A simple impression of sense causing a simple idea of sense provides an example.)

    II. A perception may be the cause of a fundamentally nonresembling perception. (An idea, either simple or complex, giving rise to a simple impression of reflection provides this example.)

Stated at this same level of generality, Hume's concession involves the acceptance of a further principle:

    III. A system of perceptions may give rise to an original perception that resembles these others, but not exactly.

Looked at this way, Hume's concession no longer strikes us as a radical departure from the fundamental principles of the *Treatise*. II reminds us that there is no *a priori* reason to suppose that those perceptions that enter into causal relations must resemble each other for, in fact, they often do not. The degree to which perceptions resemble those other perceptions they cause can only be established by an empirical inquiry. Nor is it in any way contrary to the spirit of the *Treatise* to suppose that a principle like I, in the context of other causal factors, could be modified to yield a principle like III. Indeed, the explanation of mental phenomena as the joint product of causal factors—the image of the composition of forces—is a fundamental theme of the *Treatise*. Hume's discussion of the missing shade of blue is just one of many illustrations of it.

## NOTES

1. All references to the *Treatise* are to the Selby-Bigge edition, revised by P. H. Nidditch (Oxford: Clarendon, 1978).

2. Robert Cummins, "The Missing Shade of Blue," *The Philosophical Review* 87 (October 1978): 548–65. I am indebted in many ways to this thoughtful and sophisticated article despite the fact that Cummins, it seems to me, imposes upon Hume the concerns of contemporary analytic philosophy. This comes out in the opening sentence, where he immediately gives the discussion a linguistic turn: "Hume is quite sure that blind persons cannot understand color-words." Although certain things that Hume says surely imply this, it is not something he ever says nor is it characteristic of Hume to pursue issues in these terms. For this reason I think that Cummins has offered an ingenious (and philosophically interesting) solution to a problem that Hume did not raise.

3. H. A. Prichard, *Knowledge and Perception* (Oxford: Clarendon, 1950), p. 177.

4. Barry Stroud, *Hume* (London: Routledge and Kegan Paul, 1977), p. 34.

# 5

# Hume's Worries
# about Personal Identity

In the Appendix to the *Treatise*, Hume tells us:

upon a . . . strict review of the section concerning *personal identity*, I find myself involv'd in such a labyrinth, that, I must confess, I neither know how to correct my former opinions, nor how to render them consistent. (633)[1]

Then, more specifically, he tells us:

[T]here are two principles, which I cannot render consistent; nor is it in my power to renounce either of them, viz. *that all our distinct perceptions are distinct existences*, and *that the mind never perceives any real connexion among distinct existences*. Did our perceptions either inhere in something simple and individual, or did the mind perceive some real connexion among them, there wou'd be no difficulty in the case. (636)

Well that is clear enough. Hume plainly finds his account of personal identity as presented in Book I, Part IV, Section VI of the *Treatise fundamentally* defective. What is not clear, and commentators have been sharply divided on this issue, is what precisely is bothering him. More specifically, no consensus has emerged concerning the nature of the inconsistency he here complains of. The only consensus that does exist is that Hume's own description of this inconsistency cannot be accepted at face value, for the two principles he cites are plainly not inconsistent with one another.

My previously expressed opinion was that the nature of Hume's worries cannot be established definitively simply because the text is underdetermined on the matter. The most we could do — I thought — was to offer hypotheses concerning things that Hume, on his own terms, *ought* to have been worried about and then tentatively attribute them to him if his position lacks the resources to deal with them.[2] That assessment now strikes me as unduly pessimistic. A careful reading of the text will direct us to the source of Hume's concerns, and having found the source of Hume's self doubts (as Don Garrett nicely calls them) we can characterize them with reasonable confidence.[3]

Now, very briefly, let me review the basic strategies that have been used for dealing with Hume's worries about personal identity. The first cut divides interpretations along the following lines:

1. Hume came to see that his theory demanded a real self as opposed to a fictitious self, and could find no way of supplying this need.
2. Hume found some fundamental flaw in his account of how the *fiction* of personal identity arises.

The first interpretation can be given a Königsbergean twist. It suggests that Hume came to see what Kant later said he should have seen, namely, that the manifold of experience can exist as someone's experience only in virtue of some unifying principle that runs through it, takes it up, and ties it together. What Hume needs, but cannot supply, is the "I think" that must accompany every representation. Put less teutonically, Hume constantly attributes activities to the mind, for example, comparing, combining, and separating ideas, which are actions that perceptions, bundled or unbundled, could not perform.

Since I have discussed this matter before, I will simply say, rather dogmatically, that no one to my knowledge has ever cited a text that shows Hume's worries took this form. However, there is at least one explicit text in which Hume confronts this issue and seems wholly unconcerned about it. "The mind," Hume tells us in a famous passage, "is a kind of theatre, where several perceptions successively make their appearance; pass, re-pass, glide away, and mingle in an infinite variety of postures and situations." Now this image of a theater naturally suggests that the mind is a spectator viewing its perceptions and we might wonder where such a spectator is placed within the Humean bundle of perceptions. Clearly aware of this difficulty, Hume explicitly warns his reader not to take his comparison in this light. "The comparison of the theatre," he tells us, "must not mislead us. *They are the successive perceptions only, that constitute the mind*"; (253, emphasis added). It was a central part of Hume's program to deny anything like a Cartesian ego, and I do not think that he ever went back on this.

On a second broad interpretation of Hume's concerns, his difficulties are located in giving an account of the fictitious unity and identity of the mind. This approach gains support from the exact wording of Hume's expression of his self doubts.

> [H]aving thus loosen'd all our particular perceptions, when[1] I proceed to explain the principle of connexion, which binds them together, and makes us attribute to them a real simplicity and identity; I am sensible, that my account is very defective. [footnote reference in Hume's text]

Of course, the attribution of a real simplicity and identity is, for Hume, a false attribution. Strictly speaking the bundle of perceptions lacks simplicity at a given time and identity over time. What needs explaining, according to this interpretation, are the mechanisms of association that lead us to make these false attributions to the self and, as it seems, Hume came to think that his explanation here was fundamentally defective.

On his own terms, Hume might well have worried about this problem. Broadly speaking, Hume accounts for the false attributions of simplicity and identity to both material objects and to the mind by an appeal to the associative principles of resemblance and causality. To cite just one difficulty, it is unclear, using an explanation of this kind, how an impression of sensation with a novel content gains membership in the bundle of perceptions. As an original impression, no other idea in the bundle is its cause, and if its content is sufficiently novel, then resemblance seems not to help either. I think, in fact, that this is a technical problem for Hume's program, but I do not think that it (or anything like it) is the source of Hume's worries. First, it is far from transparent that Hume's position lacks resources to deal with a problem of this kind. Second, and more to the point, the worries that Hume express in the Appendix seem to be of a global rather than of a technical kind. If Hume had had a specific worry of this kind, presumably he would have said so.

A suggestion of such a global worry has been made by Stroud in one way and Garrett in another.[4] It is that Hume came to realize that he was unable to *individuate* bundles, that is, he had no way of sorting perceptions into Smith's bundle and Jones' bundle. Or to turn to the first person, which is more characteristic of Hume's approach: there is no way, given the resources of the Humean position, to individuate a set of perceptions into my bundle as opposed to someone else's. Here an appeal to the principles of association based on the relations of resemblance and cause and effect seems not to work, for, as Stroud and Garrett see it, nothing blocks the possibility of these relations holding between perceptions in different minds.

Without going into details, it seems that Stroud and Garrett may have raised a serious problem for Hume's account of how we come to believe that mind is a unity at one time and preserves its identity over time. After all, given the explicit (theatre) statement cited above, Hume is not in a position to respond that he is only concerned with the perceptions in *his* mind, since (1) his mind is nothing beyond the perceptions that make it up, (2) there is nothing about the content of these perceptions that tag them as Hume's (or mine) rather than someone else's, and (3) perceptions in "different" minds can, as Stroud and Garrett seem to show, stand in just those relations of resemblance and causality that supposedly give rise to the unity and identity of an individual's mind.

I think that this is a deep criticism and it is suitably global. It is hard to see how Hume might go about answering it through refining his associationalist explanations. Nonetheless, I do not think that it *is* Hume's worry. Again he does not say so — admittedly a rather limited point since his own explanation of his concerns seems incoherent. More to the point, in the *Treatise* Hume is committed to a first-person introspective methodology that he accepts without question. The "mineness" of perceptions is simply something he takes for granted. In the present context he is asking "What keeps my perceptions *together*?" but he does not transpose this question into "What *makes* these perceptions mine?" That transposition is a modern innovation quite alien to Hume's way of doing business. Hume did not read Strawson.

In offering my own account of Hume's worries about personal identity, I am going to take a textual tour of Part IV of Book I of the *Treatise*. To fix our bearings, it might be useful to describe briefly how that portion of the text unfolds. The opening two sections present skeptical arguments directed, respectively, against the faculties of reason and the senses. The remainder of this part of the *Treatise* is largely an assault on the notion of substance. Section III, *Of the Antient Philosophy*, is an attack on the ancient notion of substance; Section IV, *Of the Modern Philosophy*, is an attempt to show, largely using Berkeleyan arguments, that our modern conception of material substances is no more intelligible than its ancient predecessor. Section V, *Of the Immateriality of the Soul*, is an attack on the modern/Cartesian notion of a thinking substance. Finally, in Section VI, *Of Personal Identity*, Hume offers an associationalist account of the origins of our false belief in the simplicity and identity of the self. This discussion closely parallels his earlier discussion, in Section III, of our propensity to falsely attribute simplicity and identity to material objects.

Throughout this discussion, the notions of identity and substance are closely connected. Actually, the relation of identity (over time) makes its first important appearance in the *Treatise* in Hume's discussion of the skepticism with regard to the senses. There Hume offers an associationalist account of the ingrained tendency to falsely attribute identity to distinct and interrupted perceptions—e.g., to the perception of my house in the morning and my perception of it in the evening. Here I naturally suppose that I am aware of the same thing when, in fact, I am aware of two distinct (sequences) of perceptions. Then in a marvelously original move, Hume argues that the philosopher's theory of double existence—what we now call representational realism—is an attempt to supply a surrogate for the vulgar notion of identity that sophistication has destroyed. The modern philosopher's notion of an external object is thus a fiction based on a fiction.

In the sections that follow, this same theme is developed with respect to the notion of substance. The philosopher's concept of substance is also a fiction that piggybacks on the vulgar fiction of identity over time. With material objects, inspection reveals no stability of qualities in virtue of which the object remains the same thing. The same is true of the qualities of the mind, i.e., of its perceptions. To avoid this unsettling discovery, the philosopher introduces substance as the unchanging substrate of the change. Substance, both material and mental, protects us from confronting the unbearable lightness of being.

To bring this digression to a close, setting aside the opening and closing sections, the central theme of Part IV of Book I is to deflate the metaphysical notion of substance by revealing it as a substitute, and a sorry one at that, for the vulgar fiction of identity. As such, it stands as a companion piece to Part III with its attack on the philosopher's notion of cause as a necessary connection between events. Taken together, they represent an assault on the twin pillars of rationalist metaphysics. If the destruction of rationalist metaphysics is a central theme of Book I of the *Treatise*, as it surely is, and if Hume attempts to achieve this by undermining the notions of substance and real connection, then it is clear why the two principles that Hume was unwilling to renounce in dealing with the problem of personal identity are central to his philosophical program.[5] But now back to that problem.

A clue to the correct account of Hume's worries about personal identity is given in the opening sentence of that part of the Appendix in which he expresses his dissatisfaction with his previous views on this subject:

> I had entertain'd some hopes, that however deficient our theory of the **intellectual world** might be, it wou'd be free from those contradictions, and absurdities, which seem to attend every explication, that human reason can give of the material world. (633)

This remark contains a specific allusion to an earlier discussion in the *Treatise*, but it is not to Hume's discussion of personal identity. The reference is to the section that immediately precedes it: *Of the Immateriality of the Soul*. That section begins with these words:

> Having found such contradictions and difficulties in every system concerning external objects, and in the idea of matter, which we fancy so clear and determinate, we shall naturally expect still greater

difficulties and contradictions in every hypothesis concerning our internal perceptions, and the nature of the mind, which we are apt to imagine so much more obscure, and uncertain. But in this we shou'd deceive ourselves. The **intellectual world**, tho' involv'd in infinite obscurities, is not perplex'd with any such contradictions, as those we have discover'd in the natural. What is known concerning it, agrees with itself; and what is unknown, we must be contented to leave so. (232)

This passage in turn refers back to the previous section (Book I, Part IV, Section IV, *Of the Modern Philosophy*) where Hume ends by saying that

there is a direct and total opposition betwixt our reason and our senses; or more properly speaking, betwixt those conclusions we form from cause and effect, and those that persuade us of the continu'd and independent existence of body. When we reason from cause and effect, we conclude, that neither colour, sound, taste, nor smell have a continu'd and independent existence. When we exclude these sensible qualities there remains nothing in the universe, which has such an existence. (231)

Hume opens Section V by assuring us that no like "contradictions and difficulties" will be found in examining what he calls the "intellectual world" (232). At the start of the Appendix entry we are examining, Hume specifically alludes to this passage and *specifically* reverses his position.

But the Appendix entry not only begins with an allusion to the opening paragraph in Section V, in rehearsing the arguments that induced him, as he says, "to deny the strict and proper identity and simplicity of a self or thinking being" (633), he actually repeats arguments that he previously used in Section V against those who held that the soul or self is a *substance*. Evidently Hume came to hold that the arguments that he had used against the substantiality of the self had a direct bearing on the identity and simplicity of the self as well. It will be useful, therefore, to look closely at these arguments.

In Section V, Hume maintained that contradictions arise in dealing with the intellectual world only through the imposition of philosophical categories alien to it. Thus the confident opening paragraph of this section is followed by this warning:

'Tis true, wou'd we hearken to certain philosophers, they promise to diminish our ignorance; but I am afraid 'tis at the hazard of running us into contradictions, from which the subject is of itself exempted. These philosophers are the curious reasoners concerning the material or immaterial substances, in which they suppose our perceptions to inhere. (232)

That is, we encounter contradictions in dealing with the intellectual world when—and seemingly only when—we apply the notion of substance to mental phenomena. As we shall see, in a crucial sense, Hume came to see that mental phenomena do have the status of mental substances.

In Section V, Hume offers a number of arguments against the doctrine that the soul is an individual or simple substance. Since only the first two are explicitly repeated in the Appendix, I will concentrate on them.[6]

1. In Section V Hume denies that we have an impression of a soul or mental substance and therefore concludes that we can have no idea of it either (232–233). That argument is repeated with respect to the self in the Appendix at (633) where he says that "we have no impression of self or substance, as something simple and individual. We have, therefore, no idea of them in that sense."

2. In Section V he argues that ideas themselves, strictly speaking, qualify as substances:

[S]ince all our perceptions are different from each other, and from every thing else in the universe, they are also distinct and separable, and may be consider'd as separately existent, and may exist separately, and have no need of any thing else to support their existence. They are, therefore, substances, as far as [the traditional] definition explains a substance. (233)

This argument is repeated at (634) where again Hume insists that ideas may themselves exist separately:

Whatever is distinct, is distinguishable; and whatever is distinguishable, is separable by the thought or imagination. All perceptions are distinct. They are, therefore, distinguishable, and separable, and may be conceiv'd as separately existent, and may exist separately, without any contradiction or absurdity.

In the Appendix, Hume dwells on this second argument, repeating it in a number of ways. The upshot is that, strictly speaking, individual perceptions have the status of individual substances. This is something he actually says in the process of making another point:

> Is *self* the same with *substance*? If it be, how can that question have place, concerning the subsistence of self, under a change of substance? If they be distinct, what is the difference betwixt them? For my part, I have a notion of neither, when conceiv'd distinct from particular perceptions.
>
> Philosophers begin to be reconcil'd to the principle, *that we have no idea of external substance, distinct from the ideas of particular qualities*. This must pave the way for a like principle with regard to the mind, *that we have no notion of it, distinct from the particular perception*. (635)

Read off the page, these passages do *not* say that we have no idea of mental substance: they tell us that we have no idea of mental substance *distinct* from particular perceptions that, as he has argued, themselves have the status of mental substances.

These reflections are confirmed, I think, by the following passage:

> We can conceive a thinking being to have either many or few perceptions. Suppose the mind to be reduc'd even below the life of an oyster. Suppose it to have only one perception, as of thirst or hunger. Consider it in that situation. Do you conceive any thing but merely that perception? Have you any notion of *self* or *substance*? If not, the addition of other perceptions can never give you that notion. (634)

We have to be careful in responding to the rhetorical question in this passage. I think that we are being asked whether we have any idea of self or substance *distinct from this particular perception*. The answer to that question must be no. The final sentence in the passage tell us that piling up further perceptions does not change the answer to this question. After interpolating some further considerations, Hume comes to the following summary conclusion:

> I have a notion of neither [*self* nor *substance*], when conceiv'd distinct from particular perceptions.

Now it is a plain implication of these passages that a bundle of perceptions is not strictly speaking a self but instead, strictly speaking, a bundle of selves. This follows from the fact that each individual perception is an utterly distinct existence and each individual perception — as a center of sentience — already counts as a self. Picking up Hume's own comparison, we can also say that each individual perception is, as it were, an individual substance, and, taken that way, the mind becomes a bundle of individual substances. I will call this the perception-as-substance argument.

We can now examine exactly how Hume expresses his worries concerning personal identity:

So far I seem to be attended with sufficient evidence. But having thus loosen'd all our particular perceptions, when[1] I proceed to explain the principle of connexion, which binds them together, and makes us attribute to them a real simplicity and identity; I am sensible, that my account is very defective, and that nothing but the seeming evidence of the precedent reasonings cou'd have induc'd me to receive it. [footnote reference in Hume's text]

The footnote after the word "when" refers to passages in Section VI where Hume begins to develop his positive (associationalist) account of how we falsely come to attribute a "real simplicity and identity" to the self. But before this, when he tells us that he has "thus loosen'd all our perceptions," he is referring to what I have called the perception-as-substance argument first presented in Section V. In the middle of the passage he tells us that he is sensible that his associationalist account of the "real simplicity and identity" of the self is "very defective" — though he has yet to say exactly why. Finally, he tell us that he accepted this associationalist account only because of the "seeming evidence of the precedent reasonings," where the precedent reasonings can be only what I have called the perception-as-substance argument drawn from Section V.

Hume then continues his reflections by sketching the associationalist view that he later came to think was "very defective":

If perceptions are distinct existences, they form a whole only by being connected together. But no connexions among distinct existences are ever discoverable by human understanding. We only *feel* a connexion or a determination of the thought, to pass from one object to another. It follows, therefore, that the thought alone finds personal identity, when reflecting on the train of past perceptions, that compose a mind, the ideas of them are felt to be connected together, and naturally introduce each other. (635)

Hume remarks that though "extraordinary," this conclusion "need not surprise us" since "most philosophers seem inclin'd to think, that personal identity *arises* from consciousness; and consciousness is nothing but a reflected thought or perception" (635).

So what is wrong? Hume gives his specific diagnosis of his problem in these words:

[A]ll my hopes vanish, when I come to explain the principles, that unite our successive perceptions in our thought or consciousness. I cannot discover any theory, which gives me satisfaction on this head. (635–636)

What that means is this: if our successive perceptions could be united in thought or consciousness, then we could understand how the *perceptions themselves* could be felt to be united. What now strikes Hume as incomprehensible is how perceptions themselves can be united in a single consciousness. That is mysterious for Hume because, given the clear implications of the arguments of Section V as drawn out in the Appendix, each individual perception is already a single (individual) consciousness. Furthermore, there is no such thing as consciousness independent of perceptions. That is a point that Hume makes quite explicitly earlier in the theatre passage already cited.

Notoriously, Hume describes his difficulties in these words:

In short there are two principles, which I cannot render consistent; nor is it in my power to renounce either of them, viz. *that all our distinct perceptions are distinct existences*, and *that the mind never perceives any real connexion among distinct existences*. Did our perceptions either inhere in something simple and individual, or did the mind perceive some real connexion among them, there wou'd be no difficulty in the case. (636)

Despite his exact wording, given what Hume will say later, he cannot mean that these two principles are contradictories of one another. The inconsistency he has in mind takes the following form: As Hume acknowledges, for perceptions to be associated with one another, they must be united in our thought or consciousness. Indeed, for his entire associationalist program to work, such a union of ideas in consciousness must be possible. Hume's difficulty is that the two principles he cannot renounce seem to preclude the only two ways that this could happen. Surely this is what he has in mind, for he goes on to say that someone, perhaps he himself at some later time, will hit on "some hypothesis" that will "reconcile those contradictions." If Hume's two principles were *formal* contradictories — which plainly they are not — then no hypothesis could reconcile them.

Hume's two principles raise another issue. The claim that *all our distinct perceptions are distinct existences*, in the strong sense needed for the present discussion, is the result of Hume's arguments in Section V. Where does the second principle, *that the mind never perceives any real connexion among distinct existences*, come from? That seems to be a simple transformation of an earlier claim that appears in various forms throughout the *Treatise*, namely, that the mind never perceives any real connection between distinct ideas. This, in turn, explains why causal relations, *in this context*, are not serviceable to meet Hume's demands. In Section VI Hume explained how causal relations could introduce associations, i.e., felt connections, between perceptions and thus produce the fiction of a self enduring over time. Has Hume fallen into an extraordinary state of amnesia in not recalling this earlier maneuver? No: in that earlier discussion Hume was trying to explain how individual perceptions could be felt to be connected one with another. There he held that perceptions that are constantly conjoined *in* consciousness are felt to be connected. In the present context he is asking a different and seemingly prior question: how are perceptions united in a single consciousness at all, so that, among other things, such associations can be established? A simple invocation of the earlier discussion of the role of causal associations in forming our conception of personal identity is thus out of place.

Now if we go all the way back to the beginning, we see that, in a

way, there is something right about what I have called the Königs-
bergian interpretation. What is lacking in Hume's approach, and
what he seemingly cannot get, is a single consciousness within
which associationalist principles can operate. But given his resolute
denial of anything like a Cartesian ego (which is one of the central
themes of his philosophy), the problem does not present itself to
him in this way. Instead, it emerges as a demand for a real connection between perceptions, which, as far as he can see, his own
theory cannot supply.

## NOTES

1. All references to the *Treatise* are to the Selby-Bigge edition, revised
by P. H. Nidditch (Oxford: Clarendon, 1978).

2. My earlier views, together with criticisms of competing interpretations, are found in Chapter VIII of *Hume's Skepticism in the Treatise of
Human Nature*, International Library of Philosophy (London: Routledge
and Kegan Paul, 1985).

3. Don Garrett offers a useful survey of recent positions taken on this
issue together with an interesting suggestion of his own in his "Hume's
Self Doubts About Personal Identity," *The Philosophical Review* Vol.
XC, no. 3. (1983).

4. See Barry Stroud, *Hume*, The Arguments of the Philosophers (London: Routledge and Kegan Paul, 1977), Chapter VI, and Don Garrett, *op
cit*.

5. To continue this digression in the safety of a footnote, earlier in the
*Treatise* (69) Hume divides all relations into two categories: those that
"depend entirely on ideas" and those that do not. In the second category
Hume places the relations of time and space, identity (over time), and
causation. Although the point is so obvious that someone has surely noticed it, I cannot recall anyone explicitly pointing out that the first book
of the *Treatise* is largely concerned with these three relations that cannot
be established simply through the comparison of ideas. Part II examines
the relations of space and time; causation is the central theme of Part III;
and problems concerning identity dominate the middle sections of Part
IV.

6. In his elaborate third argument, Hume challenges those who believe
that the soul is a *material* substance to explain how nonextended ideas can
be locally conjoined with an extended entity (234–239). In his fourth

argument, he challenges believers in an *immaterial* soul to explain how extended ideas — for Hume, ideas of extended things — can be locally conjoined with a soul that is nonextended. In *Hume's Skepticism* I speculated that Hume might have come to think that this problem of local conjunction could also raise difficulties concerning how these two sorts of ideas could be combined in a single bundle of perceptions. Perhaps Hume should have worried about this, but the text in the Appendix gives no suggestion that he did.

# 6

# What Hume Actually Said about Miracles

Two things are commonly said about Hume's treatment of miracles in the first part of Section X of the *Enquiry Concerning Human Understanding*:[1]

1. Hume did **not** put forward an *a priori* argument intended to show that miracles are not possible.
2. Hume **did** put forward an *a priori* argument intended to show that testimony, however strong, could never make it reasonable to believe that a miracle had occurred.

In a recent article in this journal, Dorothy Coleman calls this the "traditional interpretation," and since this characterization strikes me as correct, I shall call it that too.[2]

Antony Flew stands virtually alone in challenging the traditional interpretation, arguing, in particular, that Hume did not even attempt to provide an *a priori* argument showing that testimony can never establish the existence of a miracle. On Flew's reading, Hume's argument was intended to do no more than place a "check" on arguments put forward to establish the existence of miracles on the basis of testimony.[3] Along with others, however, Flew accepts the first part of the traditional interpretation, namely, that whatever Hume was up to, he was certainly not trying to produce a proof showing that miracles cannot exist. He endorses the first part of the traditional interpretation in these words:

"What Hume Actually Said about Miracles." *Hume Studies*, Vol. XVI, No. 1 (April 1990). Reprinted by permission of the publisher.

What [Hume] is trying to demonstrate a priori in Part I is: not that, as a matter of fact, miracles do not happen; but that, from the very nature of the concept — 'from the very nature of the fact' — there must be a conflict of evidence required to show that they do.[4]

In opposition to these united voices, I will argue that this consensus on the first part of the traditional interpretation is unfounded, for there are clear texts — at the very heart of Hume's discussion — that go dead against it.

Two passages, which occur in the same paragraph, are particularly relevant to this discussion:

Passage I. *A miracle is a violation of the laws of nature; and as a firm and unalterable experience has established these laws, the proof against a miracle, from the very nature of the fact, is as entire as any argument from experience can possibly be imagined.* (E 114, emphasis added)

Passage II. *There must . . . be a uniform experience against every miraculous event, otherwise the event would not merit that appellation. And as a uniform experience amounts to a proof, there is here a direct and full proof, from the nature of the fact, against the existence of any miracle; nor can such a proof be destroyed, or the miracle rendered credible, but by an opposite proof, which is superior.* (E 115, emphasis added in final clause)

The clause *nor such a proof be destroyed, or miracle rendered credible* in Passage II is crucial for our purposes, for it simultaneously expresses **two** claims which, for clarity's sake, I will state separately. First, when Hume speaks of *such a proof*, he is referring to the *direct and full proof, from the nature of the fact, against the existence of any miracle* mentioned in the first part of the same sentence. Thus, one thing that Hume is saying is this:

$C_1$: Nor can such a proof (against the existence of any miracle) be destroyed, but by an opposite proof which is superior.

He is also making the following claim:

$C_2$: Nor can such a miracle be rendered credible, but by an opposite proof which is superior.

Having sorted things out, it is now possible—using only direct quotations from the immediate text—to show that, contrary to the traditional interpretation, Hume does present an *a priori* argument against the existence of miracles.

### Argument One

1. *There is here a direct and full **proof**, from the nature of the fact, against the existence of any miracle; nor can such a proof be destroyed . . . but by an opposite proof, which is superior.* (E 115, from Passage II)
2. *The proof against a miracle, from the very nature of the fact, is as **entire as any argument from experience can possibly be imagined.*** (E 114, emphasis added, from Passage I)
Therefore:
3. *There is . . . a direct and full **proof**, from the nature of the fact, against the existence of any miracle.* (E 115)

The argument intended to show that the existence of a miracle can never be rendered credible has precisely the same general form.

### Argument Two

1. *There is here a direct and full **proof**, from the nature of the fact, against the existence of any miracle; nor can . . . [the] miracle be rendered credible, but by an opposite proof, which is superior.* (E 115, from Passage II)[5]
2. *The proof against a miracle, from the very nature of the fact, is as **entire as any argument from experience can possibly be imagined.*** (E 114, emphasis added, from Passage I)
Therefore:
3. *There is . . . a direct and full **proof**, from the nature of the fact, against . . . [the possibility that the] miracle [can be] rendered credible.* (E 115)

In both versions of the argument, the strong claim in the second premise that the proof against a miracle is as **entire** as any argument from experience can possibly be imagined cancels the possibility left open in the first premise that there might be *an opposite proof, which is superior.* The conclusion then follows at once. Both arguments have equal standing in the text, so it seems to me to be wholly implausible to attribute one argument to Hume but not the other, as, indeed, the traditional interpreters have done.

Since the stated text seems transparently clear in meaning, how have commentators been able to miss its plain import? The answer, I think, is that they have been misled by concentrating on an argument that appears in the paragraph immediately following the passages I have labelled Passage I and Passage II. There, at least, Hume unambiguously puts forward the thesis traditionally attributed to him:

> Passage III. *The plain consequence is (and it is a general maxim worthy of our attention), 'That no testimony is sufficient to establish a miracle, unless the testimony be of such a kind, that its falsehood would be more miraculous, than the fact, which it endeavors to establish.'* (E 115–16)

This passage does not, however, support the first thesis of the traditional interpretation, namely, that Hume did not put forward an argument intended to show that no miracle can exist; indeed, read in context, this passage goes against the traditional interpretation. It is important to see that Hume describes this thesis concerning testimony as *the plain consequence* of some other thesis, and that other thesis can only be the one just stated, namely that there is *a direct and full proof, from the nature of the fact, against the existence of any miracle.* Thus, contrary to the traditional reading, the text contains both a thesis denying the existence of miracles and a thesis denying the credibility of testimony in favour of miracles, and Hume explicitly describes the latter as a *consequence* of the former.

Flew, as noted above, distinguished himself from traditional interpreters by denying that Hume even put forward a thesis denying the credibility of testimony in favor of miracles. If it is not already clear, a very brief argument will show that he is wrong about this.

Passage III, in a way that parallels Passage II, contains the qualifying phrase, *unless the testimony be of such a kind, that its falsehood would be more miraculous, than the fact, which it endeavours to establish.* Now, I think that it would be altogether wrong, in fact would miss the whole drift of Hume's argument, to read this passage as leaving open the possibility that the falsehood of the testimony just might, on some occasion, be *more miraculous, than the fact, which it endeavours to establish*. Hume surely expects us to remember the claim made only a paragraph earlier that *the proof against a miracle, from the very nature of the fact, is as entire as any argument from experience can possibly be imagined*. Since on Hume's account the proof against the miracle derives from the same evidence that proves the law, he is surely inviting us to conclude that the falsehood of the testimony can never be more miraculous than the fact it endeavors to establish. Unpacked, this new argument differs from Argument Two only by making a specific reference to testimony rather than speaking more generally about credibility.

Having presented two arguments concerning miracles — one about their existence, the other about the credibility of the testimony on their behalf — Hume gives his argument one last rhetorical turn. Reflecting upon a possibility that runs **conceptually** counter to his previous commitments, he considers what consequences would follow **even if** the evidence on behalf of the miracle **were** superior to the evidence supporting the law. Concerning this possibility, he tells us,

> *even in that case there is a mutual destruction of arguments, and the superior only gives us an assurance suitable to that degree of force, which remains, after deducting the inferior.* (E 116)

We already know that there can be no proof of a miracle, for it is not possible for this proof to surpass the proof of the law of nature that it supposedly violates, but even if we suppose, just for the sake of argument, that the proof of a miracle did surpass the unsurpassable proof of the corresponding law, the evidence to support the existence of the miracle, Hume now tells us, could hardly have much strength once the contrary evidence that supports the law of nature is deducted from it.

What, then, did Hume actually say about miracles in Part I, Section X of the *Enquiry*? His reflections begin with the following leading premise:

> *[T]he proof against a miracle, from the very nature of the fact, is as entire as any argument from experience can possibly be imagined.* (E 114)

From this he concludes that

> *there is here a direct and full* **proof**, *from the nature of the fact, against the existence of any miracle.* (E 115)

This is Hume's first argument. He next uses this same leading premise to establish a further conclusion more narrowly focused on testimony:

> *[N]o testimony is sufficient to establish a miracle.* (E 115–16)

This follows, Hume thinks, because the evidence on behalf of a miracle can never surpass the evidence in favor of the corresponding law it supposedly violates. This is Hume's second argument. Finally, to give the argument one last turn, he notes that even if the evidence on behalf of the supposed miracle were superior to that in favor of the corresponding law, there must be a *mutual destruction of arguments* (E 116) leaving as a remainder only weak evidential support in favor of the occurrence of the miracle.

The two paragraphs spanning *Enquiry* 114–16 thus contain three distinct lines of argument: one against the possibility that a miracle can **exist**, one against the possibility of **establishing** the existence of a miracle, and one against the likelihood that an argument in support of the existence of a miracle could be **compelling**.[6] It seems to me that these three arguments appear in the text transparently. If so, the traditional reading of Hume's essay on miracles is wrong, and Flew, in rejecting the aspect of the traditional interpretation that is correct, is doubly wrong.

## NOTES

1. David Hume, *Enquiries Concerning the Human Understanding and Concerning the Principles of Morals*, ed. L. A. Selby-Bigge, 2nd ed. (Oxford, 1972). Further references ("E") will be given in parentheses within the body of the text.

2. Dorothy Coleman, "Hume, Miracles, and Lotteries," *Hume Studies* 14.2 (1988): 343, n. 4.

3. Antony Flew first put forward this view in "Hume's Check," *Philosophical Quarterly* 9 (1959): 1–18, and then developed it further in Chapter VIII of his *Hume's Philosophy of Belief* (Humanities Press: New York, 1961).

4. Flew, *Hume's Philosophy of Belief* (above, n. 3), 176.

5. The slight change in wording here and in the conclusion is forced by the lack of grammatical parallelism in Hume's own sentence. It in no way alters the sense.

6. Flew (above, n. 3), it seems, finds only the third argument in the text.

# 7

# Kant and Hume on Simultaneity of Causes and Effects

Among other things, Hume says:

> We may define a *cause* to be "An object precedent and contiguous to another, and where all the objects resembling the former are plac'd in like relations of precedency and contiguity to those objects that resemble the latter" (p. 170).[1]

Against this definition stand numerous examples of causes that are simultaneous with their effects rather than prior to them. Kant spoke of a ball resting on a cushion and thereby (simultaneously) causing a depression in it.

One strategy open to the friend of Hume is to grant the existence of these cases and then "patch up" the definition to accommodate them. But the matter is not simple. Given a regularity interpretation we must find some way of *distinguishing* cause and effect. If *A* and *B* stand in a causal relation, we must have some way of determining which is cause and which is effect. For Hume this is accomplished via the notion of priority, and if we delete this item, it is far from clear how this distinction can be restored. Speaking more generally, and a bit loosely, cases where the cause and effect are simultaneous suggest that there must be *more* to a causal relation than constant conjunction (and, perhaps, contiguity). Con-

"Kant and Hume on the Simultaneity of Causes and Effects," *Kant Studien*, Jahrgang 67, Heft 1 (1976). Reprinted by permission of the publisher.

stant conjunction and contiguity are symmetrical relations whereas causal relations are non-symmetrical.[2] Thus if we acknowledge instances where the cause and its effect are simultaneous, we will have to go beyond mere regularity to explain the directedness of this relationship. I think that this constitutes one of the deeper attacks upon Hume's position.

Hume seemed to recognize a threat from this direction, for he offered an ingenious argument intended to show that the cause must always be *prior* to its effect. This argument, as we shall see, is invalid and thus the threat remains unanswered. The task of this essay is to show that a plausible treatment of instances where causes are simultaneous with their effects is congruent (though not identical) with Hume's analysis of causal relations. In different words, I wish to show that on one reasonable approach, instances where the cause is simultaneous with its effects do not constitute a refutation of a regularity treatment of causal relations. The first task, then, is to present what I have called a reasonable account of instances where cause and effect are simultaneous.

Having cited Kant's example of the ball resting on the cushion, we can begin by examining his treatment of it:

> Now we must not fail to note that it is the *order* of time, not the lapse of time, with which we have to reckon; the relation remains even if no time has elapsed. The time between the causality of the cause and its immediate effect may be [a] vanishing [quantity], and they may thus be simultaneous; but the relation of the one to the other will always remain determinable in time. If I view as a cause a ball which impresses a hollow as it lies on a stuffed cushion, the cause is simultaneous with the effect. But I still distinguish the two through the time-relation of their dynamical connection. For if I lay the ball on the cushion, a hollow follows upon the previous flat smooth shape; but if (for any reason) there previously exists a hollow in the cushion, a leaden ball does not follow upon it.
>
> The sequence in time is thus the sole empirical criterion of an effect in its relation to the causality of the cause which precedes it.[3]

The opening sentence in this passage is disconcerting in suggesting that simultaneous events can be *temporally* ordered. Yet the remainder of the passage annuls this suggestion. The key is given in this sentence:

> The time between the causality of the cause and its immediate effect
> may be [a] vanishing [quantity], and they may be thus simultane-
> ous: . . .

Here the time in which the cause has its effect is taken as the
limit of a period of time that *precedes* (in part) the time in which
the effect takes place. Thus through a reference to a succession of
events, the causal ordering is established. This is the explicit point
of Kant's elucidation of his example:

> For if I lay the ball on the cushion, a hollow follows upon the
> previous flat smooth shape; but if (for any reason) there previously
> exists a hollow in the cushion, a leaden ball does not follow upon it.

Here the appeal to succession is transparent. The act of placing
a ball on the cushion is, in part at least, prior to the formation of
the hollow. If we now contract this event in the direction of its
completion, we arrive at the idea of the ball *being on the cushion*.
It is because the ball's being on the cushion is the terminus of its
being put there that we can treat them as similar cases and thus
bring the example under a law whose primary application is to
cases where we have a *succession* of events. About the only complaint we might have of Kant's treatment of this problem concerns
his needlessly dark suggestion that the example exhibits an order in
time without a lapse in time. He could just as well have said that
under special circumstances the direction of causation is preserved
even though temporal ordering—not just lapse—has simply van-
ished.

In the end, then, we must say something rather complicated
about cases where a cause is simultaneous with its effect. We must
first admit that sometimes a cause and its effect are cotemporary,
for here Kant's example and others like it are completely decisive.
At the same time we must admit that these cases of simultaneity
are parasitic upon cases that involve a genuine succession in time,
for without an appeal to cases of the latter sort there would be no
basis for counting one thing as a cause and another as its effect.
We must conclude, then, that causality *involves* a reference to
priority in the straightforward sense of *earlier than*, but the in-
volvement is not as straightforward as Hume's definition suggests.

I think it is also clear that an adjustment in this direction will not compromise the essential features of a Humean analysis of causal relations.

We are now in a position to examine a remarkable argument Hume presents in an effort to show that a cause and its effect are *never* cotemporary.

> 'Tis an established maxim both in natural and moral philosophy, that an object, which exists for any time in its full perfection without producing another, is not its sole cause; but is assisted by some other principle, which pushes it from its state of inactivity and makes it exert that energy, of which it was secretly possest. Now if any cause may be cotemporary with its effect, 'tis certain, according to this maxim, they must all of them so be; since any one of them, which retards its operation for a single moment, exerts not itself at the very individual time, in which it might have operated; and therefore is no proper cause. The consequence of this would be no less than the destruction of that succession of causes, which we observe in the world and indeed, the utter annihilation of time. For if one cause were cotemporary with its effect, and this effect with *its*, and so on, 'tis plain there would be no such thing as succession, and all objects must be co-existent. (p. 76)

Hume's argument, fully spelled out, looks like this:

Assumption:
Some causes *are* simultaneous with their effects.
Therefore:
All causes *could be* simultaneous with their effects.
Finally (via the "established maxim"):
All causes *are* simultaneous with their effects.

Since, in Hume's opinion, the conclusion runs counter to experience, we are invited to reject the assumption that heads the argument.

Our first instinct is to attack the argument at its final step, for there is something suspicious about the inference from *All causes could be* to *All causes are*. Yet the inference is at least plausible, for if we agree that causes have their effects *as soon as possible* (the "established maxim") then it does follow that if all causes could be simultaneous with their effects, then they would be. If we were arguing for the soundness of Hume's total argument, then we would have to exhibit more than the plausibility of this inference, but, as it is, the plausibility of the inference invites us to retreat one step to the point where a deeper conceptual issue presents itself.

The inference from the first claim to the second depends upon the assumption that simultaneous causation and successive causation are conceptually on a par. That is, we are asked to think of two *independent* kinds of causal relations, those where the cause and effect are successive and those where they are simultaneous. It is only on this assumption of conceptual independence that the generalization argument from *some are* to *all could be* is valid. But if we recall our previous conclusions — those derived from Kant — we see that this assumption of conceptual independence is false. Furthermore, the notion of a cause simultaneous with its effect is parasitic on the notion of a cause that precedes its effects, and so even if we could have a world where all causes precede their effects, we could not have a world where all causes are simultaneous with them. There could not be a world where all causes are simultaneous with their effects, for in such a world there would be no *basis* for distinguishing causes and effects.

It is now clear that the Kantian argument — or what I have called the Kantian argument — is bearing a heavy burden and it is time to examine it more closely. First a point of clarification. I am not merely saying that in such a world it would be impossible to know (or find out) which was cause and which was effect. I agree, of course, that in a world of this kind we could not obtain such knowledge, but this follows in a trivial way from the strong claim that I am making that there is nothing in the envisaged world that counts as cause or effect.

Once it is clear that my claim is not epistemological, it may seem less clear that it is true. Is it really impossible to conceive of a world where all causes are simultaneous with their effects? Consider a world of the following kind: we simply take our world — with a lead ball resting on a cushion — and stop all motion. Will it cease to be the case that the ball causes the depression in the pillow at the time of stoppage? Strangely, the answer seems to be *yes*. From the moment of universal freeze, objects that were previously falling will now hang motionlessly in the air and a ball that was about to rebound will not rebound. In sum, the law of gravity and the laws of elasticity no longer hold in the world, and once we recognize this, we simply give up the idea that the ball causes a depression in the pillow.

Another example should bring out the remaining points that need to be made. Again we can begin with our world containing a ball that causes a depression in a cushion by resting on it. We now eliminate, for all time, everything save the ball, the cushion, and the earth. These three items remain forever in their fixed relative positions. This is the only news concerning this universe. I now want to say that there is nothing *in* this universe that provides a basis for a distinction between cause and effect, and therefore, causal relations do not obtain within it. Our tendency to believe the contrary is due to treating this world as a limiting case of our own — a tendency supported by the method used for introducing the example.

We can pursue this matter further by allowing an imaginary critic to present an objection. "Even though the world you describe presents no instances of an unsupported object falling toward the earth's center, it still *might* be true that the law of gravity obtains in this world so that if an unsupported object *were* introduced into this world, then it *would* fall. We thus have a basis, albeit a subjunctive basis, for distinguishing cause and effect, so we can now say that the ball causes the depression in the cushion. It might turn out that there is no way of *finding out* whether this subjunctive claim is true, but as you yourself have pointed out, such epistemological considerations are entirely beside the point."

Yes, the epistemological consideration is entirely beside the point, and I shall not go back on this. At the same time, we can notice that the objection turns upon the following picture of things: we can place the history of a world — the news concerning the world — on one side and the laws governing it on the other. Statements about events that do not form part of the world's history, but fall under the laws pertaining to it, are expressed as contrary-to-fact conditionals. We can even imagine an empty world — one containing nothing at all — but as long as there is a set of laws pertaining to it, there will be a corresponding set of contrary-to-fact conditionals true in it.

Over against this picture there is another view, at least as plausible, that laws are completely determined by the character of the *actual* things in the world. More fully, subjunctive conditionals are derived from laws and laws in their turn are completely dependent upon the actual facts of the world. Thus the truth of a contrary-to-fact conditional, *if it be determined at all*, will be determined by reference to the actual disposition of the universe. The italics in the previous sentence mark the fact that in a given world the truth of a contrary-to-fact conditional may not be determined. "If, in our world, a rainbow were to turn into a confection, what would be the flavor of the violet band?" It would be a new form of madness to insist that the account of our world remains *incomplete* until we can determine the truth of direct answers to this question. Nor do I think that any more sanity resides in the more sophisticated claim that our world would be less deterministic if this question lacks an answer. The world is as deterministic as it can be if all the *actual* events occur in a manner conformable to law.

The above remarks are thoroughly Humean in character, and I do not expect that everyone will find them as platitudinous as I do. Yet they do not have to be accepted in order to establish the systematic point at issue: a person who holds a regularity view of causal relations will not encounter *special* problems with cases where the cause is simultaneous with its effect. He can adopt the Kantian strategy of treating those cases as conceptually dependent upon cases where the cause precedes its effect, and he can do this within the general framework of a regularity theory.

It might help to review this tortured discussion. I have represented Hume's attack against the possibility that a cause can be simultaneous with its effect in the following way:

1. Some causes *are* simultaneous with their effects. — Assumption.
2. All causes *could be* simultaneous with their effects. — A Generalization Argument.
3. All causes *are* simultaneous with their effects. — Via the "established maxim."

But since Hume holds that (3) is manifestly false, he concludes that we must deny the assumption (1) that leads to it. We may therefore conclude:

4. No cause is simultaneous with its effect.

I have two criticisms of this argument: (i) the conclusion (4) is itself manifestly false, and (ii) the inference from (1) to (2) is invalid. The inference is invalid because it presupposes the conceptual independence of causes that are simultaneous with their effects from causes that are prior to their effects. Following Kant, I have rejected this presupposition.

All this may seem a strange way of defending a Humean account of causality, but I hope it is now clear that Hume's position does not depend upon showing that *no* cause is simultaneous with its effect. Instead, Hume must reject the *possibility* that *all* causes could be simultaneous with their effects. That is, Hume must reject step (2) in the argument sketched above. It should also be clear why he must reject this possibility, for if he grants it, he would then have to admit that there is more *in the world* to causality than regularity. This *more* is needed in order to differentiate cause and effect. Thus, as it stands, Hume's argument is defective in three ways: it is invalid, it presents us with a false conclusion (4), and, most important of all, it actually grants a thesis—at step (2)—that he should be most anxious to deny. In contrast, by rejecting Hume's argument at the second step, we provide him with just the argument he needs, and we do this without departing from the general Humean framework.

Cases where a cause is simultaneous with its effect *seem* to present a challenge to Hume's account of causal relations by suggesting that there is more *in the world* to causation than regularity. I shall now take an excursion into a neighboring field in order to neutralize a related situation carrying this same suggestion.

By Boyle's Law we know that under certain limitations the pressure and volume of a fixed quantity of gas stand in the following functional relationship:

$$PV = k$$

Thus, for example, if I double the pressure, the volume will be halved or if I double the volume the pressure will be halved. Now it is easy enough to think of a way of *bringing about* a change in pressure by manipulating the volume. We can imagine a piston moving in a closed cylinder where the scale on the piston rod gives a direct reading for the volume of the enclosed gas. Now through halving the volume I bring it about that the pressure is doubled. I can also say, *quite naturally*, halving the volume *causes* the pressure to double. We should wonder about this sudden appearance of a concept of a cause, for Boyle's Law contains no explicit mention of this notion, and it is not clear where else it could come from. We will worry about this later.

The thing that will worry us first is this: although we can alter the pressure by changing the volume, there does not seem to be any way of changing the volume by altering the pressure. I cannot alter the pressure by pumping in more gas, for the law is defined for a fixed quantity of gas. Nor am I allowed to increase the pressure by heating the gas, for one of the limitations on Boyle's Law is that the temperature remain constant. In sum there does not seem to be any way of *getting at* the pressure except through moving the piston, but that, after all, is to change the pressure through changing the volume—just the reverse of what we are trying to achieve. Here Boyle's Law, in spite of its surface appearance, seems to exhibit a curious asymmetry: changes in volume can cause a change in pressure, but there is no way to bring about a change in volume through changing pressure.[4]

This presents an intolerable situation for a Humean approach to causal relations. Perhaps this is not immediately obvious, but the following considerations will bring this home. One *demand* we can make of the Humean approach to causal relations is that it account for the fact that Boyle's Law can support a claim that a change in volume will *cause* a change in pressure. In a moment, we shall see that it can perform this task. But second, if we allow this apparent asymmetry to stand, the Humean account will have to provide a reason for this as well. It is surely hard to see how this could be done, for the law itself gives no preference to volume over pressure. Thus, as long as this apparent asymmetry is allowed to stand, we seem driven to the conclusion that there is more *in nature* to a causal relation than admitted of in Hume's philosophy.

Let us go back to the original question: how can we halve the volume by doubling the pressure? Suppose that I reply in the following way: "I do just the same thing, namely *this*," and, suiting my actions to my words, I then perform physically the same operation. This is precisely the correct thing to say, and all that we need now are some therapeutic illustrations to convince us of this. We can begin by redesigning our apparatus by replacing the scale giving a reading for volume by some device that gives a reading for pressure. I then manipulate the pressure—i.e., fiddle with the rod until the right pressure is attained. In this way (via Boyle's Law), through doubling the pressure I bring it about that the volume is *in fact* halved.

Before turning an ear to the protest that these remarks might produce, I shall consider one further example. We are now to think of ourselves applying a given force to the piston rod and thereby producing a change *both* in volume and in pressure in the correlated way laid down by Boyle's Law. We thus have three cases: bringing about a change in volume by changing the pressure, bringing about a change in pressure by changing the volume, and, finally, bringing about a change in both volume and pressure by exerting a force.

What are we to say about these cases? Shall we say at least sometimes the *direction* of the causal relation is determined by our point of view? I think that we can say this provided that we do not associate it with an extravagant picture of the mind bending nature to its will. We are here dealing with a situation where the cause is simultaneous with its effect and thus (following Kant) any assertion of a cause will depend upon taking some state as the dynamical outcome of a process. But unlike the ball–cushion example, pressure and volume are functionally on a par, so we are able to view either as the attained state, and whichever we pick, it becomes the cause and the other the effect.

We can now deal with our first problem: the relationship between Boyle's Law and a singular causal judgment. If we take, say, the pressure as the attained state, then Boyle's Law provides the principle of unrestricted universality to underwrite the claim that the change in the pressure caused the change in volume. The law will, of course, provide the same service when we treat the volume as the attained state. If, however, we treat neither as an attained state, then causal notions have no application. *Boyle's Law does not assert a causal relationship.* The reason for this is that it contains no reference to *events* or any other plausible candidates for causal relationships. In particular, it does not assert a relationship of *reciprocal* causation.

Taken at face value, the notion of reciprocal causation would demand that we take both the volume and the pressure as attained states, but then they would each be candidates for a cause, but neither for an effect. To repeat, Boyle's Law does have the capacity to support singular causal judgments in either direction, but since it cannot do both at once, the notion of reciprocal causation misdescribes the situation.

Something must be said, however briefly, about these notions of *treating* something in a certain way or *viewing* something in a certain way. From the physical side, in doubling the pressure and in halving the volume, we may do the very same thing: namely this (here we do something). Yet as actions they remain distinct in their success conditions. In doubling the pressure, for example, I move the piston until a certain pressure is achieved as registered on the pressure gauge. If we note the truism that actions can be causes, then there is nothing mysterious in the fact that from the physical side the same thing happens when the pressure is doubled and the volume is halved, yet, for all that, it is the doubling of the pressure that causes the volume to be halved. To these reflections we should also add that it is not essential that we actually be doing something — manipulating an apparatus — in order to create this situation. Even for events that occur in the course of nature we speak (and think) of certain states being achieved, and then it is the logic of the situation (not a piece of lamentable anthropomorphism) that allows us to pass from a functionally symmetrical law to a directed singular causal judgment.

Even with these apologies it may still seem intolerable that the direction of causation can be determined by what we are doing or by how we view things. But why should this seem intolerable? Boyle's Law has not been compromised, for it, after all, is not a causal assertion. Indeed, nature itself has been left untouched by our apparent subjectivism. But if the direction of causation can *ever* be altered in this way, hasn't this notion of a cause lost its status as a fundamental physical category? But how was it decided that causation is a fundamental physical category anyway, and what is this supposed to mean?

## NOTES

1. All citations to Hume are to the Selby-Bigge edition of Hume's *Treatise*.

2. *A* may be constantly conjoined with *B* while *B* is not constantly

conjoined with $A$, but if $A$ and $B$ are constantly conjoined, then (trivially) $B$ and $A$ are constantly conjoined.

3. *Emmanuel Kant's Critique of Pure Reason*, translated by Norman Kemp Smith, McMillan & Co., Ltd., (London, 1953), $A$ 203, $B$ 248–49.

4. In conversation I have found that some people grant this asymmetry but insist, usually vehemently, that it goes the other way around, i.e., we cannot get at the volume directly, but only indirectly by altering the pressure.

# 8

# The Tendency of Hume's Skepticism

During his lifetime Hume was thought to be a skeptic and (both inconsistently and falsely) an atheist. In time the charge of atheism has fallen away, but for most of the two hundred years since his death, Hume's position as the leading (and almost only) British skeptic has seemed secure. Things have changed. Starting with the claim made early in this century by Norman Kemp Smith that Hume was not simply, or even primarily, a skeptic, but a naturalist instead, we now find interpreters of Hume arguing (or simply assuming) that skepticism has little or no role in Hume's philosophical position.[1] I think that this new way of reading Hume is, first of all, one-sided in ignoring a great many important texts. More deeply, I think that interpreters of Hume who downplay the skeptical moment in his position misunderstand the fundamental tendencies of his philosophy, including the naturalistic themes that they bring to prominence.

Part of the difficulty of fixing issues here is that no clear sense is attached to the claim that a philosopher is or is not a skeptic. In common parlance, skepticism is concerned with *doubt*: to say that one is skeptical about something is to express doubt concerning it. Furthermore, skepticism suggests rather strong doubt. A skeptic, then, is one who entertains strong doubts—usually about many things. In contrast, if we turn to the philosophical literature (both ancient and modern), skepticism has a different focus. A philo-

"The Tendency of Hume's Skepticism," *The Skeptical Tradition*, ed. Miles Burnyeat, University of California Press, 1983. Reprinted by permission of the publisher.

sophical skeptic deals in *arguments* and, in particular, with arguments that call in question the supposed grounds for some system of beliefs. The system of beliefs may be more or less wide and the form of challenge may vary with the subject matter. Diversity of opinion provides a specific reason for raising skeptical doubts concerning morality, but it is less effectively invoked as a skeptical challenge to mathematics. Other skeptical challenges are perfectly general — that is, they apply to any system of beliefs whatsoever. The so-called argument from the criterion (of truth) falls into this category — as does Hume's skepticism with regard to reason.

There seems to be an obvious connection between the common notion that skepticism concerns doubt and the philosophical notion that skepticism shows the groundlessness of systems of belief: when a system of belief is shown to be groundless, then we ought not to adopt beliefs of that kind.[2] But even if this connection seems obvious, it will be important for our purposes to distinguish between principles of the following kind:

1. There are no rational grounds for judgments of kind A.
2. One ought not to assent to judgments of kind A.

I shall say that a position that embodies the first principle expresses a *theoretical* skepticism and that a position that embodies the second principle expresses a *prescriptive* or *normative* skepticism. A prescriptive skepticism may be based upon a theoretical skepticism, but need not be. A person may recommend the suspension of belief on scriptural rather than theoretical grounds.[3] Similarly, one can be a theoretical skeptic without recommending suspension of belief. It might be argued that there is nothing wrong with holding beliefs for which there is no theoretical justification, or it might be argued that beliefs are not in our control and that therefore recommendations concerning them are idle.[4]

Although the difference between a theoretical skepticism and a prescriptive skepticism is perfectly clear, criticisms of skepticism have the tiresome habit of ignoring it. Hume captures this tendency in the *Dialogues Concerning Natural Religion* by having Cleanthes address Philo in these words:

> Whether your scepticism be as absolute and sincere as you pretend, we shall learn by and by, when the company breaks up: We shall

then see, whether you go out at the door or the window; and whether
you really doubt, if your body has gravity, or can be injured by its
fall; according to popular opinion, derived from our fallacious
senses and more fallacious experience. [*Dialogues Concerning Natural Religion*, p. 382][5]

Actually, this passage involves a double confusion. It first confuses
theoretical skepticism with prescriptive skepticism, and then, by
citing Philo's own behavior as evidence, it confuses prescriptive
skepticism with what we might call *practicing skepticism*. After all,
a person may sincerely believe that he ought not to believe something, yet believe it. This is just a special case of a person believing
that he ought not to do something, yet doing it.

With the distinction between theoretical and prescriptive skepticism in hand, it is possible to summarize the main tendencies of
Hume's skepticism. (1) His theoretical skepticism is, I shall argue,
*wholly unmitigated*. (2) Hume's prescriptive skepticism is less easily
described because it is variable. In moments of intense skeptical
reflection he comes as close as possible to holding that we ought
not to believe anything whatsoever, and indeed he finds himself
(for a time, at least) in a state of radical doubt. But the more
normal tendency of Hume's philosophy is to put forward a more
moderate or mitigated prescriptive skepticism of an Academic
rather than a Pyrrhonian cast. Both in daily life and in the pursuit
of science we ought to limit our inquiries to matters suited to our
limited faculties, and in these modest inquiries we ought always
to adjust our beliefs to probabilities established upon experience.[6]
(3) The final point I wish to make about Hume's presentation of
skepticism is that he offers no independent *arguments* for the moderate skepticism that generally characterizes his position. Instead,
his moderate skepticism is quite literally a mitigated Pyrrhonian
skepticism. Here Hume's skepticism and naturalism meet, for the
state of moderate skepticism is viewed as the result of two casual
factors: radical Pyrrhonian doubt on one side being moderated by
our natural (animal) propensities to believe on the other. This
causal explanation of moderate skepticism as the natural terminus
of philosophical reflection is, I believe, Hume's major contribution
to the skeptical tradition.

In what follows I shall show that the above claims can be easily documented in the text of the *Treatise*. I shall then show that the same views persist, without essential change, in Hume's later writings, including the *Enquiry Concerning Human Understanding* and the *Dialogues Concerning Natural Religion*.

## Hume's Skepticism with Regard to Reason

Each Book of Hume's *Treatise* has at least one skeptical episode. Most famously, Book I successively puts forward a skepticism concerning induction, a skepticism with regard to reason, and, finally, a skepticism with regard to the senses. Book II, which concerns the passions, provides fewer targets for skeptical tropes, but even here we find Hume insisting that reason in incapable, of itself, of influencing the passions (and therefore "ought always to be the slave of the passions"). Finally, in his treatment of morals, in Book III, we find Hume introducing skeptical arguments intended to show that reason—in a broad sense including both demonstrative and empirical reasoning—cannot determine the moral qualities of agents or actions.

In what follows I shall lay more stress than is usual on Hume's skepticism with regard to reason. There are both textual and systematic reasons for doing this. Textually, Hume's skepticism with regard to reason reveals his skeptical commitments in their most radical form. It also provides the occasion for Hume to write most explicitly about the nature and significance of his skepticism. For example, it is precisely the impact of this argument that throws Hume into his (real or feigned) funk in the concluding section of Book I: "The intense view of these manifold contradictions and imperfections in human reason has so wrought upon me, and heated my brain, that I am ready to reject all belief and reasoning, and can look upon no opinion as more probable or likely than another" (*Treatise*, pp. 268–269).[7] Systematically, the argument is important because it transcends its specific target, reason, and yields a skepticism that is wholly general. This follows at once from the general form of the argument, which has two parts. Hume first argues for the reduction of all knowledge to probability and then argues that, upon reflection, we see that any probability, however high, must reduce to "nothing." But if we begin, as Hume does, with an exhaustive distinction between knowledge and probability, reduce the first to the second, and then argue that, upon reflection, all probabilities must be reduced "to nothing," we arrive at a skepticism unlimited in its application and wholly unmitigated. We arrive at a skepticism on a par, in its way, with the classical skeptical argument from the criterion (of truth).

The first part of Hume's argument — the reduction of knowledge to probability — is launched by the following consideration:

> Now as none will maintain, that our assurance in a long numeration exceeds probability, I may safely affirm, that there is scarce any proposition concerning number, of which we have a fuller security. For 'tis easily possible, by gradually diminishing the numbers to reduce the longer series of addition to the most simple question, which can be form'd, to an addition of two single numbers; and upon this supposition we shall find it impracticable to shew the precise limits of knowledge and probability, or discover the particular number, at which the one ends and the other begins. But knowledge and probability are of such contrary and disagreeing natures, that they cannot well run insensibly into each other, and that because they will not divide, but must be either entirely present, or entirely absent (p. 181)

Hume adds to this the further consideration that if there be no error in the simple parts of a complex sum, there could be no error in the whole. By this argument Hume intends to show that the probability of error which (as no one denies) infects large computations, must — at least to some degree — infect our beliefs in the most simple mathematical truths.[8]

Hume offers a *causal* account of this tendency of the human mind to fall into error: "Our reason must be considered as a kind of cause, of which truth is the natural effect; but such-a-one as by the irruption of other causes, and the inconstancy of our mental powers, may frequently be prevented" (p. 180). This, in turn, leads Hume to assert that we must take into account the possibility of such an "irruption of other causes" in deciding upon the credibility of any knowledge claim. Such an assessment is a matter of probabilities (not simply a matter of "comparing ideas"), and thus we arrive at Hume's first major conclusion: " . . . by these means all knowledge degenerates into probability; and this probability is greater or less, according to our experience of the veracity or deceitfulness of our understanding, and according to the simplicity or intricacy of the question" (p. 180). Notice that Hume is not maintaining the weaker and certainly more plausible thesis that the consideration of the propriety of a knowledge claim will always lead us to raise probabilistic questions. He is asserting instead that the knowledge is itself reduced, by these means, to probability. I do not think that he gives any reason for offering the stronger rather than the weaker thesis. Indeed, his argument seems to muddle them together.

The second part of Hume's argument is a morass. He notices that the point made about knowledge holds for probabilities as well; that is, when we make a probabilistic judgment, we must consider the possibility that here our faculties have erred. This leads him to lay down the following principle: "In every judgment which we can form concerning probability as well as knowledge, we ought always to correct the first judgment deriv'd from the nature of the object, by another deriv'd from the nature of the understanding" (pp. 181–182). Now suppose that we have made a probabilistic judgment in the common way and then, following Hume's instructions, we have added to it a further judgment concerning the probability that the first judgment is correct. What next? Obviously, this new (second-order) judgment is itself susceptible of error, and it too must be evaluated before it is accepted. In Hume's words, "we are obliged by our reason to add a new doubt deriv'd from the possibility of error in the estimation of the truth and fidelity of our faculties" (p. 182). The infinite regress is now fair before us, but Hume gives this ancient trope a twist of his own by suggesting that these successive evaluations must progressively drive the probability of the *original* judgment down to "nothing." Hume continues his argument in these words:

> This doubt, which immediately occurs to us, and of which, if we would closely pursue our reason, we cannot avoid giving a decision. But this decision, tho' it should be favourable to our preceding judgment, being founded only on probability, must weaken still further our first evidence, and must itself be weakened by a fourth doubt of the same kind, and so on *ad infinitum*, till at last there remain nothing of the original probability, however great we may suppose it to have been, and however small the diminution of every

new uncertainty. No finite object can subsist under a decrease repeated *in infinitum*; and even the vastest quantity, which can enter into human imagination must in this manner be reduc'd to nothing. (p. 182)[9]

So Hume concludes that "all the rules of logic require a continual diminution, and at last a total extinction of belief and evidence" (p. 183). This conclusion and the argument leading up to it establish my claim that, in the *Treatise* at least, Hume accepts a *theoretical* skepticism that is wholly unmitigated.

Furthermore, Hume understands the radical character of his position with complete clarity. This comes out most forcefully in the way he deals with the old trick of trying to refute the skeptic by turning his arguments back upon themselves—the so-called *peritrope*. He responds to this challenge in these words:

> If the sceptical reasonings be strong, say they, 'tis proof, that reason may have some force and authority: if weak, they can never be sufficient to invalidate all the conclusions of our understanding. This argument is not just; because the sceptical reasonings, were it possible for them to exist, and were they not destroyed by their subtlety, wou'd be successively both strong and weak, according to the successive dispositions of the mind. (p. 186)

That is, skeptical arguments are self-refuting, but this only puts us on a treadmill, since setting aside our skepticism and returning to the canons of reason inevitably puts us on the road to yet another skeptical impasse. For Hume, skepticism is completely immune to rational refutation. Indeed, it is the fated end of all reasoning pursued without restraint.[10]

Turning next to the *prescriptive* skepticism of the *Treatise*, we can quickly tell a familiar tale. Hume does not recommend a radical suspension of belief because he thinks that it is not in the power of human beings to achieve this state. Hume develops this side of his theory by asking himself the following question: "How it happens, that even after all we retain a degree of belief, which is sufficient for our purposes, either in philosophy or common life." Of course, most people have never heard of Hume's skeptical argument, and it is the process of going through it—and not just its soundness — that induces a skeptical response. But Hume has gone through the argument and we want to know how *he* (or anyone else who appreciates its force) can retain a degree of belief sufficient for our purposes either in philosophy or in common life. Hume responds:

> I answer, that after the first and second decision; as the action of the mind becomes forc'd and unnatural, and the ideas faint and obscure; tho' the principles of judgment, and the balancing of opposite causes be the same as at the beginning; yet their influence on the imagination, and the vigour they add to, or diminish from the thought, is by no means equal. . . . The attention is on the stretch: The posture of the mind uneasy; and the spirits being diverted from their natural course, are not governed by the same laws, at least not to the same degree, as when they flow in their usual channel. (p. 185)

Later, now speaking generally about all skeptical arguments, he adds: "'Tis happy, therefore, that nature breaks the force of all sceptical arguments in time, and keeps them from having any considerable influence on the understanding" (p. 187).

Hume returns to this argument and gives it special prominence in the concluding section of Book 1.

> I have already shewn, that the understanding when it acts alone, and according to its most general principles, entirely subverts itself, and leaves not the lowest degree of evidence in any proposition, either in philosophy or common life. We save ourselves from total scepticism only by means of that singular and trivial property of the fancy, by which we enter with difficulty into remote views of things and are not able to accompany them with so sensible an impression, as we do those, which are more easy and natural. (pp. 267–268)

What, for Hume, is the point of this excursion into skepticism? In the *Treatise*, Hume's stated reason for dabbling in these skeptical arguments is that they confirm his theory of belief.

> My intention then in displaying so carefully the arguments of that fantastic sect, is only to make the reader sensible of the truth of my hypothesis, *that all our reasonings concerning causes and effects are*

> *deriv'd from nothing but custom; and that belief is more properly*
> *an act of the sensitive, than of the cogitative part of our natures.*
> (p. 183)

Hume's central idea seems to be this: If belief were fixed by processes of reasoning, then the skeptical argument just presented would drive all those who have considered it to a state of total suspension of belief. Indeed, in our closet, such skeptical reflections can come very close to inducing this extreme state. Yet when we return to the affairs of daily life, our ordinary beliefs come rushing back upon us and our previous state will now strike us (perhaps with some lingering jitters) as amusing. But this restoration of belief is not a matter of reasoning and therefore cannot be explained on any of the traditional theories of belief formation where it is assumed that the mind comes to its beliefs by a process of reasoning. Hume's own causal theory of belief formation suffers no such embarrassment. He does not, however, attempt to show that his approach is *unique* in this regard.

There is a final feature of Hume's treatment of skepticism that is at least broached in the *Treatise* and becomes an important theme in his later writings. Skeptical doubts, no matter how intense, are no match for the beliefs that come back upon us when we return to daily life, but not all the beliefs that antedated our Pyrrhonian catharsis have a like tendency to be restored. Those, for example, that are the product of mere education, indoctrination, fashion, and so forth, will not inexorably force themselves back upon us. For this reason, Pyrrhonian exercises will have a tendency to curb the *enthusiasm* that Hume so much despised. The outcome, then, of this philosophical progression, is a person who shares the opinions of the vulgar on the common topics of life—with them, he leaves by the door and not by way of an upstairs window. He may also carry his reflections beyond common life, but here he moves with caution, always adjusting his beliefs to probabilities grounded in experience. For matters that lie beyond experience, he suspends inquiry altogether. We have thus arrived at a position very close to Academic skepticism, and arrived at it, not by means of argumentation, but as a natural consequence of the interaction of philosophical reflection carried to its extreme with daily life carried on in a normal way.

## Skepticism in Hume's Dialogues
## Concerning Natural Religion

At no place in Hume's later writings do we find a commitment to skeptical principles as explicit as that found in the opening and closing sections of the fourth part of Book I of the *Treatise*. Yet if we keep in mind the distinctions introduced at the beginning of this essay, I think that we may also say that he never recants the central features of his skeptical position. In particular, he never explicitly rejects the unmitigated *theoretical* skepticism of the *Treatise*. Indeed, though his emphasis may change, particularly in the *Enquiry Concerning Human Understanding*, there is abundant textual evidence to show that (even in the *Enquiry*) he continues to accept a radical theoretical skepticism. But before turning to the *Enquiry*, I shall first look at Hume's skepticism as it emerges in the *Dialogues Concerning Natural Religion*.

Because of its form, the *Dialogues* present problems for the interpreter. Hume never speaks directly in his own person — not even in the introductory remarks that are spilt from the pen of Pamphilus — and as his correspondence indicates, he made a conscious effort to lend plausibility to the positions of the two main protagonists of the dialogue, Cleanthes and Philo. At the close of the dialogue, Hume seems to hint at his own preference by having Pamphilus aver that one of the protagonists, Cleanthes, has gotten the better of the debate, but he gives no reason for saying so. Pamphilus shows a similar preference for Cleanthes in his prefatory remarks where he describes him as a "careful thinker." By way of contrast, Demea is said to be a man of "rigid orthodoxy" and Philo is called a "careless sceptic." These remarks at the beginning and end of the *Dialogues* together with the fact that Cleanthes does, in fact, present his position from within an empiricist (and probabilistic) framework have led some commentators — I do not think the majority — to hold that Cleanthes represents Hume's position or at least comes closest to doing so. This, I think, is just wrong, and though it pretends to be daring, it entirely misses the underlying logic of the *Dialogues*. Cleanthes is a civilized "naturalist" who has never thought his principles through to the Pyrrhonian crisis they entail. Philo views the world from the other side of that gulf. Demea, of course, knows nothing of all this, and his occasional invocation of skepticism *cum fideism* is wholly superficial and does not cohere with other things he says. Except for one place where he gets in a telling blow against Cleanthes, Demea is presented as a stooge.

Perhaps another, more plausible view, is that Hume sorts his views out between Philo and Cleanthes, assigning to Philo a more radical skepticism than he himself would accept while making Cleanthes, however inconclusive his positive arguments are, closer in general orientation to his own position. I think that this is also mostly wrong, for in no place in the *Dialogues* does Philo express skeptical commitments that Hume himself had not expressed in the *Treatise*. More to the point, *the fine details* of Philo's skepticism mirror exactly the ideas developed in that earlier book. On the other hand, Cleanthes rarely expresses views that reflect the more sophisticated aspects of Hume's philosophy. The one exception to this is Cleanthes' rejection of the ontological proof offered by Demea; and here, as Cleanthes himself remarks, he is not disagreeing with Philo, merely beating him to the punch.

To see that Philo's position reflects the "fine-grained" features of the *Treatise*, we may notice first that in a single paragraph Philo alludes directly to the skepticism concerning reason and then repeats the claim of the *Treatise* that it is only the mind's natural incapacity to sustain subtle inquiry that saves us from a total lack of assurance and conviction on *any subject*.

> All sceptics pretend that, if reason be considered in an abstract view, it furnishes invincible arguments against itself, and that we could never retain any conviction or assurance, on any subject, were not the sceptical reasonings so refined and subtle, that they are not able to counterpoise the more solid and more natural arguments, derived from the senses and experience. (p. 385)

Here, of course, the word "pretend" is used in its eighteenth-century sense, and the skeptical pretensions expressed are precisely those of the author of the *Treatise*.

But Philo not only invokes the radical (theoretical) skepticism of the *Treatise* in a general way, he also shows genuine sophistication concerning it. This comes out, for example, in his response to an attack upon skepticism offered by Cleanthes. Skeptical reflections generate uneasiness when they are undertaken and have no lasting effects (good or bad) when they are terminated. So Cleanthes asks for what reason the skeptic imposes "on himself such a violence," adding that "this is a point, in which it will be impossible for him [the skeptic] ever to satisfy himself, consistently with his sceptical principles" (p. 383). Philo's response does not deny the uneasiness that skeptical reflections may produce; instead it rejects the claim that skeptical reflections will have *no* lasting effect. His answer involves a comparison with the effects of the teachings of Stoicism which, traditionally, have been subjected to the same complaint that they lose all efficacy when confronted with genuine problems of life.

> Though the mind cannot, in Stoicism, support the highest flights of philosophy, yet even when it sinks lower, it still retains somewhat of its former disposition, and the effects of the Stoic's reasoning will appear in his conduct in common life, and through the whole tenor of his actions. . . . In like manner, if a man has accustomed himself to sceptical considerations on the uncertainty and narrow limits of reason, he will not entirely forget them when he turns his reflection on other subjects; but in all his philosophical reasoning, I dare not say, in his common conduct, he will be found different from those, who either never formed any opinions in the case, or have entertained sentiments more favourable to human reason. (pp. 383–384)

Once more, Hume describes himself.

There are a number of other places in the text where Philo expresses fine points of Hume's own position,[11] but the most striking instance of Philo's adherence to the central features of Hume's skeptical position occurs, oddly enough, at the one place in the text where Cleanthes is able to silence him. Having been badly mauled by Philo's objections to the inductive inference from the supposed order in nature to the existence of an intelligent creator, Cleanthes shifts his tactics (and with it his grounds) and responds to Philo in these words:

> The declared profession of every reasonable sceptic is only to reject abstruse, remote, and refined arguments; to adhere to common sense and the plain instincts of nature; and to assent, wherever any reasons strike him with so full a force that he cannot, without the

greatest violence, prevent it. Now the arguments for natural religion are plainly of this kind; and nothing but the most perverse, obstinate metaphysics can reject them. Consider, anatomize the eye; survey its structure and contrivance, and tell me, from your own feeling, if the idea of a contriver does not immediately flow in upon you *with a force like that of sensation*. (pp. 402–403)

This passage has a number of remarkable features. In the first place, Cleanthes here shows a more sympathetic understanding of skepticism by dropping the spurious criticism that it has disastrous consequences for daily life ("Will you leave by the door or window?"). More significantly, Cleanthes shifts the grounds of his position by no longer arguing that the signs of order in the world provide *evidence* for an inductive argument showing that the world must have an intelligent being for its cause. He now puts forward a causal thesis to the effect that the contemplation of the exquisite organization of the eye, for example, immediately induces in us the idea of a being who contrived it. Hume underscores this shift in position by having Cleanthes acknowledge that this new argument is of an "irregular nature" (p. 403). More importantly, once the position is put on this footing, it becomes completely immune to the pattern of skeptical argument found in the *Treatise*. Hume's theoretical skepticism concerns arguments. In its various manifestations it shows the groundlessness of given beliefs. It is not aimed at nor does it have any tendency to diminish the force of those beliefs that spring up in us naturally. So if our conception of an intelligent creator of the universe flows immediately in upon us "with a force like that of sensation," then the groundlessness of the belief is admitted, and no argument presents itself as a target for skeptical attack. The skeptic can only affirm or deny the fact. I think that we can now understand why at this point in the *Dialogues* Hume has Pamphilus tell us that Philo falls silent: "Here I could observe, Hermippus, that Philo was a little embarrassed and confounded; but, while he hesitated in delivering an answer, luckily for him, Demea broke in upon the discourse and saved his countenance" (p. 403).

We may also be able to make some sense out of the most problematic feature of the *Dialogues*. At the close of the *Dialogues* Philo seems to undergo a remarkable conversion where he seems to agree with Cleanthes — despite the fact that he has quite demolished every particular argument that Cleanthes has presented. This seeming reversal is, it seems to me, quite inexplicable, unless we assume that Philo is here admitting that the contemplation of the wonderful contrivances of nature naturally induces in us the thought of a divine contriver. That is, it is Cleanthes' irregular argument that Philo cannot refute and may, consistently with his stated principles and consistently with the principles of the *Treatise* as well, accept. These considerations remove some of the shock from Philo's claim that "to be a philosophical Sceptic is, in a man of letters, the first and most essential step toward being a sound believing Christian" (p. 467). A man of letters will find the *reasons* adduced for religion less than compelling. More to the point, the kind of deity presented by the arguments of natural religion is hardly a fit object for our religious sentiments. This is the one forceful point that Demea makes in the *Dialogues*, and it is aimed against Cleanthes. The arguments of natural religion are not only weak, as Philo shows, but present an inappropriate object for our religious sentiments, as Demea rightly protests. The skeptic, then, is better placed to accept the doctrines of *received* religion than is the proponent of natural theology. That, I think, is what Philo is saying.

The *Dialogues* remain a problematic text, for the interpretation sketched out here is subject to criticism.[12] This much, however, does seem to be beyond dispute: the *Dialogues Concerning Natural Religion* are written in the framework of the radical theoretical skepticism of the *Treatise*, and the central core of the work is lost if this fact is ignored or suppressed.

## Skepticism in the Enquiry Concerning Human Understanding

I said at the beginning of this essay that Hume never — to my knowledge — retreats from the unmitigated theoretical skepticism of the *Treatise*. The discussion in the closing section of the *Enquiry* may seem to belie this claim, for there he comes out quite explicitly for a mitigated as opposed to a Pyrrhonian skepticism. I shall argue that no such change takes place, although there is, I think, an important shift in emphasis.

Before going into this matter directly, it will be useful to give a quick survey of the differences between the *Treatise* and the *Enquiry* on the range of skeptical discussions. The one important addition to the skeptical topics discussed in the *Treatise* is, of course, the essay on miracles. That essay has the skeptical conclusion that, by the nature of the case, we can never have sufficient inductive evidence to establish the occurrence of a miracle. The skepticism concerning induction is carried over from the *Treatise*, although in a simplified, perhaps even different, form. The skeptical arguments concerning the senses are carried over almost exactly from the *Treatise* to the *Enquiry*. The argument, which is as old as skepticism itself, calls in question inferences from our perceptions to the existence of the external world. Here, at least, there is no retreat from an unmitigated theoretical skepticism:

> This is a topic . . . in which the profounder and more philosophical sceptics will always triumph when they endeavour to introduce an universal doubt into all subjects of human knowledge and enquiry. Do you follow the instincts and propensities of nature . . . in assenting to the veracity of sense? But these lead you to believe that the very perception or sensible image is the external object. Do you disclaim this principle, in order to embrace a more rational opinion, that the perceptions are only representations of something external? You here depart from your natural propensities and more obvious sentiments; and yet are not able to satisfy your reason, which can never find any convincing argument from experience to prove, that the perceptions are connected with any external objects. (p. 126)[13]

The most curious feature of the treatment of skepticism in the *Enquiry* is the handling of skepticism with regard to reason as it appears in the second part of Section 12. It is strange in two ways: (1) the argument of the *Treatise*, which, as we saw, was intended to reduce all knowledge claims to probabilities and then drive all probabilities down to "nothing" is nowhere to be found, and (2) in its place Hume puts ancient puzzles that he claimed to solve in the *Treatise*. In particular, Hume simply trots out standard puzzles about infinity and infinite divisibility in order to show that even abstract reasoning, when left to itself, will be led into intractable difficulties. He then suggests in a footnote that it may not be impossible to avoid these absurdities.

So our comparison between the *Treatise* and the *Enquiry* comes to this. The theoretical skepticism concerning induction and the theoretical skepticism concerning the existence of the external world is the same in both. The skeptical argument concerning miracles is new to the *Enquiry*. Only the skepticism concerning reason is missing.

I think that we are now in a position to understand the "mitigated scepticism or academical philosophy" that Hume recommends at the close of the *Enquiry*. Let me comment on its nature, then on its source. In the first place, the mitigated skeptic is a fallibilist and a probabilist: "In general, there is a degree of doubt, and caution, and modesty, which, in all kinds of scrutiny and decision, ought for ever to accompany a just reasoner" (p. 132). But Hume also speaks of another *species* of mitigated skepticism that calls for "the limitation of our enquiries to such subjects as are best adapted to the narrow capacity of human understanding" (pp. 180–181). Taking the phrase from Alexander Pope, I shall call this *man's middle-state skepticism*, for it reflects the same sentiment as the following lines from his "An Essay on Man":

> Placed on this isthmus of a middle state,
> A being darkly wise, and rudely great:
> With too much knowledge for the Sceptic side,
> With too much weakness for the Stoic's pride. . . .

A similar sentiment is expressed in *Paradise Lost*, where Milton has Raphael warn Adam not to inquire into the deep mysteries of the universe, but, instead, study to become "lowly wise." Indeed, Hume here adopts one favorite religious use of skeptical arguments, namely, to curb the extent of man's inquiries and restrict it to topics fit for his state.[14] This middle-state skepticism with its call for a restriction upon the range of inquiry was characteristic of the eighteenth century; and here, at least, Hume reveals himself a man of his time.

One last question: How does one attain this state where we are suitably cautious in our assent and modest in our inquiries? Hume's answer is that this is brought about by reflection on Pyrrhonian arguments. "To bring us to so salutary a determination, nothing can be more serviceable, than to be once thoroughly convinced of the force of the Pyrrhonian doubt, and of the impossibility, that anything but the strong power of natural instinct, could free us from it" (p. 181). The clear implication of this passage is that there are no arguments that will refute Pyrrhonian skepticism and thus there can be no arguments that will justify a more mitigated version of skepticism. The mitigated skepticism that Hume recommends is thus the causal consequence of the influence of two factors: Pyrrhonian doubt on one side and natural instinct on the other. We do not argue our way to mitigated skepticism, we find ourselves there.

In sum, Hume's skepticism and his naturalism meet in a causal theory of skepticism itself.

## NOTES

1. Nicholas Capaldi's *David Hume* (Boston: Twayne, 1975) represents the extreme version of this new dispensation, but he has been followed, in varying degrees, by others.

2. As W. K. Clifford puts it, "[I]t is wrong always, everywhere and for anyone, to believe anything upon insufficient evidence."

3. See, e.g., *Ecclesiastes* 3:11.

4. Thomas Reid, whose commonsense philosophy involves a theoretical skepticism every bit as radical as Hume's, adopts the first alternative. Hume, as we shall see, largely adopts the second.

5. All citations to the *Dialogues Concerning Natural Religion* are to Vol. II of *David Hume: Philosophical Works*, ed. Green and Grose (London, 1886).

6. Notice that this moderate skepticism has two sides: (1) a limitation upon the *range* of inquiry, and (2) a limitation upon the degree of assent. The second limitation amounts to a *probabilism* or *fallibilism* and is, of course, a standard feature of Academic skepticism. The first limitation, which concerns the permissible range of human inquiry, has a long association with religious thought and may, indeed, lay claim to a scriptural basis. I shall examine such calls for limitations upon the range of permissible investigation when I consider the distinctive features of Hume's skepticism as it appears in the *Enquiry*.

7. All citations to the *Treatise of Human Nature* are to the Selby-Bigge edition (Oxford: Clarendon Press, 1888).

8. Actually, this is not much of an argument, for the source of error in performing a large sum is not likely to be a momentary lapse where we suddenly believe, say, that three plus four equals eight. Error typically

arises from such external difficulties as forgetting what number we are carrying along or not being able to read our own writing. None of this touches upon the possibility of falling into error when contemplating simple mathematical propositions.

9. The closing sentence of this passage contains an obvious mistake. Hume does not realize that an infinite series of finite diminutions can sum to a finite limit. Beyond this, the proper analysis of Hume's argument — which involves taking probabilities on probabilities — is far from obvious and may lie outside the range of standard probability theory.

10. Hume also notices the practical difficulties that would attend the lot of a person who attempted to carry his philosophical skepticism over into life. But this does not provide a reason for rejecting skeptical principles, for these pragmatic considerations are themselves subject to skeptical doubt.

11. Of particular interest is a passage that appears in the final dialogue where Philo remarks "that the Theist allows that the original intelligence is very different from human reason: The atheist allows, that the original principle of order bears some remote analogy to it. Will you quarrel, Gentlemen, about the degrees, and enter into a controversy which admits not of any precise meaning, nor consequently of any determination?" (p. 459).

W. T. Jones has suggested to me, and I am sure he is right, that this passage gives Hume's own assessment of the debate between Cleanthes and Philo, i.e., that it concerns only matters of degree, and is therefore incapable of resolution. In the fourth appendix of the *Enquiry Concerning the Principles of Morals*, Hume also examines disputes concerning matters of degree and comes to the same conclusion, calling them "verbal disputes." A similar line of argument is pursued in Hume's discussion of personal identity in the *Treatise* (p. 262). An examination of these passages will again show that Philo serves as the vehicle for expressing some of Hume's most sophisticated ideas.

12. Although I give more stress to the skeptical themes carried over in detail from the *Treatise*, much of what I have said here is a simplified borrowing from Nelson Pike's careful and insightful commentary on the *Dialogues*. See, in particular, Section Four of his edition of the *Dialogues Concerning Natural Religion* (Indianapolis: Bobbs-Merrill, 1970).

13. All citations to the *Enquiry Concerning Human Understanding* are to Vol. 4 of *David Hume: Philosophical Works*, ed. Green and Grose (London, 1886).

14. In passing, this is the central theme of a remarkable Pyrrhonistic work by Bishop Huet entitled *A Philosophical Treatise Concerning the Weakness of Human Understanding*. Huet is cited in the *Dialogues* (p. 388).

# 9

# Richard Price on Promising:
# A Limited Defense

In this essay I shall examine a work that is rarely read without
praise, but still rarely read: Richard Price's *Review of the Principal
Questions in Morals*.[1] I shall concentrate upon one specific topic:
Price's account of our obligation to keep promises. I shall show
that his concerns were essentially the same as those that have
marked discussions of promises in this century. Indeed, as we shall
see, two recent writers have revived Price's position without recognizing him as a precursor. More importantly, I shall argue that
Price's account of promising has considerable merit in its own
right. In fact, though it is somewhat underdeveloped by modern
standards, I think that it can hold its own against competitors.

Before examining Price's account of promising, let me quickly
revive the standard perplexity that any adequate account of promising must resolve. Prichard, whose contribution in this regard is
well known, put the matter this way:

> In promising, agreeing, or undertaking to do some action we seem
> to be creating or bringing into existence the obligation to do it, so
> much so that promising seems just to *be* binding ourselves, i.e.,
> making ourselves bound to do it. . . . Yet an obligation seems a fact
> of a kind which it is impossible to create or bring into existence.[2]

Prichard's point is that an obligation does not seem to be the kind
of thing that can be brought into existence *directly*. Of course, by

"Richard Price on Promising," *Journal of the History of Philosophy*, Vol XXI,
No. 3 (July 1983). Reprinted by permission of the publisher.

doing or saying certain things I can bring it about that I have an obligation. For example, by becoming the father of a family, I fall, as Prichard remarks, under the obligation "to feed and educate it."[3] But in this case my action does not directly generate an obligation: instead, it puts me into a situation where an obligation devolves upon me. In virtue of doing certain things I become the father of a family. In virtue of being the father of a family I assume certain obligations. Here my doings generate obligations, but, as Prichard wants to say, only *indirectly*. Yet promising seems to be nothing more than an act of creating an obligation (for myself). That, according to Prichard, is paradoxical. It seems no more reasonable to suppose that I can create an obligation directly than that I could have made it the case, through some action of my own, that "the square of three is odd."[4] For Prichard, this is an apt comparison, because the disability in question is not contingent: it is not an incapacity we discover through repeated failing attempts. Prichard thinks that it is sufficient to reflect upon what obligations are in order to see that they cannot be brought into existence directly by any action on the part of an agent. To become obligated, we must do something *else* in virtue of which we are obligated.

Two hundred years earlier, Hume used a parallel argument to show that our obligation to keep a promise must spring from an artificial rather than a natural source. On his moral sense theory, an obligation is explained in the following way:

> All morality depends upon our sentiments; and when any action, or quality of the mind, pleases us *after a certain manner*, we say it is virtuous; and when the neglect, or non-performance of it, displeases us *after a like manner*, we say that we lie under an obligation to perform it.[5]

But we can no more directly change our sentiments than we can change "the motions of the heavens."[6] In contrast with Prichard, Hume cites a contingent fact as a comparison. Again we arrive at the conclusion that what seems to happen in promising cannot happen, i.e., promising is not a direct act of undertaking an obligation to do something. Neither in principle (Prichard) nor in fact (Hume) may obligations be directly undertakable. The paradox that demands resolution is that in promising we seem to do precisely what we should not be able to do.

With the problem before us, we can turn to Richard Price's treatment of it. To begin with, Price shares a fundamental tenet with both Prichard and Hume. Presumably on grounds more Prichardian than Humean, he considers it impossible for an obligation to be brought into existence directly by some action, in particular, by an act of will. So, like them, he must find some alternative source for the obligation attaching to promises. But unlike them, he thinks the problem admits of an easy solution. "[F]idelity to promises," he tells us, "is *properly* a branch or instance of *veracity*."[7]

Price develops this position in terms of a contrast between the declaration of a promise and the declaration of a resolution or intention:

> By a *promise* some declaration is made, or assurance given to another, which brings us under an obligation to act or not to act, from which we should have been otherwise free. Such an obligation never flows merely from declaring a *resolution* or *intention*; and therefore a promise must mean more than this; and the whole difference is, that the one relates to the *present* the other to *future* time. — When I say I *intend* to do an action, I affirm only a present fact — But to *promise* is to declare that such a thing *shall* be done, or that such and such events *shall* happen. . . . When a person declares that he *will* do any action, he becomes obliged to do it, and cannot afterwards omit it, without incurring the imputation of declaring falsehood, as really as if he had declared what he knew to be a false past or present fact; and in much the same manner as he would have done, if he had pretended to know, and had accordingly asserted, that a certain event would happen at a certain time which yet did not then happen. There is, however, a considerable difference between this last case, and the falsehood implied in breaking promises and engagements; for the object of these is something, the existence of which depends on ourselves, and which we have the power to bring to pass; and therefore here the falsehood must be known and wilful, and entirely imputable to our neglect and guilt. . . . To *promise* then, being to assert a fact depending on ourselves, with an intention to produce faith in it and reliance upon it as certainly to happen; the obligation to keep a promise is the same with the obliga-

tion to regard truth; and the intention of it cannot be, in the sense some have asserted, to will or create a new obligation.[8]

Price's remarks stand in need of elaboration. First, whether he is right or not in saying that a declaration of a resolution or an intention is an affirmation of a present fact, he is surely right in saying that the declaration of a resolution or of an intention is fundamentally different from the declaration of a promise. Indeed, most discussions of promising begin by making just this point. But the central theme of Price's discussion is not to stress this *dissimilarity*, but, rather, to insist upon an important *similarity* between declaring a promise and making a future tense statement about one's own actions. In this latter case we are plainly bound by the principle of veracity; we should not say (falsely) that we are going to do something that we are not going to do. This, for Price, is simply a special case of the general demand that we speak the truth. Price's central claim is that our obligation to keep a promise derives from this same source. Notice that Price is not saying that a promise simply is a future tense statement about the speaker's own actions. Promising has special features that he at least alludes to. Nor is he saying that every future tense statement about the speaker's own actions is a promise. What he is saying is that the ground of the obligation in both cases is the same, i.e., the principle of veracity.

At first sight, this theory may seem merely silly. Although it does not *equate* certain future tense statements with promises, it does have the consequence that a person who utters a future tense statement about his own actions falls under an obligation to make it come true. Suppose, however, that Allen says to Brandon, "Since today is a holy day, I shall stay my hand, but tomorrow I shall return and thrash you." Having said this, for whatever reason, is Allen now under an obligation to return the next day and thrash Brandon? The answer seems to be no, but it is not immediately clear why. The most obvious (and plausible) explanation is that we read Allen's remark as the expression of a resolution or of an intention. In that case, no obligation rests on Allen to thrash Brandon. (He does, however, stand under an obligation to express his intentions accurately.) I suspect that many of the obvious counter-examples to this implication of Price's theory (i.e., that we stand under an obligation to make our statements about our future actions come true) can be met by noticing that the speaker is most naturally interpreted as expressing an intention about what he will do rather than making the assertion that he will do it.

To avoid interference from expressions of resolve or intention, let us further suppose that Allen makes it clear that his remark has no such import and is, instead, a straightforward assertion about his future actions. On the assumption that we are under an obligation to tell the truth, the following argument seems unassailable: In making his statement, Allen is under an obligation to tell the truth, and he can tell the truth only by thrashing Brandon, so he is under an obligation to thrash. There is something right and something wrong about this. What's right is this: if Allen tells Brandon that he will thrash him tomorrow and then does not, then he has lied, and lying is wrong. Of course, Allen may have other obligations and among these might be the obligation not to inflict pain upon others except for very special reasons. (The avoidance of telling a lie may or may not be among these special reasons.) Thus Allen's obligation not to thrash may override his obligation not to lie. So, if Allen says that he is going to thrash Brandon and doesn't, then he has done something wrong—he has lied. It says nothing against this that he would have done something worse if he had thrashed him.

So what seemed paradoxical to begin with no longer seems paradoxical when various interfering conditions are taken into account. If a person asserts that he will do something—where he is not merely expressing a resolve—then he *eo ipso* falls under an obligation to do so, granting, of course, that this obligation may be overridden by others.

Price's position faces a second and more difficult objection. It will be pointed out that our obligation to keep a promise cannot be grounded in the obligation to tell the truth, for in declaring a promise we are not making an assertion, i.e., we are not saying anything that can correctly be considered either true or false. Prichard put it this way:

> [W]hile everyone would allow that a promise may be made either in good or in bad faith, no one would allow that it could be either true

or false. Rather, they would insist that promising resembles asking a question or issuing an order, in that it consists not in making a statement but in doing something, in the sense in which we oppose doing to mere talking.[9]

This view has been given a more elaborate development by Prichard's student, J. L. Austin.[10]

Prichard's claim may seem sufficient to demolish Price's position—but this is not so.[11] Showing this will involve a brief excursion into the theory of performative utterances. One important function of what Austin calls *explicit performatives* is to clarify illocutionary force. Consider the imperative "Leave the room!" It could be used to formulate a command, an order, a request, a piece of advice, etc. There is, however, nothing in the expression itself that indicates in which of these ways it is being used. I shall call expressions of this kind, i.e., those that contain no explicit markers for illocutionary force, *primary utterances*. We can contrast the primary utterance: "Leave the room!" with the following explicit performative, "I command you to leave the room." In a particular context it may be clear that the use of the utterance "Leave the room!" has the force of a command, but if someone says "I command you to leave!", then there is no doubt that a command has been given instead of, say, a piece of advice. There is, however, an important similarity between the primary utterance "Leave the room!" and the explicit performative "I command you to leave the room.": in each case I issue the directive that the person leave the room. The explicit performative has a marker that indicates something left unsaid in the simple imperative—i.e., it refers to the character of the illocutionary act, but *in* saying either of these things I issue the selfsame directive.

We can now look at the explicit performative "I promise to see you tomorrow." What should we take to be the primary utterance associated with this explicit performative? Certainly not an expression of intention, for promising, among other things, stands in contrast with the mere expression of a resolve or intention. Austin makes a suggestion that will be useful for our purposes:

Let us pause then to dwell a little more on the expression 'explicit performative', which we have introduced rather surreptitiously. I shall oppose it to 'primary performative' (rather than to inexplicit or implicit performative). We gave an example: (1) primary utterance [sic.]: "I shall be there", (2) explicit performative: "I promise that I shall be there", and we said that the latter formula made explicit what action it is that is being performed in issuing the utterance: "I shall be there". If someone says "I shall be there", we might ask: "Is that a promise?" We may receive the answer "Yes", or "Yes, I promise it" . . . , whereas the answer might have been only: "No, but I intend to be" (expressing or announcing an intention), or "No, but I can foresee that, knowing my weaknesses, I (probably) shall be there".[12]

This passage from Austin will help us articulate Price's position with some precision. Both Austin and Price think that in certain contexts saying "I shall be there" can commit one to being there. Now for Austin, as I read him, if the context is right, we can indifferently use the expressions "I promise to be there" and "I shall be there" to commit ourselves to being there. This is certainly right. But beyond this, Austin seems to think that in such a context, the expression "I shall be there," despite its surface appearance, does not put forward a truth claim. It does just what the explicit performative "I promise etc." does: it commits me to doing something. In contrast, an advocate of Price's position would say that in using the explicit performative "I promise etc.," which does not have the form of a truth claim, I *eo ipso* put forward the truth claim that underlies it as a primary utterance, i.e., the assertion "I shall be there." Viewed in this way, the explicit performative "I promise that," is just one member of a large family of explicit performatives that have assertions as their primary utterances. "I swear that," "I guarantee that," "I vow that," "I pledge that," etc., are other members of this family. Price would hold, I think, that in each case the obligation that falls upon me through using these expressions is simply the obligation of veracity with respect to the assertion expressed *in* what I say.

The above considerations allow us to deal with a further criticism. There seem to be two different ways in which we can violate the principles governing promises. At the time that I make a promise I may do so knowing full well that I will not keep it.

[A] man finds himself forced by need to borrow money. He well knows that he will not be able to repay it, but he also sees that nothing will be loaned him if he does not firmly promise to repay it at a certain time.[13]

If, under these circumstances the man does promise, then he can be said to have made a lying promise. Kant dwells on this case, and Price's position applies most naturally to it. Somewhat differently, at the time that I make the promise, I may have no settled opinion whether I shall keep it or not. I may make a promise now and then wait until later to see if it is possible or worth my while to fulfill it. I do not think that we would here speak of a lying promise, but still, such a promise would be dishonest and deceitful. I can also make promises that are rash or stupid in the sense that at the time I made them I thought that I could fulfill them but should not have thought so. All these cases concern respect for truth at the time that I make the promise. But I can also make a promise in all sincerity and then, when the time comes to fulfill it, decide not to. This is not an instance of a lying promise — it is not an instance of lying at all. All the same, it is an example of deceit, for I have knowingly thwarted an expectation that I induced. I have knowingly brought it about that another's mind is infected with false belief. This may, in turn, have other bad effects, for example, his going bankrupt, but we do not have to wait upon these other effects to determine the culpability of my act.

These last remarks may not seem persuasive, for they seem to ignore what has come to be called the *direction of fit*. In making assertions, so the story goes, the task is to make our discourse fit the world, whereas with practical discourse, which is often thought to be prescriptive, the task is to get the world to fit our discourse, e.g., by following an order or *fulfilling a promise*. I have not been able to discover where the notion of direction of fit first appeared,[14] but Austin used it in 1952 in "How to Talk: Some Simple Ways"[15] and there, interestingly enough, it is not used to distinguish what he then called performatives from constatives. It is used instead to distinguish different kinds of constatives from one another. Without trying to recapture Austin's subtlety, the following example will bring out a contrast important for our purposes. We are looking at pictures of early fossils. You point to one and say "That's a trilobite." You are wrong because, in fact, it is a diatom. Here your words have not matched the world. Now suppose I ask you to point to a trilobite and you produce the same performance, i.e., you point to what in fact is a diatom and say "That's a trilobite." Again you are wrong, but there is nothing wrong with the words you picked, for if you had said, albeit truly, "That's a diatom," you would not have done what you were supposed to have done. Your error here concerned getting your deeds to match your words. Now the difference between these two cases is, roughly, the difference between *identifying* something (where my words have to match the world) and providing an *instance* of something (where my presentation of an instance has to match my words). But whatever direction the onus of fit might be, in each case I am making an assertion which will be either true or false depending upon whether the words and the world match in the right sort of way.

I believe that modern proponents of a Pricean position on promising have been less persuasive than they might have been because they have not been careful enough in specifying just what kind of assertion about the future most nearly matches the kind of assertion they think is made in the act of promising. Warnock, for one, invites criticism by constantly comparing making a promise to *predicting* one's own future behavior.[16] First of all, making predictions about one's future behavior is relatively rare and quite special. We do sometimes say such things as "I know that as soon as I am cross-examined I'll panic," but it is not the sort of remark we make very often. In contrast, we often say such things as "I'll show you our new coffeemaker." I am then expected to conform my conduct to what I have said. It is an assertion of this kind, where my future conduct is expected to *instance* my remark, that provides the best model for the assertions inherent in a promise. Once this is seen, *direction of fit* can no longer be cited as grounds for rejecting the kind of theory of promising that Price has put forward.

A further objection remains to Price's account of promising: it seems to leave out one of its essential features, its social or contractual element. Even a gratuitous unilateral promise usually waits upon acceptance and uptake before it becomes operative. Of course, most promises are not unilateral, but bilateral. They involve an agreed-upon exchange: a promise for a benefit, a promise for a promise, etc. Here the agreement strikes many as the heart of the matter, yet Price seems to ignore it altogether.[17]

Actually, I do not think that Price would have much difficulty in formulating a response to this challenge. Since promises (as opposed to threats) typically offer benefits, it is natural that they have an implicitly conditional character waiting upon acceptance. "Most offered promises are conditional on an acceptance; but when acceptance has taken place the condition is performed and the promise is no longer conditional."[18] Now on Price's theory, when a promise is made (and accepted) a person has solemnly and unambiguously said that he will do a certain thing. This creates a prima facie obligation to do that thing. Since obligations are generally burdensome, people will not, in general, say that they will do something, thus incurring an obligation, unless they are assured of some benefit in return. Consider the exchange of a promise for a present benefit or an exchange of mutual promises, the standard contractual situations. On the contractarian account, it is the agreement that creates the mutual obligations. On Price's account, it is the fact that agreement has been reached (typically through bargaining) that leads each party to say that he will do a certain thing. Here the agreement is not the source of the obligation, but the reason why each person is willing to accept an obligation through saying that he will do a certain thing. Rather than taking contractual agreement as a primitive source of obligation, as so many have, Price tries to derive it from a deeper source: our obligation to do what we say we will do.

To summarize, Price holds that our obligation to keep promises is grounded in a more general obligation to have a proper regard for truth. In his own words, it falls under that "division of rectitude . . . which has truth for its object. . . . "[19] But he also holds something stronger than this: veracity is just one subsection of this division of rectitude which has truth as its object, and our duty to keep our promises falls into this subdivision. This comes out, somewhat obscurely, in the following development in the text. Speaking about veracity he first makes this general remark: "Under this head, I would comprehend impartiality and honesty of mind in our enquiries after truth, as well as a sacred regard to it in all we say. . . . "[20] Then later he corrects this claim:

> Some of these particulars, though they belong to the division of rectitude I have now in view . . . are not properly included in the

signification of *veracity*. — But it requires our notice, that fidelity to
promises is *properly* a branch or instance of *veracity*.[21]

In other words, our obligation to keep a promise is not marginally
or merely analogically related to our obligation to speak the truth;
it is identical with it.

It is time to look more closely at Price's demand that we show a
"sacred regard to truth in all we say." What is there about truth
that makes it worthy of this regard? Price's remarks on this subject
reveal his deep Platonic commitments. They are also metaphorical
and obscure.

> The difference between truth and falsehood is the same with the
> difference between something and nothing, and infinitely greater,
> than the difference between realities and chimeras or fictions; be-
> cause the latter have a real existence *in the mind*, and so far, also a
> *possible, external* existence. . . . Now, it cannot be conceived, that
> what is *real* and what is not so, should be alike regarded by the
> mind. Truth must be pleasing and desirable to an intelligent nature;
> nor can it be otherwise than disagreeable to it, to find itself in a
> state of deception, and mocked with error. — As much error as there
> is in any mind, so much darkness is there in it; so much, if I may so
> express myself, is it less distant from non-existence.[22]

I shall content myself with two prosaic remarks about this passage. First, whatever utility (on the whole) truth may have and
falsehood lack, the primary appeal of truth is immediate and underived. This is important, for, if correct, it blocks the possibility of
tracing both our obligation to tell the truth and our obligation to
keep our promises to some deeper source (e.g., the principle of
utility or a divine command). As we shall see in the closing part of
this paper, this is important for Price's overall concerns in producing a moral theory. Secondly, these passages make it clear that
Price is primarily concerned with true and false *beliefs*. Normally,
our concern with true statements is connected with our regard for
true belief. There are, after all, times when we make statements
with no intention either of expressing a belief or trying to induce a
belief. For example, you ask what number between one and twenty
you are thinking of and I say "You are thinking of fourteen." This
remark is either true or false and, as I realize, there is a very good

chance it is false. Yet Price, for all his high Platonism, is not likely to object to it on these grounds. The situation is altogether different with lying, which Price describes in the following way:

> And the essence of *lying* consisting in using established signs in order to *deceive*, it must be disapproved by all rational beings upon the same grounds with those on which truth and knowledge are desired by them, and right judgment preferred to mistake and ignorance.[23]

Thus, whatever other bad effects, if any, an unfulfilled promise might have, it will always have the bad quality of inducing (or attempting to induce) a false belief—a darkness of the mind—in the promisee.

It should now be clear that a *full* defense of Price's account of promising will fall into two parts: (1) a defense of his reduction of our obligation to keep our promises to our obligation to conform with obligations concerning veracity, and (2) a further defense of his account of our obligations with regard to veracity itself. So far I have only concerned myself with the first task. I shall now discuss this second issue. In the process, it will become evident why I call my defense a "limited defense."

Here it will prove helpful to touch briefly upon the historical setting of Price's discussion of promises, for this will reveal the importance of his account of promising for his moral philosophy as a whole. One plainly labelled target of Price's criticism is the utility (if not quite utilitarian) account of promising developed by Hume. But he was equally anxious to reject all voluntarist theories that grounded morality in the will of a sovereign—either secular (Hobbes) or divine (Descartes).

Price is led into a consideration of voluntarism in the following way. He begins an enumeration of some of the "most important Branches of virtue, or heads of rectitude and duty" with these words:

> What requires the first place is OUR DUTY TO GOD, or the whole of that regard, subjection, and homage we owe him. These seem unquestionable objects of moral approbation, independently of all considerations of utility.[24]

Now if someone asks why we have a duty to obey and worship God, the answer, among other things, is that God was "the creator, governor, and benefactor of the whole world." If the questioner persists and asks why such a being is worthy of our obedience and worship, then there is little to be said in response. According to Price, this would be on a par with asking why "twenty was greater than two." For Price, "submission, reverence, and devotion to *such* a being as God, are . . . instances of an *immediate duty intuitively* perceived. . . . "[25]

Price spends a number of pages celebrating God's perfection in order to enforce this idea that man owes total submission to God's will. Then quite abruptly he pulls himself up with the following remark:

> It will, I suppose, scarcely be thought by the most cursory reader, that what has been now said, lays greater stress upon *will*, than is consistent with the foundations of morals I have been defending.[26]

All this talk about God's perfection and about the subordinate position it implies for man in relationship to God's will has a disturbingly Cartesian ring that demands explanation. What Price says is that "It has not been asserted that, *of itself*, [God's will] can have any effect on morality, or be an end and rule of action."[27] The reason for this—and here Price echoes Cudworth—is that a will that acted independently of antecedently given principles of action would actually be powerless:

> UNDERSTANDING is, in the nature of it, before WILL; KNOWLEDGE before POWER; it being necessary, that every intelligent agent, in exerting his power, should *know* what he does, or design some effect, which he *understands* to be possible. The general idea of *will* is applicable alike to all beings capable of design and action; and therefore, merely as will, it can never have any influence on our determinations.[28]

The reason, then, that we have an obligation to obey the will of God is that it is *God's* will that we are obeying, i.e., the will of a being who is our creator, sustainer, and master. It is sufficient to know that God wills us to act in a certain way to know that this is the way that we ought to act, but, even so, it is not God's will that makes it obligatory for us to act in this way.

Returning to promises, I think that we can now see why Price is anxious to reject any voluntarist account of the obligation that attaches to them. If a person could bring an obligation upon himself simply by an act of will, then the idea that an obligation can be created by an act of will would at least make sense. But if obligations could be generated in this way, then it would be impious to deny this capacity to God. Once this capacity is attributed to God, we must assign it to Him in the fullest and most extensive way. Starting with the assumption that one can create an obligation for oneself by an act of will, there is thus a strong temptation for the reverent to conclude that all obligations are grounded in the will of God. Promising seems to provide the model for a voluntaristic account of the origin of moral obligation. By rejecting this interpretation of promising, Price blocks the road to ethical voluntarism on a cosmic scale.

On the assumption that I am right in identifying the two chief targets of Price's attack—a Humean utility theory on one side and a Cartesian (and perhaps Hobbesian) voluntarism on the other—we can ask, in conclusion, how successful he is in presenting a theory that refutes them. As I said earlier, a *full* defense of Price's position must have two parts: (1) a defense of his reduction of our obligation to keep a promise to our obligation to tell the truth, and (2) a further defense of his account of the obligation to tell the truth. This essay has been almost wholly dedicated to the first task, and I hope that I have shown that there are no modern linguistic arguments that refute Price's position on this matter. On the contrary, I believe that our current theories about performatives can be used to defend this position.

Price's defense of our obligation to tell the truth is much more problematic. In fact, Price hardly defends it at all. For him there is an *"immediate rectitude in veracity,"*[29] and whatever other benefits it may have, its primary worth lies there. It is open to a utilitarian to deny this. There are, of course, times when benefits are derived from false beliefs—where ignorance is bliss—but the utility value of true beliefs is so obviously high that a utilitarian will have little trouble in explaining the high (instrumental!) value we assign to them and the strong social sanctions we apply to guarantee their production. In sum, I think a utilitarian could accept, and might even welcome, Price's reduction of our obligation to keep our promises to our obligation to tell the truth, for he could accept this much and then offer a utilitarian account of our obligation to speak the truth.

The voluntarist (such as the Cartesian and the contractarian) will not be silenced either. At one point Price dismisses his Cartesian opponents in these words:

> [T]he intention of [a promise] cannot be, in the sense some have asserted, to will or create a new obligation; unless it can be pretended that the obligation to veracity is *created* by the mere breath of men every time they speak, or make any professions.[30]

This is, of course, tendentious, for no one would suggest that the *mere breath* of man's speech brings about our obligation to speak the truth. Yet it has been maintained that every assertion (at least) carries with it an implicit promise to tell the truth. W. D. Ross adopted just this position.

> While we are concerned with the duty of fulfillment of promise, it is worth while to consider the relation of this duty to that of telling the truth. These are apt to be thought of as distinct and complementary duties, the one a duty to say what is true, the other a duty to make true what one has said. But the relation between the two is more complex than this; the two are connected in the following way. You can break a promise without telling a lie (for it is only when the promise is made with the *intention* of breaking it, that a lie is told); but you cannot tell a lie without breaking a promise. . . . If someone asks me whether John is alive or dead, and I think he is alive, it can be a duty for me to say 'John is alive' only in virtue of a pre-established expectation that when I make this noise I shall be thinking of him to be in the state which we usually express by saying that he is alive . . . [for] . . . it *must* be supposed that there is a general convention that we shall not without notice use words in a meaning other than in which they are generally used. . . . But, there being this convention or understood promise, I am guilty of a breach of promise if I say he is dead when I think he is alive.[31]

This, of course, simply reverses Price's position. For Ross, our obligation to tell the truth is not immediate and underived, but our obligation to keep our promises is. It is very hard to see what would count as a compelling reason for choosing one of these positions over the other. And there is no reason why a voluntarist could not press his case and argue, as R. H. Robins has argued, that in every case in which we are *morally* bound to perform some future act, we are so through an act of the will.[32] If we ask, as Prichard asked long ago, how it is possible for a *moral fact* to come into existence in this way, the answer is that this is a primitive and underived source of moral obligation.

The upshot of this investigation thus seems both clear and disappointing. On the positive side, I think that a strong defense can be made of Price's reduction of our obligation to keep our promises to our obligations to veracity. If so, then Price can be credited with solving a puzzle concerning promising. But if we shift our gaze to the issues that lie behind Price's account of promising, we see that Price's opponents — both the utility theorists and the voluntarists — can renew their claims with respect to our obligation to veracity itself. In that case, Price's *reduction* will not have the general significance he seemed to attribute to it. In the end, all the old combatants remain in the field with their strength neither increased nor diminished.

## NOTES

1. Richard Price, *Review of the Principal Questions in Morals*, 3rd ed. (London: T. Cadell in the Strand, 1787).

2. H.A. Prichard, "The Obligation to Keep a Promise," *Moral Obligation* (Oxford: Clarendon Press, 1949), p. 169.

3. *Ibid.*, p. 170.

4. *Ibid.*, p. 169.

5. David Hume, *Treatise of Human Nature*, Selby-Bigge editor, second edition revised by Nidditch (Oxford: Clarendon Press, 1978), p. 517.

6. *Ibid.*, p. 517.

7. Price, *Review*, p. 258.

8. *Ibid.*, pp. 258–60.

9. Prichard, *Obligation*, p. 171.

10. See J.L. Austin, *How to Do Things with Words*, J.O. Urmson, editor (Oxford: Clarendon Press, 1962).

11. In an exchange in the *Philosophical Quarterly*, C.G. New raised essentially this objection to a position similar to Price's defended by Pall

Ardal. The rejoinder given above favors Ardal's side of the controversy, although he does not use this specific response. See Ardal's "'And That's a Promise,'" *Philosophical Quarterly*, Vol. 18, 1968, pp. 225-237, and "Reply to New on Promising," *Phil. Quarterly*, Vol. 19, 1969, pp. 260-262, and also New's "Ardal on Promises as Statements," *Phil. Quarterly*, Vol. 19, 1969, pp. 159-160. A position similar to Price's and Ardal's is also maintained by G.J. Warnock, in his *The Object of Morality* (London: Methuen, 1971).

12. Austin, *Words*, p. 69. In this passage Austin shifts from speaking of primary *performatives* to primary *utterances*. The expression "primary utterances" will serve our present purposes better.

13. Kant, *Foundations of the Metaphysics of Morals*, trans. by Lewis White Beck (Indianapolis: Liberal Arts Press, 1959), p. 40.

14. Writers often cite Section 32 of G.E.M. Anscombe's *Intentions* when discussing this topic, but the central idea is much older. See, for example, the passage cited later in this article from Ross's *Foundation of Ethics*.

15. J.L. Austin, *Philosophical Papers* (Oxford: Oxford University Press, 1961 and 1970), pp. 134ff.

16. Warnock, *The Object of Morality*, pp. 102-11.

17. D. Daiches Raphael raises this objection in his introduction to his edition of Price's *Review* (Oxford: Clarendon Press, 1948), p. xxxvii.

18. Arthur L. Corbin, *Corbin on Contracts* (St. Paul: West Publishing Co., 1952), p. 215.

19. Price, *Review*, 259-260.

20. *Ibid.*, p. 257.

21. *Ibid.*, p. 258.

22. *Ibid.*, p. 257.

23. *Ibid.*, p. 258.

24. *Ibid.*, p. 231.

25. *Ibid.*, p. 233.

26. *Ibid.*, p. 246.

27. *Ibid.*, p. 246.

28. *Ibid.*, p. 246.

29. *Ibid.*, p. 259.

30. *Ibid.*, p. 262.

31. W.D. Ross, *Foundations of Ethics* (Oxford: Clarendon Press, 1939), pp. 112-113.

32. M.H. Robins, "The Primacy of Promising," *Mind*, LXXXV, 1976, pp. 321-328.

# 10

# Hamilton's Quantification of the Predicate

Hamilton's theory of the quantification of the predicate has found few friends. When mentioned at all, it is usually dismissed on grounds used long ago by Hamilton's antagonist Augustus De Morgan.[1] Although Hamilton made innumerable mistakes in the exposition of his position (and thereby made himself an easy mark for criticism), his central theory has been unfairly treated. To show this, my discussion will move through three phases: (I) an informal examination of Hamilton's classification of propositions giving what I take to be their correct interpretation, (II) a more rigorous treatment of his position showing that it embodies a coherent advance in logical theory, and (III) some general remarks about Hamilton's contribution to the theory of the syllogism together with some suggestions about why he has been so consistently misunderstood.

## I

Where traditional theory found four basic propositions, Hamilton found eight. He expressed them in the following schematic forms:

| | | |
|---|---|---|
| 1. All A is all B. | (toto-total) |
| 2. All A is some B. | (toto-partial) |
| 3. Some A is all B. | (parti-total) |

"Hamilton's Quantification of the Predicate," *Philosophical Quarterly*, 26 (1976). Reprinted by permission of the publisher.

| | |
|---|---|
| 4. Some A is some B. | (parti-partial) |
| 5. Any A is not any B. | (toto-total) |
| 6. Any A is not some B. | (toto-partial) |
| 7. Some A is not any B. | (parti-total) |
| 8. Some A is not some B. | (parti-partial) |

The first problem is to decide what these schemata are intended to say. This is not an easy job, for not one of them corresponds to a sentence form in the English language. In fact, since these constructions are artificial — and badly explained by Hamilton himself — it is easy to misunderstand them and through this misunderstanding accuse Hamilton of simple errors.

As a guide to getting things right, I wish to employ the traditional notion of the *distribution* of a term or, to use Hamilton's preferred word, the *extension* of a term.[2] Traditional logic made the following rulings concerning the distribution of terms in the basic *A E I O* propositions: the subject term is distributed in universal propositions (*A* and *E*); the predicate term is distributed in negative propositions (*E* and *O*); the remaining terms are undistributed. These rulings are backed by explanations which, as Peter Geach has shown, are typically incoherent.[3] Later on I shall show that Hamilton's use of the notion of distribution (extension) admits of a coherent development that may meet Geach's basic criticisms. For now, however, I shall simply take over this traditional doctrine as if it were unproblematic.

In order to generate a correct reading of Hamilton's eight basic propositions, I shall raise the following question: by what traditional propositions or combination of traditional propositions can we capture the correct distributional relationships for the eight Hamiltonian propositions? Hamilton marked the distributional character of the individual terms by the expressions in parentheses next to each proposition. His intention, I take it, is obvious. When the question is raised in this form, there is no difficulty answering it. The traditional counterparts of the Hamiltonian propositions are as follows:

1. All A is B and all B is A.
2. All A is B.
3. All B is A.
4. Some A is B.

5. No A is B.
6. Some B is not A.
7. Some A is not B.
8. Some A is not B or some B is not A.

De Morgan, in fact, gave just this interpretation for the first seven Hamiltonian propositions. He departed from it only with proposition (8), and it is this proposition that has been the constant source of confusion. More strongly, without a proper reading of proposition (8), it is impossible to develop a coherent representation of Hamilton's position. Here is De Morgan's reading of this problematic proposition:

> 8. Some X is not some Y. This is not in ordinary use. It means that some of the Xs are not some of the Ys, even if there be others. To contradict it we must affirm that there is but one X and one Y, and that X is identical with the Y. (p. 257)

I do not deny that, taken in isolation, "Some X is not some Y" might be read in this way. It has, after all, no natural reading. But Hamilton plainly intends (8) to be the contradictory of (1), so the fair interpretation is just to *make* it that, for notice that this interpretation does yield the correct distributional assignments.

On the assumption that we have captured the intent of Hamilton's propositions, we can consider De Morgan's criticisms of this system:

> That Hamilton really believed the above system to be in *common thought*, and not the deduction of a postulated extension, is manifest. To this we object: but our greatest objection is to the system itself. We have not seen any defence of the following which has a single respectable element, except the character of its producers. The introduction 1, of a complex proposition; 2, of a proposition which is not simply contradicted by any *one* other proposition; 3, of a proposition which cannot be contradicted at all in the system; 4, of a proposition compounded of two others *already in the system*. (pp. 257-8)

In Part III I shall comment upon Hamilton's belief that his propositions occur implicitly in common thought. This will also be the occasion to remark upon Hamilton's robust ability to fly in the

face of the ordinary use of such words as "any" and "all." Here I
shall consider De Morgan's systematic criticisms.

   1. Of course Hamilton's first proposition appears *complex* relative to the traditional classification of propositions: it conjoins
two *A* propositions. But this complexity is *essential* only on the
assumption that the traditional theory is legislative for the classification of propositions—something that Hamilton would deny.
More deeply, the traditional classification and the Hamiltonian
classification are founded on totally different principles. The traditional theory cross-classifies propositions by *quantity* and *quality*,
yielding a 2-by-2 matrix of four propositions. The theory of distribution is then rather disparately tacked on. In contrast, Hamilton
starts out from the notion of distribution (extension), which he
cross-classifies with the quality of a proposition, yielding a 4-by-2
matrix of eight propositions. I have used the first system as a
provisional aid for expounding the second, but to use it as a means
for criticizing the second system shows a misunderstanding of its
intentions.

   2 and 3. De Morgan is just wrong in suggesting that the system
of propositions do not pair up into proper contradictories. The
following list of contradictories is complete and exhaustive: (1) and
(8); (2) and (7); (3) and (6); (4) and (5).

   4. De Morgan's claim that proposition (1) is compounded of two
other propositions *already in the system* is answered in much the
same way as his first criticism. Traditional theory only takes the
*negation* of other propositions already in its system. For Hamilton's purposes, *conjunction* (and, derivatively, *disjunction*) are also
implicitly used.

   Some points of clarification are in order. Following the tradition, Hamilton develops his theory of universal propositions on an
existential (rather than a Boolean) interpretation. That is, he assumes that he is not dealing with empty classes when he speaks of
all As or of all Bs. (And if he is to construct complement classes
freely, he must also assume that he is not dealing with the universal
class.) I do not think that a theory embodying the existential interpretation of universal propositions can be developed in a manner
that is both complete and coherent. There is, however, no need to
go into this difficult matter, since it does not touch upon the fragment of quantification theory developed by Hamilton. Anyway,

this is not a problem special to Hamilton's theory of quantifying over the predicate.

The question of existential import is, however, related to another question of some importance in interpreting the text. One difference between the existential interpretation and the Boolean interpretation of quantifiers is that subalternation holds in the first case, but not in the second. That is, we may infer *Some A is B* from *All A is B* on the first interpretation, but not on the second. Hamilton, in fact, held complicated views on the quantifier *some*. He thought that it sometimes meant *some but not all* and at other times meant *some perhaps all*. Obviously, subalternation holds on the second reading (given an existential interpretation), but not on the first reading (even with an existential interpretation). Various writers have averred that Hamilton accepts the first reading (*some but not all*) and that this helps to generate his eightfold way with propositions.[4] This, however, is a mistake. Hamilton acknowledges both interpretations of the quantifier *some*, but only insists that each interpretation must be examined in order to capture all the everyday inference patterns a logician should study. A correct theory of the quantifier *some but not all*, as he says, "though it may not supersede, ought, I think, to have been placed alongside the other" (p. 281). Hamilton thus develops his eightfold system of propositions for both readings of *some*. He then goes on to explore the relationships between propositions on each interpretation and, beyond this, he explores the logical relationships that obtain between these two systems of propositions.[5]

## II

On the assumption that Hamilton classified propositions by combining the idea of the quality of a proposition with the distribution of its terms, I have interpreted Hamilton's basic propositions by associating them with ordinary propositions that exhibit the right quality and the right distributional patterns. I think that this account is plainly correct for the first seven Hamiltonian propositions. It pays special dividends in generating what I take to be the correct interpretation of proposition (8). The task of this section is to document this reading more closely in the text and them to give it a more rigorous development. I shall begin with Hamilton's *analysis of propositions* (including his doctrine of *simple convertibility*), and then consider the *theory of syllogisms* he constructs upon this analysis.

## The Analysis of Propositions

Hamilton's leading idea about the status of propositions is given in these words:

> [A] proposition is simply an equation, an identification, a bringing into congruence, of two notions in respect to their Extension. (p. 271)

Here Hamilton seems to forget negative propositions, but his later discussion takes them into account. More seriously, it is hard to see how this approach could be extended to many things we call propositions (e.g., "I believe that it is raining"). But I propose to waive this criticism, take Hamilton on his own terms, and ask how this account can be applied to his own system of basic propositions.

We may notice in the first place that Hamilton's suggestion makes no sense if taken quite literally. The logical form of the proposition "All men are mortal" is not "$\varphi = \theta$." Only singular terms can fill the two places in this sentence frame. It literally makes no sense to say "All men are identical with some animals." But if we look at Hamilton's intentions rather than abusing him for his clumsy mode of speech, it becomes clear that he is treating categorical propositions as propositions with quantifiers ranging over identities or nonidentities. I can bring this out in the following way. We can imagine certain identities holding between the members of two classes $A$ and $B$. For example, if all As are Bs, then for *anything* in $A$ there is *something* in $B$ with which it is identical. Notice that as soon as we make explicit reference to this identity relationship, a quantifier must appear governing the predicate term as well as the subject term. It is in this way that Hamilton's belief that propositions are equations or identifications is related to his belief in the implicit quantification of the predicate.

At this point it is easy enough to generate grammatically coherent translations of Hamilton's eight basic propositions where the distributed term is uniformly governed by the quantifier *any* and the undistributed term is *uniformly* governed by the quantifier *some*:

1. All A is all B.            All A is B and all B is A.
   Anything that is an A is identical with something that is a B and anything that is a B is identical with something that is an A.
2. All A is some B.          All A is B.
   Anything that is an A is identical with something that is a B.
3. Some A is all B.          All B is A.
   Anything that is a B is identical with something that is an A.
4. Some A is some B.         Some A is B.
   Something that is an A is identical with something that is a B.
5. Any A is not any B.       No A is B.
   Anything that is an A is not identical with anything which is a B.
6. Any A is not some B.      Some B is not A.
   Something that is a B is not identical with anything that is an A.
7. Some A is not any B.      Some A is not B.
   Something that is an A is not identical with anything that is a B.
8. Some A is not some B.     Some A is not B or some B is not A.
   Something that is an A is not identical with anything that is a B or something that is a B is not identical with anything that is an A.

Some comments. If we look at this list, we see that Hamilton was not extravagant in elaborating his system of propositions. If anything, he was a bit of a piker. Once the logical form of his analysis is clear, we see that tinkering with quantifiers and negation will allow us to construct a much wider system of propositions from the base propositions (1)–(8). To cite one example, we can construct the following proposition:

Anything that is an A is identical with anything that is a B.

This amounts to saying that there is exactly one thing that is A, one thing that is B, and these things are identical. This, you may recall, is the proposition that De Morgan mistakenly hit upon when searching for the proper contradictory of (8). Without realizing it, he had found a contrary of (8). Until the logical form of Hamilton's analysis is clarified, such mistakes are easy enough.

## Simple Convertibility

On the traditional theory, only the $E$ and the $I$ propositions converted simply; the $O$ proposition could not be converted at all; and the $A$ proposition could only be converted *per accidens*. Hamilton held that this traditional theory was deeply confused, based, as he thought, on two cardinal errors. The first error is this:

> That the quantities are not converted with the quantified terms. For the real terms compared in the Convertend, and which, of course, ought to reappear without change, except of place, in the Converse, are not the naked, but quantified terms. (p. 257)

The second error is not making the quantification of both terms explicit so that we are able to recognize the correct form of conversion (*ibid.*). According to Hamilton, once these errors are overcome, it is evident that *simple* conversion holds for all categorical propositions.

I can illustrate Hamilton's position using the $A$ proposition "All A is B." On the traditional theory this cannot be converted simply into "All B is A," but can only be converted *per accidens* into "Some B is A." Hamilton does not object to the validity of this inference (which is easily captured in his own system); his complaint is that the tradition has failed to recognize the correct converse of "All A is B." In Hamilton's system "All A is B" is rendered "All A is some B." The proper converse of this latter expression is "Some B is all A." Hamilton seemed to think that the principle of simple convertibility becomes obvious once both quantifiers are made explicit, for, on the assumption that categorical propositions are *equations* or *identifications*, simple convertibility follows at once from the symmetry of identity. To repeat, categorical propositions are not equations, but even so, just a bit deeper, Hamilton's theory of simple conversion does depend upon the symmetry of identity. For example, the conversion of "All A is some B" into "Some B is all A" can be justified in the following way: if it is possible to pair all the members of one class with some of the members of another class under the identity relation, then, telling the story in reverse, it is possible to pair some of the members of the second class with all of the members of the first class under the identity relation. The remaining simple conversions (which hold without exception) can be justified in similar trivial ways.

## The Theory of the Syllogism

Hamilton's theory of the simple convertibility of his propositions at once introduces a simplification into his theory of the syllogism; figure is wholly inessential to the validity of syllogisms as he constructs them.[6] We need only concern ourselves with the moods of the syllogism, for — and this is a nice result — every valid mood in one figure is valid in all others.

Hamilton announces that on his approach the theory of the syllogism can be reduced to a single principle:

> General canon. — What worse relation of subject and predicate exists between either of the two terms and a common term, with which one, at least, is positively related; that relation subsists between the two terms themselves. (p. 285)

Whether we treat this as a single canon or a number of canons is not important. It turns on nothing more than whether we count up complete sentences or include in our count relative clauses. Although I am not sure about this, it also seems that Hamilton counts the distribution of the middle term as *definitive* of a syllogism and thereby avoids stating another rule. Since this makes no difference to the structure of Hamilton's position, I have not had the patience to straighten this out. Given the normal definition of a syllogism (that it has two premises, three terms, etc.), Hamilton's rules for quality and distribution have the following form.

1. The middle term must be distributed at least once.
2. There are no valid syllogisms with two negative premises.
3. An extreme term can bear no better relationship to an extreme term than it bears to the middle term.

We can shortcut some of Hamilton's discussion by merely stipulating that being particular is worse than being universal and being negative is worse than being affirmative. I shall not explain the reason for this way of speaking, although it may be obvious enough.

A specific example will explain this rather shorthand way of speaking. Consider the following valid syllogism.

| All A is all B. | (toto-total) |
| All B is some C. | (toto-partial) |
| ∴ All A is some C. | (toto-partial) |

The relation in extension that C enjoys to the middle term is toto-partial, so this is the best relation that it can enjoy to the extreme term A. Since A stands in a toto-total relationship to the middle term, it make things no worse. So A stands in a toto-partial relationship to C. Finally, since both relations are affirmative, they are no worse than affirmative, so the conclusion may be affirmative as well. Since rules 1 and 2 are also satisfied, the syllogism is valid. Suppose, now, that we deny one (but only one) of the premises. Then a term in the premises enjoys this worse relation to the middle term and so must enjoy this worse relation to the other extreme term (i.e., a syllogism with one negative premise must have a negative conclusion).

At first sight, it may seem that Hamilton has only formulated an alternative (and clumsy) way of insisting that a term distributed in the conclusion must also be distributed in the premises. Actually, if we examine only the Hamiltonian counterparts of traditional syllogisms. this way of stating the quantity rule will be sufficient. But the rule is not, by itself, sufficient for correctly evaluating Hamilton's extended system of syllogisms. Consider the following argument:

| All A is all B. | (toto-total) |
| Some B is all C. | (parti-total) |
| ∴ All A is all C. | (toto-total) |

Here the middle term is distributed at least once and the terms distributed in the conclusion are both distributed in the premises. Nonetheless, the argument is invalid. (If this is not obvious at once, return to the translations of these propositions suggested in Part I.) The argument is, indeed, declared invalid by Hamilton's general canon. The worse relation enjoyed by an extreme term to a middle term is the parti-total relationship between B and C, so this is the best relationship that A can bear to C. The correct conclusion to the proposed syllogism is "Some A is all C."

This last result has an important consequence. Not only do Hamilton's procedures generate a system of syllogisms more extensive than the traditional enumeration, but the system of rules used to evaluate traditional syllogisms is unable to evaluate Hamilton's extended system. In this way, Hamilton has made a genuine advance beyond traditional theory.[7]

I shall state, without going through the proof, that Hamilton's general canon (including the law of distributed middle) yields the correct analysis of all the argument forms his system generates. We could prove this in two ways: (1) somewhat superficially, go back to Part I and put the initial translations into symbolic form and then (with existential import in force) check every possible derivation; (2) more deeply, translate the analyses of these propositions into symbolic form and again (with existential import in force) check every possible derivation. This, needless to say, proves to be excruciatingly boring.

Rather than offering such a proof, I think that I can give a better insight into the character of Hamilton's position by considering a criticism which, though easy to answer, casts Hamilton's position in a different light. The criticism is this: there must be something wrong with Hamilton's position, for moods that are valid in some figures are not valid in others and, after all, Hamilton's position includes the traditional position. Consider the *AAA* mood: this is valid in the first figure, but not in the second. Here are the specimen syllogisms in traditional notation:

| | | | |
|---|---|---|---|
| All B is C. | (*A*) | All C is B. | (*A*) |
| All A is B. | (*A*) | All A is B. | (*A*) |
| ∴All A is C. | (*A*) | ∴All A is C. | (*A*) |

Why, then, is there not a shift in validity from the first to the second figure on the Hamiltonian approach? The answer becomes evident when we apply the Hamiltonian translations and labels to these syllogisms:

All B is some C.  (2)            All C is some B.  (2)
All A is some B.  (3)            All A is some B.  (2)
∴ All A is some C.               ∴ All A is some C.

Now both the figures and the moods are different. But what justifies labeling the same proposition (3) in one syllogism and (2) in the other? When we answer this question, "light dawns slowly over the whole." The classification of propositions in the Hamiltonian system does not apply to propositions in isolation, but, instead, to propositions as they establish a relationship to a middle term within an argument. It is for this reason that Hamilton does not attach a label to the conclusion of the syllogism in specifying moods.

This yields another important result: Hamilton's procedure does not yield *more* moods than the traditional approach, for the concept of a mood has been completely redefined. There are more things called Hamiltonian moods than there are things called traditional moods, but there is no univocal sense of "moods" such that Hamilton has more of them than the tradition. Hamilton misled others — and may even have misled himself — by not making it clear that his conception of mood was not commensurate with the traditional conception.

Let me sketch, very briefly, the reasoning that shows that there are exactly thirty-six Hamiltonian moods valid for all figures. We can enumerate the *affirmative* moods of the Hamiltonian syllogisms by noticing that we can generate a valid syllogism every time the middle term is distributed at least once. Hamilton hit upon an elegant way of representing all such relations. I shall not impose upon the typesetter by using his full notation, but the following comes close to it. A bar "−" represents a copula between two terms.[8] A comma "," indicates that a term is not distributed; a colon ":" indicates that it is distributed. A specimen argument form in this symbolism looks like this:

$$A, \text{---} :M, \text{---} :B$$
$$, \text{------} :$$

This corresponds to:

Some A is all M.
Some M is all B.
∴ Some A is all B.

The argument is valid.

Once we become comfortable with Hamilton's methods, it is easy to trace out their central features. There are just three ways in which the middle term can be distributed:

:M:    ,M:    :M,

In each case there are only two affirmative propositions that can fit into the right-hand side of this pattern and only two affirmative propositions that can fit into the left-hand side of this pattern. So each middle yields four Hamiltonian moods and the three middles together yield a total of exactly twelve Hamiltonian moods. It is idle to list them.

The negative moods can also be enumerated in a mechanical way. Take any Hamiltonian pattern, e.g.:

A: —— :M, —— ,C

We can negate either proposition but not both, so two negative moods arise which we indicate by slashing the bar:

A: — / — :M, —— ,C    A: —— :M, — / — ,C

In each case, however, the same conclusion may be validly inferred:

A, — / — ,C

Thus there are twelve affirmative Hamiltonian moods and, corresponding to each, two negative Hamiltonian moods. We thus arrive at his announced result that there are exactly thirty-six valid Hamiltonian moods. I shall claim, again without going through the proof, that all thirty-six moods (and only these thirty-six moods) of the Hamiltonian system are valid. Furthermore, Hamilton's procedures are adequate for making these evaluations.

Before closing this discussion with some general remarks, let me say something about the perennial problem of subaltern moods. These are moods with a weakened conclusion, for example:

All B is C.
All A is B.
∴ Some A is C.

The validity of this syllogism depends upon an existential interpretation of the $A$ proposition, so we might expect to find it in the traditional list of valid syllogisms, but not in a list of Boolean syllogisms. In fact, it is missing from traditional lists as well. How can we explain this? If we start from the traditional theory of distribution, this seems like a mere blunder. That we can assert a stronger conclusion should have nothing to do with the *validity* of a syllogism that asserts, instead, something weaker.

The Hamiltonian approach provides a rationale for this exclusion. A syllogism represents the extensional relationships between extreme terms through a middle term. For the syllogism just examined, this relationship is represented by the proposition "All A is C" or, in Hamilton's lingo, "All A is some C." Of course, we can infer "Some A is C" (or "Some A is some C") from the conclusion of this syllogism, but this weaker conclusion does not represent the extensional relationships between the extreme terms through the middle term. That is what a syllogism is supposed to do. This, I think, is another nice result.

# III

From my reading of De Morgan's criticisms of Hamilton, I am convinced that, despite the bitter controversy between them, De Morgan made an honest effort to understand Hamilton's position. Yet he failed to do so and commentators since have hardly done better. There are various reasons that might explain this. Part of the problem, as I have already noticed, is that Hamilton continually takes up words from our common vocabulary and uses them with little regard for their regular employment. This led De Morgan to remark that "Hamilton had the faculty of fastening upon his whole species any use of language into which he had drilled himself" (p. 276). This made Hamilton's work an easy mark for criticism. He exchanges an "all" for an "any" without a blush and continually expects us to grasp the meaning of a construction that has no standard employment. Part of the task of this reconstruction of his position is to bring order out of this linguistic chaos.

Another difficulty is harder to explain in a few words. Hamilton announces what he calls a logical postulate: "*To state explicitly what is thought implicitly*" (p. 250). This may seem a useful and perfectly innocent principle, but in Hamilton's hands it has a problematic result. Hamilton noticed that in the evaluation of a syllogism we are sometimes concerned with the extension of the predicate term. This led him to say that a reference to the extension of the predicate term must be *implicit* in the very meaning of the proposition and therefore it ought to be made *explicit*. That he was clumsy in doing this is true, but I claim to have corrected this clumsiness. A deeper question arises when we ask whether the Hamiltonian analysis of a categorical proposition (even when linguistically correct) actually captures the *meaning* of this proposition. The answer to this is, I think, no. The assertion that all men are mortal is not an assertion *about* the extension of classes, even though the rules governing the assessment of inferences involving this assertion may themselves concern the extension of classes. By including a reference to these rules in the very meaning of the propositions under analysis, the meaning of these propositions is altered. Of course, there is nothing wrong with doing this provided that we know what we are doing and realize that at some point we must stop. Remember "what the Tortoise said to Achilles."

Finally, I think that Hamilton has been misunderstood because he himself did not realize how radically he had departed from the standard treatment of the syllogism. He thought of himself as completing and perfecting the traditional theory:

The New Analytic is intended to complete and simplify the old: — to place the keystone in the Aristotelic arch. (p. 249)

This is wrong. By introducing an entirely different system of classifying propositions in virtue of their potential roles in syllogisms, Hamilton made a radical departure from traditional theory.

If we do not see this, it is easy to proceed on the mistaken assumption that Hamilton has classified propositions in virtue of the extensional relationships between two classes. This is the standard interpretation — or misinterpretation — of his position, and if we follow it, his position will seem a botch.

Looked at from a modern point of view, Hamilton's achievement may not seem important. It is easy to say — and of course it is true — that he merely developed a fragment of quantification theory without laying the basis for a general account. But looked at from the perspective of traditional logic, his achievement is considerable:

1. He developed a theory for arguments involving quantified propositions that was wider than the traditional theory while containing it.
2. He developed a system of rules for evaluating such arguments that went beyond the traditional system.
3. By separating questions of quantity and quality, he thought through the theory of distribution in a clear-headed way.
4. He produced a system with all the symmetry and beauty he claimed for it.
5. He produced a system that worked.[9]

## NOTES

1. Hamilton had taught the theory of quantifying the predicate before 1840, but did not publish his ideas until 1846 — and then only as a prospectus entitled "A New Analytic of Logical Forms." Originally appended to Hamilton's edition of Reid's philosophy, it was later included as Appendix V to the Mansel-Veitch edition of Hamilton's *Lectures on Logic*, Vol. 2 (Edinburgh, 1860). All citations are from this edition.

Peter Heath gives a fine account of the bitter controversy occasioned by Hamilton's threat to charge De Morgan with plagiarism unless he acknowledged an indebtedness to Hamilton's prior work. De Morgan indignantly refused and combined a reply to this charge with a systematic criticism of Hamilton's position. See *On the Syllogism and Other Logical Writings*, edited by Heath (London, 1966). Citations of De Morgan are from this edition.

2. Hamilton contrasts the *extension* of a term with what he calls its *intension*, adopting a new spelling for his purposes. He then goes on to speak of both extensive and intensive syllogisms. In this essay I am only concerned with his theory of extensive syllogisms.

3. Geach, P. T., *A History of the Corruptions of Logic* (inaugural lecture, Leeds, 1968); *Reference and Generality* (Ithaca, 1962). Many of Hamilton's criticisms of the traditional theory of distribution parallel Geach's (see, for example, p. 273n).

4. This suggestion is made by W. Bednarowski in his article "Hamilton's Quantification of the Predicate," *PAS*, 56 (1955–6), p. 218.

5. This is given in an elaborate table on p. 284 of the *Lectures on Logic*.

6. There may be other, perhaps epistemological, grounds for distinguishing the figures of the syllogism. Hamilton, I think, holds such a view, but it need not concern us here.

7. Some of Hamilton's immediate syllogisms can be reflected in a series of syllogisms in the traditional system (i.e., through the use of sorites, immediate inference, etc.). Hamiltonian syllogisms involving his eighth proposition cannot, however, be mirrored in this way.

8. Hamilton uses a directional symbol to mark subject and predicate and thus is able to indicate the figure of a syllogism when he chooses to. But since his theory of simple convertibility makes figure inessential to the evaluation of extensional syllogisms, I shall ignore this nicety.

9. My colleague Frederick Oscanyon has been very useful in helping me formulate this interpretation of Hamilton's position.

# Hamilton's Theory of Quantifying the Predicate— A Correction

My account[1] of Hamilton's theory of the quantification of the predicate contains a fundamental mistake. Following De Morgan (and others who have written on Hamilton), I interpreted the proposition "All *A* is all *B*" to mean "All *A* is *B* and all *B* is *A*." This, after all, produces the correct distributional assignments, i.e., both terms are distributed. I next treated Hamilton's eighth proposition "Some *A* is not some *B*" to be the denial of the first proposition, interpreting it as "Some *A* is not *B* or some *B* is not *A*." Again this yields the correct distributional assignments, i.e., neither term is distributed.

Although these interpretations seem plausible and in line with Hamilton's intentions, they in fact render his system inconsistent. To see this, consider the following argument that the Hamiltonian system declares valid.

> Some P is not any M
> Some S is some M
> ∴ Some S is not some P.

On the proposed interpretation, this argument becomes:

"Hamilton's Theory of Quantifying the Predicate—A Correction," *Philosophical Quarterly*, 26 (1976). Reprinted by permission of the publisher.

Some P is not M
Some S is M
∴ Some S is not P or some P is not S.

Using a Venn diagram, it is easy to see that this argument is invalid. The upshot of this is that there must be something wrong with Hamilton's system or something wrong with my interpretation of it.

The fault lies with my interpretation of the proposition "All *A* is all *B*." The leading idea of the second part of my paper is that Hamilton treated categorical propositions as quantified statements involving identity. On this approach, the most natural interpretation of "All *A* is all *B*" is this:

Anything that is an *A* is identical with anything that is a *B*.

Taken literally, this means that there is but one thing that is an *A*, one thing that is a *B*, and these things are identical. This is the correct interpretation of this proposition. The correct interpretation of the proposition "Some *A* is not some *B*" is the denial of this proposition. As noticed in the paper, De Morgan actually offers this interpretation of Hamilton's eighth proposition. My own position was thus doubly wrong: first in accepting De Morgan's analysis of the first proposition, and second in rejecting De Morgan's analysis of the eighth proposition.

The correct interpretations of propositions (1) and (8) are as follows:

1. Anything that is an *A* is identical with anything that is a *B*.
8. Something that is an *A* is not identical with something that is a *B*.

The remaining six propositions are interpreted as before.

Returning to the argument that raised the initial problem, we see that it now gets the following interpretation:

Some P is not M
Some S is M
∴ There is at least one S and at least one P that are not identical.

A Venn diagram will show that this argument is valid.

I believe that by giving the correct interpretation to both the first and the eighth Hamiltonian propositions, the mystery of that system is finally resolved. It is also possible to answer De Morgan's criticism more directly. In any case, the system is saved from inconsistency.

## NOTE

1. *The Philosophical Quarterly*, 26 (1976), 217–28.

# 11

# Wittgenstein on Identity

Identity gives rise to challenging questions which are not altogether easy to answer.[1]

With this remarkable understatement Frege introduced a series of questions that have occupied philosophy for ninety years. In this essay I shall examine Wittgenstein's long struggle to exorcise the problems raised by Frege's challenging questions.

## 1.

Since I have discussed these matters in detail elsewhere,[2] I shall give only a brief account of Wittgenstein's views on identity as they appeared in the Tractarian (and pre-Tractarian) period. In the *Notebooks*, Wittgenstein became concerned with identity because of its connection with so-called existence propositions:

> The question about the possibility of existence propositions does not come in the middle but at the very beginning of logic. All the problems that go with the Axiom of Infinity have already to be solved in the proposition "$(Ex)(x = x)$".[3]

Wittgenstein had a number of objections to the emergence of "$(Ex)(x = x)$" as a theorem of logic. In the first place, he held that

"Wittgenstein on Identity," *Synthese*, Vol 56 (1983). Reprinted by permission of the publisher.

logic is autonomous: logical questions are never settled by an appeal to an independent reality. "Logic must take care of itself."[4] Yet, if truths of logic could make existence claims, then it would seem that the truth of a proposition of logic would depend upon the state of things in the world.

If Wittgenstein had only been concerned with the emergence of existence propositions as *truths* of logic, he might have sought ways of blocking such propositions from the status of theoremhood. This is the way of the free logician. Wittgenstein's deeper commitments forced him to seek a more radical solution. He held that every proposition is a truth function of elementary propositions, where each elementary proposition indicates that objects are disposed to one another in a determinate way. It seems wholly implausible to suppose that such existence propositions as *there are objects*, *there are* 100 *objects*, and *there are infinitely many objects*, could be expressed as truth functions of elementary propositions indicating how *objects are disposed to one another*. For this reason Wittgenstein declares:

> One cannot say, for example, 'There are objects', as one might say 'There are books'. And it is just as impossible to say 'There are 100 objects', or, 'There are $\aleph_0$ objects'.[5]

Yet if the identity sign is introduced into a standard (and otherwise acceptable) notation of quantificational logic, these things *can* be said. The only way out of this impasse, as Wittgenstein saw it, was to banish the identity sign from a properly constructed conceptual notation.

To the best of my knowledge, no one has seriously adopted Wittgenstein's suggestion for the abolition of the identity sign. The reason for this, I suppose, is that few philosophers have been impressed with the problem of the *expressibility* of existence propositions that it was intended to solve. Yet the question remains whether Wittgenstein's suggestion works. Does it allow him to express those propositions that he (and all of us) think should be expressible, while at the same time excluding those propositions that he (at least) thinks should be excluded? Wittgenstein's general strategy for achieving this result is given in the following passage:

Identity of object I express by identity of sign, and not by using a sign for identity. Difference of objects I express by difference of signs.[6]

Consider how this strategy will work in translating a proposition he would consider legitimate: "There are at least two books." Where Russell would translate this as

$$(Ex)(Ey)(Bx \ \& \ By \ \& \ x \neq y),$$

Wittgenstein would simply say

$$(Ex)(Ey)(Bx \ \& \ By).$$

It seemed to Ramsey that Wittgenstein's method could shadow Russell's, capturing the force of a numerical assignment wherever the objects are described under some nonlogical predicate.[7] If this is so, Wittgenstein has the right to say:

The identity-sign, therefore, is not an essential constituent of conceptual notation.[8]

At the same time, it does not seem possible to produce counterparts for those existence propositions [e.g., "$(Ex)(x = x)$"] that Wittgenstein placed on the Index.

To see the force of Wittgenstein's position, it will be useful to see how he would reply to an ingenious series of criticisms by an able Wittgenstein scholar, James Bogen. In print Bogen has argued that "$(Ex)(Ey)(Fx \ \& \ Fy)$" is not an adequate analysis of the proposition that there are at least two things with the property $F$. Appealing to standard logical procedures, he notes that "$Fa \ \& \ Fa$" would be true in a world containing just one thing (viz., $a$) that is $F$, but from this we may derive the formula "$(Ex)(Ey)(Fx \ \& \ Fy)$." Therefore, Wittgenstein's symbolism does not capture the force of the remark that there are at least two things that are $F$.[9] In correspondence,[10] Bogen has added the important qualification that this symbolism would be inadequate unless Wittgenstein further held that "the same name cannot be substituted for different variables bound in the same general proposition." This principle (I shall call it $P$)

blocks Bogen's criticism. Furthermore, it is also Wittgenstein's explicitly stated position, for I take it that this is just what he is saying at 5.53 when he states that "difference of objects I express by difference of signs."

In this same correspondence, Bogen provides some reasons for rejecting this saving principle *P* itself:

> (i) I think '$(x)(Fx) \supset (Ey)(Fy)$' ought to count as a logical truth. But suppose every object has *F*. That makes every value of '*Fx*' true. *P* prohibits the substitution for *y* of all names substituted for '*x*'. So there are no names left to substitute into '*Fy*'.
>
> (ii) Somewhere in *Methods of Logic*, Quine says, rightly, I think, that (1) 'There is at least one philosopher whom all philosophers contradict' entails (2) 'There is at least one philosopher who contradicts himself', where '*F*' is 'is a philosopher' and '*G*' is 'contradicts'. . . . According to *P*, once I substitute '*a*' for '*x*' in '*Fx*', I can't substitute '*a*' for '*y*' in '*Fy*' or in '*Gyx*'. This makes (1) false and prevents *a* from contradicting himself! That's a real piece of luck for *a*.

To answer Bogen's first criticism of *P*, I think that it is sufficient to note that although "$(x)(Fx) \supset (Ey)(Fy)$" does not formulate a logical truth in Wittgenstein's system, as it does under Russellian conventions, it is possible to formulate the self-same truth in Wittgenstein's notation simply by using the variable *x* throughout. It is not true, then, that Bogen has produced a logical truth that can be expressed in Russell's notation but not in Wittgenstein's. Russell simply provides more ways of saying the same thing.

Turning to Bogen's second objection to *P*, how would Wittgenstein express the claim that there is at least one philosopher whom all philosophers contradict in a way that captures the entailment to the proposition that at least one philosopher contradicts himself? Nothing could be easier:

$$(Ex)[(Fx) \ \& \ Gxx \ \& \ (y)(Fy \supset Gyx)].$$

In many cases, as in this one, the Wittgensteinian translations will be more cumbersome than their counterpart Russellian translations. Sometimes they are less cumbersome. In any case, I see no reason to suppose that Wittgenstein cannot shadow Russell's use of the identity sign in his own identity-sign-free notation, except, of course, where it is the point of his theory not to do so.

## 2.

Although, as remarked earlier, Ramsey accepted Wittgenstein's claim that a sign for identity is not needed in (what we now call) predicate logic, he still held that *identity* was needed for a full development of the foundations of mathematics. Here Ramsey was driven by a number of commitments. (1) Following Wittgenstein, he rejected Leibniz's definition of identity. He thought that the principle of the identity of indiscernibles was a proposition with a sense, hence, not a tautology, and therefore out of place in logic or the foundations of mathematics.[11] But excluding identity seems to leave us with only predicate functions for the specification of classes, and

> mathematics then becomes hopeless because we cannot be sure [for example] that there is any class defined by a predicate function whose number is two; for things may all fall into triads which agree in every respect, in which case there would be in our system no unit classes and no two-member classes.[12]

(2) Ramsey also had a strong commitment to extensionality in mathematics. What he means by this comes out in the following passage:

> I do not use the word 'class' to imply a principle of classification, . . . but by a 'class' I mean any set of things of the same logical type. Such a set, it seems to me, may not be definable either by enumeration or as the extension of a predicate. If it is not definable we cannot mention it by itself, but only deal with it by implication in propositions about all classes or some classes. The same is true of relations in extension, by which I do not merely mean the extensions of actual relations, but any set of ordered couples. That this is the notion occurring in mathematics seems to me absolutely clear from

. . . Cantor's definition of similarity, where obviously there is no need for the one–one relation in extension to be either finite or the extension of an actual relation.

Mathematics is therefore essentially extensional, and may be called a calculus of extension, since its propositions assert relations between extensions.[13]

To put matters simply, Ramsey agreed with Wittgenstein in holding that identity is not needed to give the cardinality of a class defined by predicate function. (As we have seen, there is no need for the identity sign in formulating the proposition that there are two books.) But he further held that it was improper for mathematics to restrict itself to only those classes that can be defined by enumeration or by a predicative function. (More strongly, he thought that he could provide examples of classes that cannot be defined in either of these ways.)[14]

Ramsey thought that the only way that logic could deal with *all* classes (and not just those that could be either defined predicatively or by enumeration) was through the use of a symbolic device with the power of a standard identity sign. But since, with Wittgenstein, he rejected the standard definition of identity, he could not simply help himself to this notion. In essence, he found a way to mimic Leibniz's definition of identity without committing himself to the identity of indiscernibles. For this purpose he introduced what he called a "propositional function in extension," which he explained in the following way:

Such a function of one individual results from any one-many relation in extension between propositions and individuals; that is to say, a correlation, practicable or impracticable, which to every individual associates a unique proposition, the individual being the argument to the function, the proposition its value.

Thus $\phi$(Socrates) may be Queen Anne is dead,

$\phi$(Plato) may be Einstein is a great man;

$\phi\hat{x}$ being simply an arbitrary association of propositions $\phi x$ to individuals $x$.

A function in extension will be marked by a suffix $e$ thus $\phi_e\hat{x}$.

Then we can talk of the totality of such functions as the range of values of an apparent variable $\phi_e$.

Consider now $(\phi_e) \cdot \phi_e x \equiv \phi_e y$. This asserts that in any such correlation the proposition correlated with $x$ is equivalent to that correlated with $y$.

If $x = y$ this is a tautology (it is the logical product of values of $p \equiv p$).

But if $x \neq y$ it is a contradiction. For in one of the correlations some $p$ will be associated with $x$, and $\sim p$ with $y$.

Then for this correlation $f_e \hat{x}, f_e x$ is $p$, $f_e y$ is $\sim p$, so that $f_e x \equiv f_e y$ is self-contradictory and $(\phi_e) \cdot \phi_e x \equiv \phi_e y$ is self-contradictory.

So $(\phi_e) \cdot \phi_e x \equiv \phi_e y$ is a tautology if $x = y$, a contradiction if $x \neq y$.

Hence it can suitably be taken as the definition of $x = y$.

$x = y$ is a function in extension of two variables. Its value is tautology when $x$ and $y$ have the same value, contradiction when $x$, $y$ have different values.[15]

To see how Ramsey's procedure works, suppose that the world contains only Plato and Socrates and one of the correlations is established in the way that Ramsey suggests. Then one instantiation of $(\phi_e) \cdot \phi_e x \equiv \phi_e y$ will be "Queen Anne is dead if and only if Einstein is a great man." This proposition is not self-contradictory. But since we are dealing with *all* such correlations, the following will be among them:

$\phi$ (Socrates) is Queen Anne is dead.
$\phi$ (Plato) is Queen Anne is not dead.

With respect to this correlation, we get the following instantiation of Ramsey's formula:

Queen Anne is dead if and only if Queen Anne is not dead.

But since $(\phi_e) \cdot \phi_e x \equiv \phi_e y$ is simply the logical product of such biconditionals and one of these biconditionals is self-contradictory, the logical product is also self-contradictory.

It is also easy to see that all true identity statements will emerge as tautologies under this definition. With each correlation, the *individual* (how or whether it is named is irrelevant) is assigned a single proposition. Thus each element in the logical product corresponding to $(\phi_e) \cdot \phi_e x \equiv \phi_e y$ will have the form "$p \equiv p$." In this way Ramsey's definition mirrors the formal structure of the standard definition of identity.

The two are here compared with respect to their corresponding logical products:

| Leibniz | Ramsey |
|---------|--------|
| $Fa \equiv Fb$ | $p \equiv p$ |
| $Ga \equiv Gb$ | $q \equiv q$ |
| $Ha \equiv Hb$ | $r \equiv r$ |
| $Ia \equiv Ib$ | $s \equiv s$ |
| . | . |
| . | . |
| . | . |

The striking feature of Ramsey's proposal is that the propositions that make up its logical product are the result of a wholly arbitrary set of correlations between propositions and individuals they need not concern. In any event, we thus arrive at the result that all true identity statements are tautologies and all false identity statements are contradictions. They have thus become suitable for inclusion in a logic conceived along Tractarian lines. Furthermore, a formal counterpart for the notion of identity has been found that allows us to deal with classes in a purely extensional way. "Only so," says Ramsey, "can we preserve [mathematics] from the Bolshevik menace of Brouwer and Weyl."[16]

Wittgenstein rejected Ramsey's proposal. Some of his reasons for doing so are, however, perplexing. Waismann records the following remarks by Wittgenstein on Ramsey's definition:

> Ramsey explains identity in this way:
> '$x = x$' is a tautology.
> '$x = y$' is a contradiction.
> I.e., the symbol ' . . . = . . . ' is a tautology if there is *the same* letter on both sides.[17]

Wittgenstein seems further to suppose that Ramsey would hold that the symbol " . . . = . . . " would be a contradiction if there are *different* letters on each side of the identity sign. He then goes on to complain that on this approach the identity sign could not be used to express the "intersubstitutability of two different signs."[18] This, however, is a misunderstanding of Ramsey's position. His definition is not formulated in terms of *letters* at all. To repeat what he said:

> $x = y$ is a function in extension of two variables. Its value is tautology when $x$ and $y$ have the same value, contradiction when $x$, $y$ have different values.[19]

More deeply, Wittgenstein seems to miss the point of Ramsey's definition. In his further criticisms he seems to think that Ramsey is trying to provide an adequate definition of the identity of individuals. In a letter to Schlick (and transmitted to Wittgenstein by Schlick), Ramsey rejects this reading:

> I never really meant to suggest that $Q(x, y)$[20] was a way of saying that $x$ and $y$ are identical. I imagined that Wittgenstein had shown that it was impossible to say any such thing. I only proposed $Q(x, y)$ as a substitute for the symbol $x = y$, used in general propositions and in defining classes.[21]

Here Ramsey is not backing down from his previous position, nor is he even clearing up some misleading suggestion he may have given concerning his position. In the "Foundations of Mathematics," he made it clear that he accepted Wittgenstein's claim that the identity sign could be eliminated from predicate logic. He also drew the same conclusion from the possibility of this elimination that Wittgenstein had:

> [Wittgenstein's] convention is slightly ambiguous, but it can be made definite, and is then workable, although generally inconvenient. But even if of no other value, it provides an effective proof that identity can be replaced by a symbolic convention, and is therefore no genuine propositional function, but merely a logical device.[22]

This comment helps put Ramsey's proposal in a clearer light. It too is a *logical device* intended to achieve a particular purpose. In particular, it returns to logic the formal power lost when Wittgenstein banished the identity sign. Speaking with light irony, Ramsey puts it this way:

> In thus preserving the form while modifying the interpretation, I am following the great school of mathematical logicians who, in virtue of a series of startling definitions, have saved mathematics from the sceptics, and provided rigid demonstrations of its propositions.[23]

As far as I can see, Wittgenstein's criticisms of Ramsey's proposal either misstate it or attribute to it purposes that Ramsey was careful to exclude. Nonetheless, some of Wittgenstein's comments are revelatory of his own views on the philosophy of mathematics. They show, for example, that still (in 1927) he objected to the identity sign because it allowed the formulation of existence propositions:

> You are aware of the fact that the supposition of there being no individuals makes
>
> $$(Ex) \cdot x = x \qquad E$$
>
> 'absolute nonsense'. But if '$E$' is to say 'There is an individual', '$\sim E$' says: 'There is no individual'. Therefore from '$\sim E$' [it] follows that '$E$' is nonsense. Therefore '$\sim E$' must be nonsense itself, and therefore again so must be '$E$'.[24]

He then adds, repeating a Tractarian doctrine, that the legitimate use of the symbol "$(Ex)$" *shows* that there are individuals — and this can just as well be shown by the legitimate use of the symbol "$\sim (Ex)$."[25] Ramsey, in response, claims not to disagree with this, nor need he.[26]

There is one surprising feature of Wittgenstein's treatment of Ramsey's proposal that is worth pondering. As we have seen, Ramsey's central concern was to find a way of establishing mathematics as a "calculus of extensions." His introduction of an identity-sign surrogate (as we might call it) was intended specifically and wholly for that purpose. Now how, we might wonder, did Wittgenstein deal with this problem that motivated Ramsey? The answer is that it does not come up in Wittgenstein's initial criticisms of Ramsey's position.

It is possible, but it does not seem likely, that Wittgenstein was simply unaware of Ramsey's systematic reasons for trying to reintroduce a counterpart of the identity sign. A more plausible suggestion is that Wittgenstein knew what Ramsey was about, but did not share his commitment to the extensionality of mathematics. In fact, we have independent grounds for asserting that he was against it. Already in the *Tractatus* we find an underdeveloped but clear commitment to an antiextensionalist view of mathematics:

> The theory of classes is completely superfluous in mathematics.
> This is connected with the fact that the generality required in mathematics is not *accidental* generality.[27]

I suspect that the same antiextensionalist commitments expressed in these statements are the underlying basis for Wittgenstein's rejection of Ramsey's innovations. This is reinforced by later remarks that Wittgenstein makes concerning Ramsey's definition in his *Philosophical Grammar*, where he does explicitly attack the idea of specifying a function via an arbitrarily assigned extension. Again, Wittgenstein misrepresents Ramsey's position by attributing to him the view that any statement formed by flanking an identity sign with different letters must be self-contradictory. Beyond this, he suggests that Ramsey's definition is simply an arbitrary correlation between signs.

> Now what exactly is the specification of a function by its extension? Obviously, it is a group of definitions, e.g.,
>
> $$fa = p \text{ Def}$$
> $$fb = q \text{ Def}$$
> $$fc = r \text{ Def}$$
>
> These definitions permit us to substitute for the known propositions "$p$", "$q$", "$r$" the signs "$fa$", "$fb$", "$fc$".[28]

From this he draws the conclusion that "$fa$," "$fb$," and "$fc$" are not of a function–argument form. It is not hard to imagine how Ramsey would reply to this criticism. He would simply deny that the specification of a function in extension would consist of a group or list of definitions relating certain signs to others. To repeat, the correlation is not between signs at all, but between individuals and propositions. For these same reasons, Ramsey would have little patience with the following remark about infinite extensions:

> Moreover, the purpose of the introduction of functions in extension was to analyse propositions about infinite extensions, and it fails of this purpose when a function in extension is introduced by a list of definitions.[29]

It is hard not to conclude that Wittgenstein was simply confused about the nature and purpose of Ramsey's definition. We can, however, get a more just understanding of Wittgenstein's concerns by examining a remarkable passage that occurs both in the *Philosophical Remarks* and the *Philosophical Grammar*:

> Ramsey's theory of identity makes the mistake that would be made by someone who said that you could use a painting as a mirror as well, even if only for a single posture. If we say this we overlook that what is essential to a mirror is precisely that you can infer from it the posture of a body in front of it, whereas in the case of the painting you have to know that the postures tally before you can construe the picture as a mirror image.[30]

Here I think that the relationship between the mirror and its images is a metaphor for the internal relationships between a function and its values for various arguments. For Wittgenstein, it is essential to a mathematical function that its values are the results of its application. Thus it is a mistake, or rather a conceptual confusion, to identify a function with its extensional counterpart.

Once more it must be repeated that Ramsey was not guilty of the simple misunderstandings attributed to him by Wittgenstein. All the same, his wildly nonconstructive definition of an extensional counterpart for identity, and, indeed, the very motivation for the production of such a definition exemplifies a commitment to an *unordered generality* that Wittgenstein rejected in the *Tractatus* and never ceased to reject.

## 3.

Even though Wittgenstein's philosophical position underwent profound changes from its early to its later stages, his distrust of identity statements, in particular, statements of self-identity, remained unchanged. This comes out, for example, in an unlikely setting in the *Blue Book*. Wittgenstein is attacking those who would "model the use of the word 'I' on the demonstrative 'this person' or [on] 'he.'" In the midst of this discussion he inserts the following parenthetical remark:

> This way of making the two expressions similar is somewhat analogous to that which one sometimes adopts in mathematics, say in the proof that the sum of the three angles of a triangle is 180°.

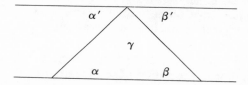

> We say "$\alpha = \alpha'$, $\beta = \beta'$, and $\gamma = \gamma$". (The first two equalities are of an entirely different kind from the third.)[31]

Although it is interesting in its own right, I shall not comment on the aptness of Wittgenstein's analogy. For our purposes, it is sufficient to ask why he thought that the third equality was of an entirely different kind from the other two. The answer, I think, is that the equality claims in the first two equations are substantial elements in the proof, whereas the third equation, although it expresses something important for the proof, could have been eliminated by a convention. A rule could be introduced to the following effect: two angles are equal if their nonshared components are equal. Under this convention, the assertion of $\gamma$'s equality with itself could have been replaced with the assertion that $\gamma$ is a shared component of the two larger angles. As it is, the assertion of $\gamma$'s self-equality reduces the proof to the standard pattern of adding up the values on two sides of a set of equations.

A more significant reference to self-identity occurs in the *Philosophical Investigations*.

"A thing is identical with itself."—There is no finer example of a useless proposition.[32]

This remark occurs in one of the most important, and certainly most difficult, parts of the *Philosophical Investigations*: the discussion of following a rule. Here Wittgenstein is trying to dispel the notion that a rule (say, for producing a series) antecedently fixes the steps that will satisfy it. Wittgenstein saw that no matter how a series is continued, there will be endlessly many functions, and hence endlessly many interpretations of the rule, that will sanction the step. From this it follows that there is a fundamental openness to rules that cannot be closed by interpretation alone:

> What this shews is that there is a way of grasping a rule which is *not* an *interpretation*, but which is exhibited in what we call "obeying the rule" and "going against it" in actual cases.[33]

Wittgenstein imagines someone trying to reject this line of argument by appealing to the notion of self-identity:

> But isn't the same at least the same? We seem to have an infallible paradigm of identity in the identity of a thing with itself. I feel like saying: "Here at any rate there can't be a variety of interpretations. If you are seeing a thing you are seeing identity too."

To this Wittgenstein replies:

> Then are two things the same when they are what *one* thing is? And how am I to apply what the *one* thing shews me to the case of two things?[34]

Now to follow a rule is to do the *same again*, for example, each time we add two. Of course, in following a rule we rarely do exactly the same thing over and over again—although we add two each time, we continually write down a new number. To use traditional language, we constantly do the same thing, but only in a given *respect*. It should, however, be clear that the infallible paradigm of self-identity will be of no use in determining whether a rule generates a series that is always the same in some respect. Again, whatever step is taken, there will be endlessly many interpretations of the rule that will show that the same thing has been done again and also endlessly many interpretations of the rule that will show that it has not. The appeal to self-identity will have no capacity to adjudicate between these competing interpretations.

More deeply, Wittgenstein not only rejects the idea that self-identity can help us fix the notion of the *same again*, he denies the very meaningfulness of statements of self-identity. (On his account of meaning, the uselessness of the proposition guarantees its meaninglessness.) Yet philosophers have been drawn to the proposition that everything is identical with itself, for it seems to exemplify that rock-hard relationship in reality that it has been philosophy's special business to articulate. Here we can become captured by the picture of a series being a limited instance of the law of identity. Each step in a series is connected with its predecessor and successor, in some respect, with the same rigidity that each thing is related to itself. This, in turn, can further the illusion that the series has an antecedently given structure that our symbolism merely traces out. In other words, a misuse of the notion of identity, in particular, a mesmerized fascination with the notion of self-identity, can lead one into a Platonism in the philosophy of mathematics and theory of meaning of the kind that Wittgenstein was most anxious to reject.

## NOTES

1. Frege, Gottlob. "On Sense and Reference," *Translations from the Philosophical Writings of Gottlob Frege*, edited by Peter Geach and Max Black (Oxford: Basil Blackwell, 1952), p. 56. I have translated "Gleichheit" as "identity" to reflect Frege's interpretation of equality as strict identity.

2. Fogelin, Robert J., *Wittgenstein* (London: Routledge and Kegan Paul, 1976), pp. 60ff.

3. Wittgenstein, Ludwig, *Notebooks, 1914–1916* (Oxford: Basil Blackwell, 1961), p. 10.

4. *Ibid.*, p. 2.

5. Wittgenstein, Ludwig, *Tractatus Logico-Philosophicus*, translated by David Pears and Brian McGuinness (London: Routledge and Kegan Paul, 1961), #4.1272.

6. *Ibid.*, #5.53.

7. See Ramsey, F. P., *The Foundations of Mathematics* (London: Routledge and Kegan Paul, 1931), pp. 31ff.

8. Wittgenstein, Ludwig, *Tractatus*, #5.533.

9. Bogen, James, "Recent Wittgenstein," *Teaching Philosophy*, 4:1, January 1981, n. 73–74.

10. Received by author, dated 7-13-82.

11. Ramsey, F. P., *Foundations*, p. 50. (See also Wittgenstein's *Tractatus*, #5.5302.)

12. *Ibid.*, p. 50.

13. *Ibid.*, p. 15.

14. *Ibid.*, pp. 50ff.

15. *Ibid.*, pp. 52–53.

16. *Ibid.*, p. 56.

17. Wittgenstein, Ludwig, *Wittgenstein and the Vienna Circle*, conversations recorded by Friedrich Waismann, edited by Brian McGuinness, translated by Joachim Schulte and Brian McGuinness (Oxford: Basil Blackwell, 1979), p. 189.

18. *Ibid.*, pp. 190–191.

19. Ramsey, F. P., *Foundations*, p. 53. It is important to remember that Wittgenstein thought that the symbol " = " has a legitimate employment in *equations*; indeed, for him, this is its paradigmatic employment. Furthermore, he rejected Frege's idea that equations are identity statements; instead he treated them as rules expressing the intersubstitutability of signs. Perhaps this explains why Wittgenstein constantly speaks of the definition of signs where Ramsey is concerned with the correlation of individuals with propositions. I do not think that Ramsey supposed that this definition bore upon the occurrence of the symbol " = " in equations.

20. "$Q(x, y)$" represents Ramsey's "$(\phi_e) \cdot \phi_e x \equiv \phi_e y$."

21. Wittgenstein, Ludwig, *Vienna Circle*, p. 191.

22. Ramsey, F. P., *Foundations*, pp. 31–32.

23. *Ibid.*, p. 56.

24. Wittgenstein, Ludwig, *Vienna Circle*, pp. 191–192.

25. *Ibid.*, p. 191.

26. *Ibid.*

27. Wittgenstein, Ludwig, *Tractatus*, #6.031.

28. Wittgenstein, Ludwig, *Philosophical Grammar*, edited by Rush Rhees, translated by Anthony Kenny (Oxford: Basil Blackwell, 1974), pp. 315ff. [See also *Philosophical Remarks*, edited by Rush Rhees, translated by Raymond Hargreaves and Roger White (Oxford: Basil Blackwell, 1975), pp. 141ff.]

29. *Ibid.*, p. 317.

30. *Ibid.*, p. 315; *Philosophical Remarks*, p. 143.

31. Wittgenstein, Ludwig, *The Blue and Brown Books* (Oxford: Basil Blackwell, 1958), p. 68. (Cf. *Philosophical Grammar*, p. 317.)

32. Wittgenstein, Ludwig, *Philosophical Investigations*, 3rd ed., trans-

lated by G. E. M. Anscombe (Oxford: Basil Blackwell, 1958), #216. A parallel discussion occurs in the *Remarks on the Foundations of Mathematics* where Wittgenstein comments on Frege's assertion that "it is impossible for human beings . . . to recognize an object as different from itself." *Remarks on the Foundations of Mathematics*, edited by G. H. von Wright, R. Rhees, G. E. M. Anscombe, translated by G. E. M. Anscombe (Oxford: Basil Blackwell, 1967), pp. 41 and 183.

33. Wittgenstein, Ludwig, *Investigations*, #201.

34. *Ibid.*, #215.

# 12

# Negative Elementary Propositions

## I

When asked by Russell whether there are any *negative* elementary propositions, Wittgenstein replied with a terse, "Of course no elementary proposition is negative" (*NB*, p. 130). The tone of this reply and the lack of an accompanying justification suggest that Wittgenstein thought the question rather stupid. I think that most commentators would follow Wittgenstein in this opinion. In fact, Russell's question is searching in its implications and, in the end, a tentative affirmative answer is perhaps more justified than Wittgenstein's dogmatic denial.

We can begin naively by considering a candidate for a negative elementary proposition; i.e., the denial of an elementary proposition. An elementary proposition, we are told, "consists of names. It is a nexus, a concatenation, of names" (4.22). Taking *A, B, C,* and *D* as names, an elementary proposition might look like this:

$$ABCD \qquad (1)$$

The denial of this proposition has the following form:

$$-(ABCD) \qquad (2)$$

"Negative Elementary Propositions," *Philosophical Studies*, Vol. 24 (January 1974). Reprinted by permission of the publisher.

From the Tractarian standpoint, it seems obvious that this cannot be treated as an elementary proposition, since it contains three expressions (the negation sign, the left-hand parenthesis, the right-hand parenthesis) that are not names. Forgetting for a moment about the parentheses (which is *not* an unimportant matter), we may simply recall that it is a "fundamental idea" of the *Tractatus* "that the 'logical constants' are not representatives" (4.0312). Thus the second proposition cannot be called elementary since it contains at least one expression — the negation sign — that is not a representative, i.e., not a name.

I think that there is a strong temptation to let matters rest here as clearly settled, but the situation becomes difficult again when we consider Wittgenstein's positive account of the role of logical constants in propositions. Logical constants (so-called) are not representatives; they do not stand for things as names do. Their actual status in propositions can be exhibited through the manner in which they are defined. Logical constants are defined truth-functionally.

We can bring out the distinctive features of Wittgenstein's truth-functional definition of the logical constants by contrasting his manner of definition with that typically found in elementary textbooks on logic. A regular truth-table definition of conjunction looks like this:[1]

| $p$ | $q$ | $(p \& q)$ |
|---|---|---|
| T | T | T |
| T | F | F |
| F | T | F |
| F | F | F |

Wittgenstein would use a different format:

| "$p$ | $q$ | " |
|---|---|---|
| T | T | T |
| T | F | F |
| F | T | F |
| F | F | F |

These formats are different in two striking ways: (1) no sign for conjunction appears in the second format, and (2) the second format is enclosed within quotation marks. The first feature of his definition Wittgenstein cites as part of his evidence that there are no logical objects. If we are tempted to think that the sign for conjunction is the name for some object or substantive relation, then this temptation should be dispelled by noticing the complete eliminability of this sign in a perspicuous notation. In the proposed definition, the conjunction sign disappears, leaving no namelike expression to take its place.[2]

The quotation marks are introduced to indicate that the expression *as a whole* is a propositional sign. It is a propositional sign that expresses a true proposition just in case both propositional signs "*p*" and "*q*" express true propositions and a propositional sign that expresses something false otherwise. In sum, we can construct new propositional signs out of old ones simply by giving a complete assignment of truth values to the combinations of truth assignments for the base propositions. We might say that logical constants do not occur *in* propositions, but operate *on* them.

We can now return to the original question: are there negative elementary propositions and, in particular, is the denial of an elementary proposition itself an elementary proposition? We may first notice how the expression "−(*ABCD*)" will look in our new and more adequate notation:

| " (*ABCD*) | " |
|:---:|:---:|
| T | F |
| F | T |

Following one of Wittgenstein's conventions, we may also use a more compact notation that assumes that the left-hand column is fixed and we merely report the assignments in the right column: "(FT) (*ABCD*)".[3] This is just the proposition that is true when the proposition expressed by "*ABCD*" is false and false otherwise.

At this point, what grounds can we invoke for saying that the denial of an elementary proposition is not itself an elementary proposition? The first thought might be this: we will not allow a proposition to be called an elementary proposition if it is a truth-function of some proposition. This move, however, does not square with one of the central claims of the Tractarian system:

> 5. A proposition is a truth-function of elementary propositions. (An elementary proposition is a truth-function of itself.)

Proceeding further, if we now ask what truth-functional relationship an elementary proposition bears to itself, we may express this in the following way: "(TF) (*ABCD*)." I think that it is just at this point that we begin to wonder whether there is any good *systematic* reason for saying that the denial of an elementary proposition is not an elementary proposition. At least the original idea that the denial of an elementary proposition contains a sign of the *wrong kind* has now been defused. In a proper notation, an elementary proposition looks like this:

$$(TF)\ (ABCD)$$

and the denial of this proposition looks like this:

$$(FT)\ (ABCD)$$

Here we see at once that there is no basis for distinguishing the two cases relative to *content*.

I am not denying that a distinction can be drawn along the lines that Wittgenstein seems to intend. We can just say that a proposition is elementary if, in canonical notation, it has the form "(TF) $(A_1 \ldots A_n)$," where the items in the right-hand parentheses are just names forming a single combination. The denial of such a proposition differs only in the *order* of the truth values given in the left-hand parentheses. If we like, we can just take this feature of order as definitive of elementary propositions, but it is hard to see what the point of this would be. The term "elementary" should stand in some relationship with its regular use, and it is far from clear how the mere commutation of ingredients should make one thing elementary and another thing not.

It thus seems that Wittgenstein has drawn the distinction between elementary and nonelementary propositions at a clearly defined, yet *unnatural*, place. The notion of something being elementary usually stands in contrast with its being complex, and for this reason it seems more natural to draw the distinction between elementary and nonelementary with respect to the structure of the items in the right-hand parentheses. We can insist that the names in the right-hand parentheses constitute a *single* combination of names rather than two (or more) distinct combinations of names. In this way the proposition "(TF) (*ABCD*)" is rightly called elementary whereas the proposition "(TFFF) (*ABCD, EFGH*)" is not. I think that this is just the kind of result we anticipate when we draw the distinction between elementary and nonelementary propositions.

At this point I think that the most plausible thing to say—if we wish to reflect the systematic character of the *Tractatus*—is that there *are* negative elementary propositions and the denial of what Wittgenstein would offer as an example of an elementary proposition provides the instance of this. I think that it is also tempting to say that Wittgenstein was misled in this area because he failed to see the full import of his own treatment of logical constants.

# II

Things are more complicated than this. If we treat both "(TF) (*ABCD*)" and "(FT) (*ABCD*)" as elementary propositions, we will have to be dimwitted not to wonder about the other truth combinations that might occur in the left-hand parentheses. There are two: "(TT) (*ABCD*)" and "(FF) (*ABCD*)."

First we can get clear what these two expressions come to. The first presents the proposition that is *true* whether or not the picture component agrees with reality; the second presents the proposition that is *false* whether or not the picture component agrees with reality. In short, the first presents a tautological construction; the second presents a contradictory construction. At this point there is no way of avoiding the following result: if we stand by our previous reasoning we must call these newly formed propositions elementary as well.

As we shall see in a moment, this result will run squarely against the stated text and leads to complicated considerations that will mute the conclusion drawn in the first part of this paper. But before taking up these difficult issues, it will help to dismiss one line of reasoning that may naturally spring to mind. When we think of a contradiction, we normally reflect upon a proposition of the following kind: "($p$ & $-p$)." Here the appearance of a conjunction sign may seem to exclude elementarity straight off, but the reasoning here is no more persuasive than the original reasoning with respect to the negation sign. In canonical notation, this proposition is rendered as: "(FF) ($p$)," and again we notice that there is no complexity in the right hand parentheses.[4] So once more if we take seriously Wittgenstein's notion that logical constants express operations *on* propositions rather than name constituents *in* propositions, we see that the mere appearance of a logical constant is not, *eo ipso*, a sign of complexity.

The idea that tautologies and contradictions constructed on the base of a single proposition are to be treated as elementary so plainly runs against the stated text of the *Tractatus* that it hardly needs documentation. Now, in fact, we have already departed from the text by treating the negation of an elementary proposition as itself an elementary proposition:

> 4.211 It is a sign of a proposition's being elementary that there can be no elementary proposition contradicting it.

The suggested treatment of tautologies and contradictions is explicitly ruled out by the following passage:

> 6.3751c (It is clear that the logical product of two elementary propositions can neither be a tautology nor a contradiction. . . . )

On the proposed account this is violated just in case both elementary propositions are tautological or at least one of them is contradictory. The situation relative to the text is, then, perfectly clear. Given the four propositions:

$$(1)\ (TF)\ (p) \qquad (2)\ (FT)\ (p)$$
$$(3)\ (TT)\ (p) \qquad (4)\ (FF)\ (p)$$

the text indicates that only the first may be treated as elementary. I do not wish to deny this! I have argued that Wittgenstein *should* not have drawn this distinction as he does, for if we take his own account of logical constants seriously, then it seems more natural to accept all four constructions as elementary.

At this point I think we can see that features of the *Tractatus* push us in different directions. If we think of elementary propositions as being *simple* and insist on the point that logical constants, since they are not representatives, have no direct bearing upon simplicity, then we arrive at the kind of position that I suggest *ought* to be presented in the *Tractatus*. In contrast, if we want our elementary propositions to be the counterparts of the *independent* possible states of affairs that make up reality, then we get the theory actually presented in the *Tractatus*.

We might also say that the demands of the *picture theory* have taken precedence over the demands of the logical theory; it might be interesting to imagine how the position will be worked out with the priorities reversed. In the first place, all the talk about independence can be preserved with only minor notational changes. We merely distinguish between various kinds of elementary propositions — i.e., the four kinds previously noted — and, where needed, simply specify that we are speaking of elementary propositions of the form "(TF)*p*." In this area nothing very interesting takes place.

Systematic questions do arise when we ask the question whether we wish to admit elementary propositions that are tautologies or contradictions. To answer this question, we must inquire into the status of such constructions within the Tractarian framework. In fact, their status is rather anomalous. If we concentrate upon the picture theory, it is surely most natural to say that tautologies and contradictions are not propositions at all. In contrast, if we concentrate upon the thesis of truth-functionality, i.e., the claim that propositions are truth-functions of elementary propositions, then we are virtually forced to treat both tautologies and contradictions as propositions.

I shall spell this out in a bit more detail. At 4.5 Wittgenstein tells us that the general form of a proposition is: "This is how things stand." Now, of course, a tautology tells us nothing about how things stand, for its truth remains constant however the things of the world are disposed toward one another. Thus if propositions are pictures in some nondegenerate sense, then tautologies ought not to be considered pictures. In contrast, at 6, Wittgenstein makes the following declaration:

> 6. This general form of a truth-function is [P, $\bar{\xi}$, N($\bar{\xi}$)]. This is the general form of a proposition.[5]

This definition implies that every truth-function of elementary propositions will count as a proposition and since both tautologies and contradictions *straightforwardly* meet this demand, there can be no question of their propositional status. Wittgenstein solves this difficulty by admitting tautologies and contradictions to propositional status while at the same time describing them as "limiting cases—indeed the disintegration—of the combination of signs" (4.466).

What is important for our present purposes is that tautologies and contradictions have a problematic status in the *Tractatus* as a whole, and that their position is finally settled with respect to the theory of truth-functionality. That is, the demands of the picture theory are finally relaxed in favor of the demands of the logical theory. So now if we ask whether *elementary* propositions must be pictures, it is really far from obvious what we should say. At some point in the *Tractatus* a decision has to be made about those propositions whose representational capacity is cancelled by a truth-functional assignment of all Ts or all Fs in the left-hand parentheses. This can be done effectively in a variety of ways, but it seems to me that the most perspicuous way of doing this in conformity with the basic ideas of the *Tractatus* would be as follows. The general form of a proposition is this:

$$(V_1, \ldots, V_{2^n})(C_1, \ldots, C_n)$$

Here the items in the left-hand parentheses are truth-value assignments; the items in the right-hand parentheses are name combinations (e.g., "*ABCD*") corresponding to possible object combinations.[6] Questions of elementarity turn upon the structure of the right-hand component. In particular, in an elementary proposition there is only one name combination in the right-hand component.

Questions concerning the contingent, tautological, or contradictory status of a proposition are settled by the structure of the left-hand component. It is thus possible to have a tautological elementary proposition. Wittgenstein chose not to proceed in this manner. Elementary propositions operate under a double constraint: they must be *simple* in the right-hand component and *affirmative contingent* in the left-hand component. As far as effectiveness is concerned, there can be no complaint about drawing the distinction in this way. But of course, the demand for effectiveness can be met in endlessly many arbitrary ways. I think that the shortcoming of Wittgenstein's method of classification is that it combines ideas of a totally disparate character. It mixes things up and therefore the internal structure of the *Tractatus* stands out much less clearly than it might have.

## III

There is another possible reason why Wittgenstein may have dismissed Russell's suggestion out of hand. Speaking a bit loosely, in an elementary proposition, a combination of names represents a combination of objects. In contrast, we cannot represent a *non*combination of objects through the noncombination of names, for noncombined names will not constitute a proposition at all. So once more we encounter an asymmetry in favor of the positive.

Now of course the *Tractatus* shows a bias in favor of combined names over uncombined names, yet, if what I have said already is correct, this should not bear upon the question of whether elementary propositions can be negative as well as positive. We can call the second component in the expressions "(TF) (*ABCD*)" and "(FT) (*ABCD*)" the *pictorial component*. I have argued that it makes sense both *intrinsically* and *relative to the basic structure of the Tractatus* to draw this distinction between elementary and nonelementary propositions solely with respect to the pictorial component. A negative elementary proposition, then, is not faced with the impossible task of asserting the noncombination of objects by means of a noncombination of names.

# IV

I have not argued that the text of the *Tractatus* contains a doctrine of negative elementary propositions. I have argued instead that on a consistent development of its basic principles it *should have*. Among other things, this gives us a natural way of understanding the following important passage:

> 4.0621c The propositions '*p*' and '−*p*' have opposite sense, but there corresponds to them one and the same reality.

More simply, there seems to be no reason why simplicity or elementarity should be affected by truth-functional considerations and this is something that seems *especially* true on Wittgenstein's treatment of logical constants.

## NOTES

1. Wittgenstein actually uses a truth-functional definition of *material implication* in his example. I have turned to conjunction because it is a more natural and less problematic notion. (See 4.442.)

2. Of course, the argument depends upon the claim that the Ts and Fs are not, contrary to Frege's position, names.

3. Using the same convention, the construction for conjunction is "(TFFF) (*p, q*)."

4. It is not difficult to avoid the pseudo-complexity of expressions like "(FFFF) (*p, p*)." It is never necessary to have redundant occurrences of a proposition in the right-hand parentheses and we shall therefore insist that they always be eliminated. Again, however, this is a matter of decision, and if we so choose we can effectively draw a distinction between elementary and nonelementary propositions that cuts between "(FF) (*p*)" and "(FFFF) (*p, p*)." It's just hard to see the point of doing this. [The tautology "(TTTT) (*p, q*)" is not reducible in this way and is not an elementary proposition.]

5. I shall not both to explain this symbolism for this is done quite adequately by Russell in his introduction to the *Tractatus*.

6. This formulation might be challenged because of its finitist implications, but that is not something at issue in the present discussion. The $2^n$ values in the left-hand parentheses correspond to the number of truth-combinations of the *n* propositions in the right-hand parentheses.

# 13

# Wittgenstein and Intuitionism

In this essay I shall discuss one important strain that runs through Ludwig Wittgenstein's *Remarks on the Foundations of Mathematics*[1]: his commitment to themes characteristic of the intuitionistic movement in mathematics. Chief among these are his attacks upon the unrestricted use of the Law of Excluded Middle,[2] his distrust of nonconstructive proofs,[3] and his impatience with the idea that mathematics stands in need of a foundation.[4]

There is a well-known historical connection between Wittgenstein and the intuitionistic movement. Presumably a person with Wittgenstein's interests would have encountered this movement before 1928, but in any case we know that he heard Brouwer lecture in March of that year. In von Wright's cautious words, "It is rumoured to have been this which stirred him to take up philosophy again."[5] But I shall not here undertake the monumental task of tracing the connections between what Wittgenstein heard in 1928 and what he ultimately wrote in the 1940s. Instead, I shall content myself with exploring these themes as they reach maturity in the *Remarks on the Foundations of Mathematics*.

Broadly speaking, these intuitionistic motifs combine Ramsey's notions of the *normativity* of logic and mathematics with the intuitionists' implicit *modal* conception of mathematical propositions. This synthesis constitutes one of Wittgenstein's most important achievements, for it allows him to bring together a wide range of those commitments that give his later philosophy its characteristic physiognomy. Seeing this will illuminate more than his philosophy of mathematics.

"Wittgenstein and Intuitionism," *American Philosophical Quarterly*, Vol. 5, No. 4 (October 1968). Reprinted by permission of the publisher.

# I

Virtually everything that Wittgenstein says about mathematics forms part of a critique of Platonism (or Realism) in that field; most of the remainder is a criticism of unsuccessful attempts to avoid Platonism. There is something inherently compelling about the following reasoning:

> "5 × 5 = 25" expresses a true proposition. Thus, there must exist a domain of objects that it is true of. Furthermore, it expresses a necessarily true proposition, hence these objects must be ideal, not empirical, objects.

Under the influence of this reasoning (which admits of a much stronger statement) we come to think of mathematics as the natural history of mathematical objects,[6] except that it is not really a natural history since the relevant objects are not natural objects and the method of investigation is not experimental.

Wittgenstein's critique of Platonism goes as deep as possible: he calls into question the root notion that mathematical judgments express assertoric propositions. We can notice some of the things he says on this matter:

> Of course, we teach children the multiplication tables in the form of little *sentences*, but is that essential? (I, 143)

> We are used to saying "2 times 2 is 4," and the verb "is" makes this into a proposition, and apparently establishes a close kinship with everything we call a "proposition." Where it is a matter only of a superficial relationship. (I, Appendix I, 4)

If mathematical constructions are only superficially related to other things that we call propositions, what, in fact, are they like? On this score, Wittgenstein says two things that, at first glance, may seem unrelated. First of all, he says that mathematics is normative:

> The proposition proved by means of a proof serves as a rule — and so as a paradigm. For we *go by* the rule. (I, Appendix II, 4)

What I am saying comes to this, that mathematics is *normative*. But "norm" does not mean the same thing as "ideal." (V, 40)

Mathematics forms a network of norms. (V, 46)

Paralleling these passages are others that speak about our *mode of acknowledging* a mathematical expression:

One might, so to speak, preface axioms with a special assertion sign.

We give an axiom a different kind of acknowledgment from any empirical proposition. . . . An axiom, I should like to say, is a different part of speech. (III, 5)

On one occasion he brings these two strands together:

I am trying to say something like this: even if the proved proposition seems to point to a reality outside itself, still it is only the expression of acceptance of a new measure (of reality). (II, 28)

Thus if we say straight out what we in fact acknowledge, mathematical expressions undergo the following transformation: "5 × 5 = 25" (acknowledged as a law) becomes "It is a law that 5 × 5 = 25." That Wittgenstein had something very like this in mind is brought out by the following striking passage:

The opposite of "there exists a law that *p*" is not "there exists a law that −*p*." But if one expresses the first by means of *P*, and the second by means of −*P*, one will get into difficulties. (IV, 13)

We might put it this way: mathematical propositions are modal propositions with their modal aspects suppressed.

We can bring these reflections into sharper focus by sketching a modal logic for the operator "It is a rule that . . . " In the style of Fitch,[7] we shall lay down natural deduction rules for the introduction and elimination of an *R*-operator. The introduction rule will employ the following subproof format:

The top "*R*" flags the column to its right as a *rule subproof*. We shall call "$\phi$" the strict reiterate of "*R$\phi$*" and then insist that items may be introduced into a rule subproof only by strict reiteration. We then say:

"*R$\phi$*" is a direct consequence, by *rule introduction*, of any rule subproof that has no hypothesis and has "$\phi$" as an item.

The elimination rule has the following form:

"$-R-\phi$" is a direct consequence of "*R$\phi$*" by rule elimination.

The system so constructed has obvious analogies with modal system *D*. The plausibility of this analogy should further emerge as we go along.

Our leading idea is this: *at work* the mathematician suppresses the modal character of his propositions, or, as we can now say using Fitch's perspicuous format, he operates within a rule subproof without attending to the logical surroundings. At the same time, an essential feature of mathematical practice is captured by the introduction rule we have adopted. Why, in particular, is it not simply perverse for the mathematician to exclude an empirical proposition from his derivation when the empirical proposition is quite beyond any sensible doubt? The Platonist answers this by saying that mathematics is not about empirical objects, but about a domain of objects of its own. The present approach offers a viable alternative to Platonism. Empirical propositions are excluded from the mathematician's proofs because his proofs are modal proofs (albeit, with their heads and tails missing).

We can now see why Wittgenstein challenges the application of the Law of Excluded Middle to mathematical expressions. In order to derive "$P$ v $-P$" (where "$P$" and "$-P$" are mathematical expres-

sions in their normal guise), we would have to produce "*Rp* v
*R −p*" as the last step of a completed proof, and this is not a
theorem of the system we have created by taking Wittgenstein's
suggestions seriously. The upshot of this is that the acceptance of
"*P* v *− P*" as an instance of the Law of Excluded Middle is nothing
more than a mistake due to the lack of perspicuity of our mathematical language.

> [T]he understanding of a mathematical proposition is not guaran-
> teed by its verbal form, as is the case with most non-mathematical
> propositions. (IV, 25)

These purely formal results tally exactly with Wittgenstein's comments about the Law of Excluded Middle. The discussion turns
upon the following question: Does the pattern $\phi$ (a particular arrangement of digits, e.g., "770," "777," and sometimes "7777")
occur in the infinite expansion of $\pi$? Of course, we do not know
the answer to this question.

> But what are you saying if you say that one thing is clear: either one
> will come on $\phi$ in the infinite sequence, or one will not?
>
> It seems to me that in saying this you are yourself setting up a rule
> or postulate. (IV, 9)

The second passage is crucial for an understanding of Wittgenstein's position; why should adopting this principle amount to
setting up a rule or postulate? Do we have any right to assume that
the expansion rule either *prescribes* or *proscribes* the occurrence of
such an arrangement within the expansion?

> What if someone were to reply to a question: "So far there is no
> such thing as an answer to this question?"
>
> So, e.g., the poet might reply when asked whether the hero of his
> poem has a sister or not − when, that is, he has not yet decided
> anything about it.
>
> I want to say: it *looks* as if a ground for the decision were already
> there: and it has yet to be invented. (IV, 9)

Why should it even *look* as though "the ground for the decision were already there?" Essentially, this is an illusion generated by a faulty analogy with the finite case.

"But surely all the members of the series up to 1,000th, up to the $10^{10}$th, and so on, are determined." This is correct if it is supposed to mean that it is not the case that, e.g., the so-and-so-many'th is *not* determined. But you can see that *that* gives you no information about whether a particular pattern is going to appear in the series (if it has not appeared so far). *And so we can see* that we are using a misleading *picture.* (IV, 11)

For an expansion of finite length, we can simply generate it and see if the pattern occurs. If it does occur, then it is obviously prescribed by the expansion rule; if it does not occur, then it is proscribed in virtue of the fact that the rule of expansion permits *only* the one sequence that it in fact generates. But there is nothing corresponding to this in the infinite case; no sense attaches to the notion of running through the *whole* of an infinite sequence in order to assure ourselves that a given pattern does *not* arise. Nothing, then, rules out the possibility that the rule of expansion simply does not cover the case.

But isn't Wittgenstein just wrong about all this? Couldn't we perhaps produce a nonconstructive proof showing that the sequence "777" occurs in the expansion of $\pi$ even though it does not show where it occurs? Wittgenstein responds directly to this possibility.

Well, proved in this way this "existential proposition" would, for certain purposes, not be a *rule.* But might it not serve, e.g., as a means of classifying expansion rules? It would perhaps be proved in an analogous way that "777" does not occur in $\pi^2$ but it does occur in $\pi \times e$, etc. The question would simply be: is it reasonable to say of the proof concerned: it proves the existence of "777" in this expansion? This is simply misleading. (V, 34)

We have thus come to Wittgenstein's second "intuitionistic" theme: his distrust of nonconstructive proofs.

Nonconstructive proofs come in various forms, but the simplest paradigm is an indirect proof concerning existence. In its classical employment such indirect proofs take two forms: (1) we assume the denial of a proposition, derive a contradiction, and in virtue of this assert it; and (2) we assume a proposition, derive a contradiction, and in virtue of this assert its denial. Wittgenstein's commitments lead to a different treatment of these two proof patterns.

His challenge to the first pattern of proof follows immediately from what we have said about the Law of Excluded Middle. When the classical mathematician attempts to establish "*P*" by assuming "*−P*," he is *misapplying* the rule of indirect proof by assuming the *contrary* − not the *contradictory* − of the proposition to be established. Schematically, his proof looks like this:

$$R - p \qquad \text{Assumption}$$
$$\cdot$$
$$\cdot$$
$$\cdot$$
$$q \,\&\, -q$$
$$Rp \qquad \text{Conclusion}$$

In fact, it should have the following form:

$$-Rp \qquad \text{Assumption}$$
$$\cdot$$
$$\cdot$$
$$\cdot$$
$$q \,\&\, -q$$
$$Rp \qquad \text{Conclusion}$$

Formally, this replacement of the contradictory by the contrary amounts to accepting the following modal principles:

$$-Rp \rightarrow R - p$$

For other quite natural reasons, the classical mathematician tacitly accepts the entailment in the reverse direction, and as a result, takes over a reduction axiom that altogether destroys the modal character of mathematical propositions. After this move, how can he distinguish mathematical propositions from empirical propositions? For want of a modal distinction, a material distinction is invoked, i.e., mathematical propositions are assigned a special subject matter. Once more we are back to the Realist's conception of mathematics as the not quite natural history of not quite natural objects. This is one important way in which Platonism and the classical employment of an indirect proof are inextricably bound together.

Given a modal interpretation of mathematics, the second pattern for the indirect proof fares a bit better. We can establish something of the form "$-Rp$" by assuming "$Rp$" and deriving a contradiction from this assumption. Schematically, such a proof would have the following form:

$$Rp \qquad \text{Assumption}$$
$$\cdot$$
$$\cdot$$
$$\cdot$$
$$q \,\&\, -q$$
$$-Rp \qquad \text{Conclusion}$$

What does such a proof establish? Our overriding idea is that mathematical propositions are elliptical for expressions having the form "$Rp$," and, of course, the derived conclusion does not have this form. We have not established a mathematical proposition by this proof, but a metamathematical proposition to the effect that a given rule cannot be introduced without an attendant loss of consistency. This is precisely Wittgenstein's position:

> What an indirect proof says, however, is: "If you want *this* then you cannot assume that: for only the opposite of what you do not want to abandon would be compatible with *that*." (IV, 28)

Thus an indirect proof, even when employed properly, cannot be used to *extend* a system. Its only legitimate use is limiting; it shows that the introduction of a new rule would engender a loss of consistency.

How does all this square with Wittgenstein's repeated claim that he leaves mathematics just as it is and only changes our way of viewing it?[8] Hasn't he here, at least, called into question the very *validity* of a standard method of proof? I do not think that Wittgenstein speaks directly to this specific question, but from what he says about the Law of Excluded Middle, it should be clear what his response must be. Through the use of an indirect proof, the mathematician does establish something *about* a system: he shows that the introduction of "*Rp*" will lead to inconsistency. If in virtue of this he goes on to treat "*R* − *p*" (or " − *P*") as a theorem, he has, in effect, *laid down a new rule* or *made a new decision*. Looked at in this way, the method of indirect proof becomes an engine of creation and not, as the Platonists believe, a device for discovering new mathematical facts. Alternatively, we can say that the classical mathematician accepts a second order rule to the effect that anything is a rule if the introduction of the contrary rule leads to inconsistency. We can call this the principle of mathematical growth.

Wittgenstein's remarks about indirect proofs are connected with another important theme in his philosophy of mathematics. For him, a perspicuous direct proof traces a pathway within our conceptual system. The proof *creates* this pathway and *eo ipso* creates a new mathematical concept that exhibits *internal relationships* within the system.

> If the proof registers the procedure according to the rule, then by doing this it produces a new concept.

> With this is connected the fact that we can say that proof must show the existence of internal relations. For the internal relation is the operation producing one structure from another, seen as equivalent to the picture of the transition itself − so that now the transition according to this series of configurations is *eo ipso* a transition according to those rules for operating. (V, 51)

In contrast, if what we have said in following Wittgenstein is correct, an indirect proof (as it is normally employed) is not like this at all; it does not exhibit the process of evolving one structure from another. In essence, the method of indirect proof is a rule for stipulating new rules under special constraints. With such a proof pattern the conceptual pathway is abruptly broken by this stipulation and thus we are not edified by seeing something new unfold out of the old.

Thus the formal side of Wittgenstein's theory, that mathematical expressions are suppressed modal propositions, ties into an important philosophical theme, that mathematics is a creative activity. A perspicuous direct proof presents an extension of mathematics from *within*; an indirect proof (in its classical employment) simply adds to the stock of theorems without enhancing our conceptual understanding. To see the full significance of this difference and to get further insight into the "deontic" aspect of Wittgenstein's modal picture of mathematics, we must now attend to his remarks concerning the *application* of mathematical propositions.

## II

In a crucial passage Wittgenstein ties mathematical discourse to empirical discourse: "Concepts which occur in 'necessary' propositions must also occur and have a meaning in non-necessary ones" (IV, 41). And less abstractly:

> I want to say: it is essential to mathematics that its signs are also employed in *mufti* [in Zivil].
>
> It is the use outside mathematics, and so the meaning of the signs that make the sign game into mathematics. (IV, 2)

The numeral "2" occurs in the empirical proposition "There are 2 horses on the elevator" and also in the necessary proposition "2 + 2 = 4"; Wittgenstein here insists that without significant occurrences in expressions of the first sort, the numeral "2" could not have significant occurrences in expressions of the second sort.

Wittgenstein's reflections on this point have a curious form: he repeatedly considers the possibility that calculating is an experimental procedure, i.e., in calculating we set out to discover what results from applying certain rules to, say, given numbers. This view, however unattractive it is in every other respect, is at least hard-headed:

> It looks like obscurantism to say that a calculation is not an experiment. . . . But only because people believe that one is asserting the

existence of an intangible, i.e., a shadowy, object side by side with what we can all grasp. (II, 76)

The experimental analysis of calculation blocks Platonism by treating mathematical propositions as statements *about* a human activity. But this will not do, just because mathematical propositions are not statements about what people do.

We say, not, *"So that's* how we go!," but *"So that's* how it goes!" (II, 69)

The same thing can be seen by reflecting upon the difference between the result of an experiment and the result of a calculation. Getting the *right* result is part of doing a calculation correctly, but it cannot be part of doing an experiment correctly. *"There are no* causal connexions in a calculation, only the connexions of the pattern" (V, 15). In an experiment we do something and then *await* the result; in a calculation we produce the result itself.

But if we abandon the experimental interpretation of calculation, how do we avoid falling back into Platonism?

"To be practical, mathematics must tell us facts." But do these facts have to be mathematical facts? But why should not mathematics instead of "teaching us facts" create the forms of what we call facts? (V, 15)

For arithmetic to equate two expressions is, one might say, a grammatical trick.

In this way arithmetic bars a particular kind of description and conducts description into other channels. (And it goes without saying that this is connected with facts of experience.) (V, 3)

These passages contain the core of Wittgenstein's conception of how mathematical propositions find application: (1) the vocabulary of mathematics provides us with *modes of description*, and (2) the laws of mathematics supply us with *rules for the identity of descriptions*. I shall examine these points separately.

1. A quotation from Wittgenstein should adequately illustrate the first point:

"It is interesting to know *how many* vibrations this note has." But it took arithmetic to teach you this question. It taught you to see this kind of fact.

Mathematics — I want to say — teaches you, not just the answer to a question, but a whole language-game with questions and answers. (V, 15)

This does not commit Wittgenstein to the position that the note did *not* have so many vibrations before people learned to count. This is worth saying if only to block an overly Kantian interpretation of the text.

2. The second idea, that the laws of arithmetic supply us with rules for the identity of descriptions, is more difficult to make articulate. As a start, we can consider the simple identity statement: "$5 \times 5 = 25$." This expression can play a double role in our mathematical activities. For one thing, it is an item we learn as part of the multiplication table and is used, more or less mechanically, when working out complex products. Here it is much like a rule for decoding — given these signs, we write down others under the governance of a rule. If we attend to just this use of the expression, we shall be led in the direction of a pure conventionalism, a position that Wittgenstein rejects as strongly as he rejects Platonism.

Beyond this, the expression relates two ways of describing a collection of things. The sense of the numeral "25" is grounded — or was originally grounded — in the practice of counting. The sense of the expression "$5 \times 5$" is grounded in a more complex practice: roughly, through counting we put things into equinumerous batches of a certain number and then count up the batches. The identity statement lays down the principle that where one mode of description is correct, so too is the other.

How do we *know* when two modes of description are so related? Suppose I try to convince someone that five times five equals twenty-five by having him count out five batches each containing five items and then have him count up the total. Is it obvious that he will come up with the expected result? To vary one of Wittgenstein's examples, suppose he counts out the batches this way:

```
×  ×  ×  ×  ×  1.
×  ×  ×  ×  ×  2.
×  ×  ×  ×  ×  3.
×  ×  ×  ×  ×  4.
×
5.
```

Has he done what we told him to do? *Of course he has*; what he did fits our description perfectly. Yet he has not done what we *wanted* him to do; he has yet to master the technique that underlies *our* use of this expression and since our use is part of the instituted practice, he has yet to grasp the role of the expression "5 × 5" in *mufti*.

Even after the student has mastered the appropriate techniques he can still come up with the wrong answer. To say that a person knows how to count does not mean that he cannot miscount. Miscounting is not a skill, knack, or achievement, but still, it presupposes skills, knacks, and achievements. Thus it is simply wrong to say that mathematical identity statements predict the result that a person will reach when he carries out a certain computation. Yet we do insist that they predict what he will get if he carries out these activities *correctly*. We now want to know how inserting the word "correctly" can make this difference. Wittgenstein's answer runs something like this: although our training in mathematics consists — at least in part — of checking results, the outcome of this activity is not a generalization about what turns up when people count things, group things, etc., but instead, we are led to view the result of our exercise as a paradigm for carrying out future computations. Once we elevate a specific result to the status of a paradigm, the language of correct and incorrect computation find its place. For the upshot of our instruction is not the conclusion:

1. *This time* the product of five times five is twenty-five,

nor even:

2. *In general* the product of five time five is twenty-five,

but instead:

3. *It is a rule* that the product of five times five is twenty-five.

We are thus back to the "modal picture" of mathematics discussed in the first part of the paper.

All this still seems somehow unsatisfactory, for pushing things back one step, we now want to know why one computation should be given the status of paradigm and thus made the measure for others to follow. We make this move with reasons—indeed, with very good reasons—but if we entertain skeptical doubts concerning the understanding, these reasons simply evaporate. To return to our student, after he has mastered the requisite techniques and, in fact, has arrived at the required result, he may still feel dissatisfied and protest that he does not see that the result *has to* come out in this way. In short, nothing *compels* the student to adopt the results of his exercises as paradigmatic. Here we have an echo of Hume's skeptical doubts concerning causality—and it is this side of Wittgenstein's position that many have emphasized. There is nothing that can put this move to a paradigm out of reach of every possible criticism. It is only from *within* mathematics, i.e., only under the guidance of assumed paradigms, that mathematical expressions appear internally connected. From the outside they appear both "separate and loose."

Thus expressions of the form "It is a rule that *p*" can be given either an *inner* or an *outer* acknowledgment. We can say (from the outside) that it is a rule for this primitive tribe that $7 \times 7 =$ many, but we can also say (from the inside) that it is a rule (for us) that $7 \times 7 = 49$. Speaking from the inside involves what Wittgenstein has called entering into a form of life. Nothing necessitates the adoption of a form of life, for necessity (internal relatedness) emerges only *after* the adoption of a form of life.

The comparison between Hume and Wittgenstein goes deeper: Wittgenstein not only presents skeptical doubts, he also offers a skeptical solution to these doubts.[9] It is a fact about human beings that we sometimes raise things to the status of a paradigm as the result of a proof:

> For it is a peculiar procedure: I *go through* the proof and then accept its result.—I mean: this is simply what we *do*. This is use and custom among us, or a fact of our natural history. (I, 63)

Thus there is no wholly external way of justifying a proof: "It is not something behind the proof, but the proof that proves" (II, 42). And if the whole procedure of acceptance from proof is called into question, there is no way of meeting the challenge:

> The danger here, I believe, is one of giving a justification of our procedure where there is no such thing as a justification and we ought simply to have said: *that's how we do it.* (II, 74)

We can now double back upon a previous point and again ask why a perspicuous direct proof enjoys a privileged status for Wittgenstein. At first glance, the Humean motifs in Wittgenstein's writings may seem to undercut our previous reflections. If mathematical propositions are separate and loose, aren't the results of a direct proof every bit as external as the results of an indirect proof? From a spectator's standpoint, the answer to this question must be *Yes*, but for a person working under the guidance of paradigms, the difference remains striking. Our original paradigms grew from the soil of application, and a perspicuous direct proof conserves this applicability and thus leads us to adopt a new paradigm. In contrast, if an indirect proof involves a new decision or stipulation, it will not bestow upon its conclusion a linkage with previous paradigms and through them a linkage with application.

Finally, we can notice why Wittgenstein was impatient with the idea that mathematics stands in need of a foundation. His attitude here is simply one instance of his general critique of foundational studies. In the sense that philosophers have used the term, Wittgenstein came to think that *nothing* stands in need of a foundation.

> What does mathematics need a foundation for? It no more needs one, I believe, than propositions about material objects — or about sense impressions, need an *analysis*. What mathematical propositions do stand in need of is a clarification of their grammar, just as do these other propositions. (V, 13)

Mathematics has its foundation in human practice and needs no other.

As far as work that goes under the heading of studies in the foundations of mathematics, he flatly denies that this *portion* of mathematics is the underpinning for the rest of the mathematical edifice.

> The *mathematical* problems of what is called foundations are no more the foundations of mathematics than the painted rock is the support of the painted tower. (V, 14)

In back of this attitude is the doctrine that the proposed systems derive whatever sense they have from the system they are intended to support, and not the other way around. For example, in the decimal notation we have a "short" calculation and corresponding to it in the Russell notation we have an extraordinary long calculation. Does the long calculation either justify or elucidate the "short" calculation? According to Wittgenstein, no![10]

In even a less charitable mood, Wittgenstein views foundational research as an exemplar of reasoning carried on with the connection to application totally ignored.

> The question, "What was it useful for?" was a quite essential question. For the calculus was not invented for some practical purpose, but in order "to give arithmetic a foundation." But who says that arithmetic is logic, etc. (II, 85)

And problems within the foundations of mathematics can also arise through this severance from application. We start out with principles that are both intelligible and plausible through their connection with ordinary discourse, then later we get into trouble by extending the system in ways initially never dreamed of. We introduce a predicate such as "heterological" and then a contradiction is found, but how is the notion of a heterological predicate connected with the initial reasons for setting up the calculus?

> What Russell's "$-f(f)$" lacks above all is application, and hence meaning. (V, 8)

Why not, following Wittgenstein's suggestion, just call the derived contradiction a *true* contradiction and note, perhaps with satisfaction, that it is part of our system (V, 21)?

The worry, of course, is that the presence of the contradiction will render the system useless. Here, belatedly, a recognition of the importance of application reappears. We are now set the task of *sealing off* the contradiction while at the same time preserving the features of the system that we want. If we cannot accomplish this, this merely shows that our system is not transparent to us; we do not know our way about.

> But how is it possible not to know one's way about in a calculus: isn't it there, open to view? (II, 80)

Wittgenstein seems to suggest that this would not happen if we stayed in touch with application at every stage in the development of the system:

> I would like to say something like this: "Is it usefulness you are out for in your calculations? — In that case you do not get any contradiction. And if you aren't out for usefulness — then it doesn't matter if you get one." (II, 80)

This suggestion is not farfetched. In effect, it amounts to the demand that every extension of a system be accompanied by a relative consistency proof within the domain of intended application. Anyway, these passages clarify Wittgenstein's supposedly *laissez-faire* attitude toward contradictions:

> "Then you are in favor of contradiction?" Not at all; any more than of soft rulers. (IV, 12)

# III

The sympathetic commentator on Wittgenstein can do one of two things: either say again what he has said in the hope that someone will listen, or reconstruct the position in a way that reveals its systematic coherence. Using the intuitionistic themes as a starting point, I have here attempted the second approach. This is not a Wittgensteinian way of doing business, but perhaps this loss of purity will be repaid by a new appraisal of Wittgenstein's contribution to the philosophy of mathematics.

## NOTES

1. Ed. by G. H. von Wright, *et al.* (Oxford: Basil Blackwell, 1956).
2. E.g., IV, 9–13, 17–20.
3. E.g., IV, 26–27, 46.
4. E.g., II, 18, 46–48, 53, 85; IV, 24; V, 13.
5. See G. H. von Wright's "Biographical Sketch," in Norman Malcolm, *Ludwig Wittgenstein: A Memoir* (London: Oxford University Press, 1958), pp. 12–13.
6. This is one of Wittgenstein's favorite phrases. See, for example, I, Appendix II, 10, and III, 11–13.
7. Frederic B. Fitch, "Natural Deduction Rules for Obligation," *American Philosophical Quarterly*, Vol. 3 (1966), pp. 27–38.
8. E.g., I, Appendix II, 18; II, 81–82; IV, 52; V, 16.
9. I am using the phrase "sceptical solution" in precisely the way that Hume uses it in Sect. V of *An Enquiry Concerning Human Understanding*.
10. For this argument see especially II, 18.

# 14

# Wittgenstein and Classical Scepticism

6.51 Scepticism is *not* irrefutable, but obviously nonsensical, when it raises doubts where no question can be asked.

It is generally thought that one of Wittgenstein's contributions to philosophy is to have said something important against scepticism. The passage cited comes from the *Tractatus Logico-Philosophicus*, his earliest philosophical work, but it captures, I believe, an approach to scepticism that persisted through his long, complex, and changing philosophical career. Wittgenstein's central idea, in simple words, is that the sceptic's questions may be dismissed because they lack meaning. The exact form of this criticism will vary as his position undergoes radical change, but in this area at least — the critique of scepticism — Wittgenstein's position shows a remarkable continuity through all stages of its development. In this essay I shall concentrate upon Wittgenstein's treatment of scepticism as it appears first in the *Tractatus* and then again in the collection of notes written near the end of his life and published by his executors under the title *On Certainty*.

## The *Tractatus*

Returning to the quotation that heads this essay, we may notice in the first place that it has a verificationist ring, and this may suggest

"Wittgenstein and Classical Scepticism," *International Philosophical Quarterly*, Vol. XXI, No. 1 (March 1981). Reprinted by permission of the publisher.

a commitment to logical positivism. But I take it that few, by now, give the *Tractatus* a positivistic reading. Wittgenstein was not a logical positivist because he was not a positivist, for his position was wholly free of a narrow empiricism, be it British or Machian. When writing the *Tractatus*, Wittgenstein followed the high *a priori* road laid out by Frege and treated all questions of epistemology as matters of empirical psychology and, as such, out of place in philosophical discussions (*TLP* 4.1121). The *Tractatus* contains a verificationist doctrine, but it is pure, i.e., it is a theory of meaning that is independent of the particular ways that we, as human beings, go about ascertaining whether a given proposition is true or false. This view, stated quite generally, is that for a statement to be meaningful or, more accurately, for a sentence to express a statement, there must be some determinate way of fixing its truth value.

The meaningfulness of questions is derived from the meaningfulness of counterpart statements. This comes out in Wittgenstein's explanation of just why the sceptic's question must be called meaningless:

> 6.51 For doubt can exist only where a question exists, a question only where an answer exists, and an answer only where something *can be said*.

This passage contains three important claims.

1. Doubt is not merely a mental state on a par, say, with a sensation: it is an expression of a propositional attitude. The standard forms of speech are these: "A doubts that . . . , " "A doubts whether . . . , " and, somewhat oddly, "A doubts if. . . . " A creature who could not comprehend propositions could not doubt.

2. The passage further indicates that there is an internal connection between questions and answers: "A question exists only where an answer exists." Of course Wittgenstein is not saying that in order for a question to exist its answer must be known, by someone at least. Speaking more carefully in the previous entry, he puts it this way: "6.5 If a question can be framed at all, it is also *possible* to answer it." To illustrate this point, perhaps no one at the moment can answer the question: "How many full- and part-time students are enrolled in Fordham University?" Yet *if these concepts are well defined*, there must be some determinate answer to it, be it

known or unknown. To contrapose this, if there is no determinate answer to the question, then the concepts do not have a determinate sense. In his Tractarian period Wittgenstein held that such indeterminacy of sense would itself constitute a sufficient reason for saying that an expression lacks meaning. Under the influence of Frege, Wittgenstein then thought that to be a sense at all, a sense must be wholly determinate. This, of course, is one of the fundamental areas where Wittgenstein changed his mind. For suppose that no determinate sense does attach to the phrase "full- or part-time student at Fordham." Perhaps because of varying practices across the University no specific number can be assigned to those entities (i.e., students) falling under this concept. But even if the meaning of the phrase is underdetermined in this way, the concept it expresses will still place constraints on possible answers. For example, the answer 10,000 is better than the answer 3.6 or 10 to the eighteenth. It is a better answer—closer to the truth—even though there is no determinate answer that it is closer to. Thinking through the far-reaching consequences of the existence of such objective vagueness is one of the important features of Wittgenstein's later philosophy. But I digress.

3. Finally, this passage concerning the sceptic's questions relates what can count as an answer to what *can be said*. To shortcut a great deal of technical material, for Wittgenstein the only thing that can be said is that certain contingencies obtain in the world. This is the only thing that can be put *into* words. The primitive insight that lies behind this claim is that in forming a proposition, we put signs together one way rather than in another. ("Brutus stabbed Caesar," vs. "Caesar stabbed Brutus.") What is said, then, by every significant proposition, is that things stand to each other in one way rather than in another. One determinate sign structure out of others pictures one possible contingent combination of objects out of others. Thus what is said by every significant proposition is, in Wittgenstein's words: "This is how things stand" (4.5). One consequence of this position is that the noncontingent (i.e., necessary) cannot be expressed *in* language. Attempts to do so lead either to tautologies, which are empty of sense (*sinnlos*), or to metaphysical pronouncements, which are nonsensical (*unsinnig*).

If this is the primitive picture that motivates the Tractarian system, the task of that complex work is to show the structure that any system of represention must have in order to exemplify it. Wittgenstein maintains, again I speak in broad terms, that all significant language—i.e., all that concerns *that which can be said*— must rely for its representational character on basic or elementary propositions. These elementary propositions stand in an immediate picturing relationship to the basic structure of reality, states of affairs (or atomic facts). All other propositions are logical constructs (in particular, truth functions) of these elementary propositions.[1] In principle, then, the truth of every proposition must hitch back to the truth (or falsehood) of elementary propositions. If this is not possible (at least in principle) then no genuine proposition has been expressed. For Wittgenstein, the range of truth functions of elementary propositions, the range of propositions with a determinate truth value, the range of significant propositions, and the range of that which can be said are one and all coextensive. The attempt to express anything beyond this yields only nonsense.[2]

Now let us return to the sceptic's questions. Wittgenstein maintains that they are nonsensical when they raise doubts where no question can be asked. Given his theory, this means that they are nonsensical when they ask questions for which there is no possible answer whose truth can be determined by an appeal to elementary propositions. Less technically, the sceptic's doubts are pseudo-doubts when there is no way, even in principle, of resolving them by an appeal to the contingent distribution of things in the world.

To see if this is a just criticism of scepticism let us reflect for a moment upon the character of sceptical questions. The sceptic, when he appears in plain clothes, often challenges commonly held beliefs on the grounds that they are not supported by sufficient evidence. Thus the sceptic may challenge the reliability of current cosmological theories or of theories concerning child rearing. Wittgenstein has no complaint against (or philosophical interest in) scepticism of this kind. But scepticism, when it dons philosophical clothing, does not depend upon such (merely) factual considerations. The classical sceptic (and here I shall take the Pyrrhonian scepticism of Sextus Empiricus as my example) generally moved at a higher level of abstraction. He was not interested in the plain man's natural and unpretentious beliefs. As long as a person remained content with modestly reporting how things struck him, then the sceptic had nothing to say against him. The object of the sceptic's attack was the philosopher, in particular, the philosopher of a dogmatic cast who attempted to maintain that his opinions enjoyed a special status above those of others.

The Pyrrhonian sceptic had a practical goal and laid down specific procedures for attaining it. The sceptic's goal was peace of mind. He thought that he could reach this goal if he could free himself from philosophical anxiety. This, as it turns out, can be attained by reaching a state of suspension of belief or noncommitment (*ataraxia*) concerning philosophical subjects. (As we shall see later, Wittgenstein sometimes expresses very similar sentiments.) The Pyrrhonian used various techniques to attain suspension of belief. Sometimes he tried to reach a state of equipolence by pairing off opposing dogmatic views. (For example, Plato held that there were transcendent forms, Aristotle denied this.) But the Pyrrhonians also developed quite general procedures that were serviceable against any philosophical position concerning any subject matter whatsoever. I shall call these the procedures of *general scepticism*.

The method of general scepticism can be illustrated by the five modes leading to the suspension of belief attributed to the later sceptic Agippa: disagreement, relativity, hypothesis, circularity, and infinite regress.[3] The dogmatist, we said, is one who goes beyond an expression of how things seem to him to the claim that his beliefs have a privileged status. The sceptic first meets this claim by pointing out that disagreement exists on this matter and therefore the dogmatist must bring forth reasons to prefer his claim over others or be discredited. (Even if no disagreement exists among men on a certain subject, the sceptic can still invoke the mode of relativity and argue that there is no reason to take universal consent as a guarantee of truth, for why should mankind be the measure of all things?) Now once enquiry is started, the remaining three modes, hypothesis, circularity, and infinite regress, are intended to stop it from terminating. If the dogmatist refuses to give any reason for supporting his supposedly objective claim, then he has merely put forward a hypothesis that has no claim upon our assent. If, on the other hand, he does put forward some reason, then that reason can be challenged. He will then fall into the terminating net, for inevitably he must either

1. given no reason
2. repeat some previous reason
3. always give a new reason

The mode of hypothesis blocks the first response, the mode of circularity the second, and the third, needless to say, generates a bad infinite regress.

It seems to be part of our philosophical heritage to treat this sort of argument with contempt. After all, it is not very different from the kind of sceptical argument that is produced by undergraduates trying to cause trouble. It is also boring, since it runs down the very same grooves no matter what the subject matter might be. All the same, it seems incumbent upon philosophy to say something decisive about it in order to clear its pedigree.

The standard response to a general sceptical argument is to turn it back upon itself—the so called *peritrope*. A piece of reasoning that shows that no reasoning is adequate shows itself to be inadequate and may therefore be rejected. Having produced this argument, the critic of scepticism rarely stays for an answer, but the ancient sceptics knew about it and said, I believe, the right thing in response. First they admitted that sceptical arguments are self-undercutting, but they saw no embarrassment in this, since they never claimed to be able to establish anything by reasoning. More to the point, the dogmatist can gain no comfort from this result, since the burden falls upon him to find something wrong with a pattern of argument that proceeds from principles he himself accepts. He may notice its self-refuting quality, but this merely puts him on a treadmill, for with reason restored, the very same canons of reasoning will lead him back to a sceptical cul de sac. David Hume put the matter this way:

> If the sceptical reasonings be strong, say they, 'tis proof, that reason may have some force and authority; if weak, they can never be sufficient to invalidate all the conclusions of our understanding. This argument is not just; because the sceptical reasonings . . . would be successively both strong and weak, according to the successive dispositions of the mind.[4]

Since the standard refutation is no good, scepticism, then, is the skeleton in the philosophical closet. I think that one of the reasons that Wittgenstein's philosophy seems attractive is that it gives a systematic response to the sceptic's challenge. It is not hard to see how this works out within the system of the *Tractatus*. Any question with a sense must have an answer whose truth is, at least in principle, determinable by an appeal to the contingent combination of things in the world. By its very intention, however, the system of sceptical challenges generates a nonterminating system of questions. But by the principles of the *Tractatus*, such a system of nonterminating questions must lack sense. General scepticism thus becomes nonsensical just because it is in principle invulnerable.

I think that this response to scepticism is an advance over the standard use of *peritrope*. But the response carries with it the implication that many other questions are meaningless as well. Here are some examples:

1. Does God exist?
2. Does anything exist?
3. Are some things better than others?
4. Is the universe finite or infinite?
5. Is meaningful thought or language possible?

Now the very same reasoning that led us to say that the sceptic's questions are meaningless must now lead us to say that all of these questions are meaningless.[5] For Wittgenstein none of these questions could be settled (even in principle) by an appeal to the contingent combinations of objects in the world.

Wittgenstein, of course, recognized these consequences of his position. In particular, he saw that the meaninglessness of question 5 (How is meaningful thought or language possible?) implies the meaninglessness of the whole Tractarian system which, after all, was intended to answer it. In a fashion strikingly similar to that of the ancient sceptics, Wittgenstein ends by acknowledging the self-annihilating character of his position:

> 6.54 My propositions serve as elucidations in the following way: anyone who understands me eventually recognizes them as nonsensical, when he has used them — as steps — to climb beyond them. (He must, so to speak, throw away the ladder after he has climbed up it.)

The closing remark is an allusion to Sextus Empiricus, indeed an allusion to Sextus's own response to peritropic refutation. One embraces it. That is, neither Sextus nor Wittgenstein thought that the self-destroying character of their positions showed something wrong *within* them. Wittgenstein held, I'm sure, that any correct inquiry into the theory of meaning would lead to his own position. Its self-annihilating character, far from being a defect, is revelatory of the subject matter itself. It turns out that a theory of meaning is an attempt to express the inexpressible, and this becomes clear in the terminal stages of a correctly developed theory of meaning.

I assume that by now a striking parallel should have appeared between sceptical reflection on reasoning and Wittgenstein's reflections on the character of meaning. The ancient sceptics thought (and Hume repeated this) that a rational inquiry into reasoning would be self-destructive, whereas Wittgenstein held that a correct theory of meaning must, in the end, be seen to be meaningless. They both recommended that we must go beyond their explicit statements and, in surmounting them, finally see the world aright.

But the *Tractatus* seems to contain an escape hatch from these nihilistic consequences. It seems that things that cannot be said can sometimes be made known in another way:

6.522 There are, indeed, things that cannot be put into words. They *make themselves manifest*. They are what is mystical.

Included in the mystical is the fact that a world exists at all (6.44), and "feeling the world as a limited whole" (6.45). Other remarks seem to concern the mystical as well, for example:

5.621 The world and life are one.
5.63 I am my world. (The microcosm.)
6.431 . . . at death the world does not alter, but comes to an end.

It is plain that the truth of none of these propositions is grounded in the contingent facts within the world, for they all concern the world as a whole. For that reason, they are misfiring attempts to say that which cannot be said. Yet somehow they are able to make themselves manifest, perhaps in their very misfiring. This, it seems to me, brings us to one of the mysteries of the *Tractatus*—not the doctrine that the mystical can somehow make itself manifest, that is *supposed* to be mysterious—but Wittgenstein's decision to forward particular mystical avowals rather than others. He clearly favors a mystical vision of the world that reveals its wholeness and one's communion (or identity) with it. Here, it seems to me that Wittgenstein is uncharacteristically superficial. Indeed, he seems not to recognize the full force of one of his own remarks:

> 6.521 The solution of the problem of life is seen in the vanishing of the problem.
>
> (Is not this the reason why those who have found after a long period of doubt that the sense of life became clear to them have then been unable to say what constituted that sense?)

Of course, Wittgenstein is right. Mystics often complain of the inadequacies of language to capture the quality of their experience, and the defect is often considered so radical that they are tempted to say one thing together with its opposite and thus fall into paradox. In contrast, Wittgenstein's onesided preference for certain mystical pronouncements over others (e.g., their denials) suggests that he does, after all, assign to them a kind of (or degree of) literal meaning. But, of course, on his own theory they have no literal meaning at all—not even a defective or inadequate literal meaning.

Let us now return to scepticism. Wittgenstein is right: given the canons of meaning laid down in the *Tractatus*, the sceptic's wholly generalized non-terminating questions make no sense. But the same can be said about the propositions of the *Tractatus* itself. Furthermore, Wittgenstein agrees on the central point of ancient scepticism: philosophy is not possible as a theoretical, discursive, or rational discipline. But even that cannot be said; it too must make itself manifest. A proper understanding of scepticism suggests that the sceptic's pronouncements be placed side by side with Wittgenstein's own mystical remarks. This, it seems to me, both coheres better with the system of the *Tractatus* and shows a better understanding of mysticism.

## *On Certainty*

The work that his executors entitled *On Certainty* is a compilation of notes written by Wittgenstein during the last year and a half of his life (1949–1951). Here Wittgenstein reflects upon G. E. Moore's attempts to invoke common sense to refute various philosophical positions. Most famously, Moore argued that those who denied (or expressed doubts about) the existence of material objects could be refuted by displaying a right hand and then a left hand, thus showing to anyone who would look that the world contained at least two material objects. Similarly, Moore claimed to know (and know with certainty) that the world had existed for many years before his birth and this, he thought, was sufficient to show that those who maintained that time is unreal must also be mistaken.[6]

Wittgenstein thought that Moore's refutations were ineffective against the targets at which they were aimed. Of course, he did not side with the idealists nor did he deny the common sense propositions put forward by Moore. Instead, he expressed his reservations this way:

> 19. The statement "I know that here is a hand" may . . . be continued: "for it's *my* hand that I'm looking at." Then a reasonable man will not doubt that I know. — Nor will the idealist; rather he will say that he was not dealing with the practical doubt which is being dismissed, but there is a further doubt *behind* that one. That this is an *illusion* has to be shewn in a different way.[7]

This, I think, is a key passage for understanding one of the central themes of *On Certainty*. Moore, at least as Wittgenstein reads him, supposes that philosophers often maintain (or hold positions that imply) propositions that are contrary to plain matters of fact. He rejects such philosophical claims on the grounds that anything that asserts or implies a falsehood is false. Wittgenstein replies that the idealist will not disagree with Moore at the level of common sense. He will hold instead that his denials or doubts come at quite another level. An idealist doubting whether material objects exist is nothing like a naturalist doubting whether the Ivory Billed Woodpecker still survives in the swamps of Louisiana. Moore's mistake is to suppose that they are on the same level. Wittgenstein wishes to reject the idealist position as well but, unlike Moore, he sees that their doubts are second order—or hyperbolic. Wittgenstein's position is that these second-order or hyperbolic doubts are illusions and a proper refutation of dissolution of idealism involves exposing these illusions.

Wittgenstein's thought underwent a profound alteration between the time he completed the *Tractatus* on the Eastern front in World War I and that time, near the end of his life, when he sat down in Norman Malcolm's house in Ithaca, New York, to collect his thoughts about Moore's "refutations." By then Wittgenstein had long since given up the theory of elementary propositions, atomic facts, eternal objects, logical space, etc.; that is, the whole elaborate picture of an ideal logical framework underpinning our language and mirroring an *a priori* structure in reality had been abandoned. Nor was anything of a like kind put in its place. Instead, Wittgenstein's later philosophy is an interrogation of those features inherent in our language which lead us—inevitably, but still misguidedly—to philosophize in the first place. The task of philosophy is to expose and neutralize these tendencies.

But even if the *Tractatus* is a specimen of the very kind of philosophy that Wittgenstein came to reject, there are certain themes in it that were carried over and amplified in his later philosophy. The most important carryover is the thought that an expression can have a meaning without *standing* for anything. In the *Tractatus* this insight was largely limited to logical and mathematical notions. "My fundamental idea," he said, "is that 'logical constants' are not representatives;" (4.0312). Much of Wittgenstein's later philosophy is an elaboration on this theme that meaning is not fixed merely by word–thing correlations. A second important theme common to both the early and later stages of his philosophy is that meanings are internally related to one another. This may seem contrary to Wittgenstein's so-called atomism, but in the Tractarian period, Wittgenstein was an atomist with respect to contingent truth, but he was a holist with respect to meanings. Meaning does not come in isolated chunklets, it is always embedded in a system. In the *Tractatus* that system was the sublime structure of elementary propositions systematically connected in logical space. In the later philosophy the idea of a single all-embracing system is abandoned in favor of the idea of a plurality of systems or contexts. Wittgenstein usually refers to these contexts as "language games" and in a few rare pretentious moments as "forms of life." An expression only has a meaning when it is employed in some particular language game. We may understand its meaning when we see what use it has in a particular language game. An expression that has no such use is meaningless.

Now let us return to the matter of doubt. Someone says "I doubt that" and we ask ourselves what he means. Our first temptation is to say that he is telling us something about his own mental condition. Though this may be right in part, it cannot be the whole story or even the most important part of it. For notice, it always makes sense to ask a person *why* he doubts and here our request is for reasons, not causes. The person is then expected to point to some more or less definite lack, something which, if dealt with, will satisfy, not just relieve, the doubt. (I can satisfy a craving with a drug, but not a doubt.) This is not to say that the doubt must always be clearly articulable — that is a Tractarian prejudice. We may simply think that things are fishy and then be satisfied when we realize that certain odd features of the situation are, after all, extraneous. A doubt that cannot meet even this minimal demand is at best pathological and *in extremis* no doubt at all. (Can one be mistaken about being in doubt? Yes.)

In *On Certainty*, Wittgenstein expresses these ideas in the following way:

3. If, e.g., someone says "I don't know if there's a hand here" he might be told "Look closer". This possibility of satisfying oneself is part of the language game. Is one of its essential features.

Or again

24. The idealist's question would be something like: "What right have I not to doubt the existence of my hands?" . . . But someone who asks such a question is overlooking the fact that a doubt about existence only works in a language-game. Hence, that we should first have to ask: what would this doubt be like?, and we don't understand this straight off.

More specifically, we do not understand the character of the doubt until we understand the grounds for doubt — and this the idealist and the sceptic resolutely refuse to specify.

It is important to see that Wittgenstein is doing more than challenging the sincerity of the idealist; he is not just saying they do not really *feel* doubt. (Nonsense is often maintained with complete sincerity.) His point is conceptual: the expression of a doubt that in principle admits of no answer would make no move in a language game. It would stand in no systematic connection with the other elements in the language game and therefore would lack meaning. Although the surrounding philosophical position is radically changed, in essence this is the line that Wittgenstein took in the *Tractatus*, criticizing the sceptics who raise doubts where no question can be asked (because no answer can be given).

The closing sentence of the passage just cited contains one of Wittgenstein's most important ideas. As philosophers we tend to take the meaningfulness of a question for granted and then set directly about answering it. For surely, we want to say, we know what it is to doubt, and we know what it is to have hands, so surely we know what it would be to doubt whether we have hands. It seems obvious that we can raise such a doubt and in most cases settle it. This is Moore's standpoint, and for that reason he will attempt to refute the idealist by showing him his hands. Against this Wittgenstein holds that the idealist's doubts cannot be answered because they make no sense.[8] Not only that, he holds that Moore's responses to their questions seem curious in their own right.

> 481. When one hears Moore say "I *know* that that's a tree," one suddenly understands those who think that that has by no means been settled.
>
> The matter strikes one all at once as being unclear and blurred. It is as if Moore had put it in the wrong light.

Is Wittgenstein suggesting that Moore, sitting in a park in broad daylight, does *not* know that there is a tree before him? Is he suddenly granting some point to the sceptic's doubt? No, what Wittgenstein is indicating is that knowledge claims are also context bound and play quite a particular role within a language game:

"11. We just do not see how very specialized the use of 'I know' is." If we look at typical contexts in which people claim to know things, we discover that they respond to actual or potential doubts. One can always be asked "How do you know?" and that calls for reasons. The character of these reasons will be a function of the particular matters at issue. The difficulty with answering the sceptic's question is that the reasons I give are no better than the claim that I am trying to defend and it is part of the sceptic's tactics to raise questions of just this kind. But where doubt is wholly indeterminate, nothing can be cited to resolve it. Here a knowledge claim will be out of place, useless, and thus, for Wittgenstein, without meaning.[9] We thus arrive at the position that meaningful doubts can be raised, questions asked, answers given, etc., only within the context of a particular language game. The guile of the sceptic and the error of those who try to refute him directly is to ask questions and seek answers completely outside of the context of some particular language game.

But now the following question naturally arises: if the activities of asking questions and answering them (raising doubts and settling them) are justifiable only in the context of a language game, what justifies the language games themselves? Wittgenstein's answer is Nothing. This is a persistent theme in Wittgenstein's later philosophy: "166. The difficulty is to realize the groundlessness of our believing."

This does not mean, of course, that all my particular beliefs are groundless. I think, for example, that Wittgenstein knew something about the philosophy of C. S. Peirce through conversations with F. P. Ramsey. *That's* the kind of thing that can be established by citing evidence. But if you asked me to prove that Wittgenstein existed, I'm not sure what I would say. I can remember when I first heard of Wittgenstein, but at that time no one paused to prove to me that there was such a person. Furthermore, if I now tried to produce such a proof, it might strike me as not particularly persuasive. I could cite the constant references to him by Moore, Russell, and others, but do I have any better reason for thinking that Moore and Russell existed than I have for thinking that Wittgenstein existed? (Suddenly my attempt to prove Wittgenstein's existence seems as superficial as Moore's attempted proof of material objects.)

Here it is tempting to cite coherence as my grounds for believing in Wittgenstein's existence. That is, I believe this because it fits in so well with all the other things that I believe. There is, I think, something right about this appeal to coherence, but I do not think that coherence is the *ground* for my belief in Wittgenstein's existence. On first hearing him spoken about, I simply took it for granted that there was such a person. I have taken a great many other things for granted as well and they form a framework — or better, a set of frameworks — within which I try to settle problematic issues.

341. . . . the *questions* that we raise and our *doubts* depend on the fact that some propositions are exempted from doubt, are as it were like hinges on which those turn.
342. That is to say, it belongs to the logic of our scientific investigations that certain things are *in deed* not doubted.
343. . . . if I want the door to turn, the hinges must stay put.
344. My *life* consists in my being content to accept many things.

Three things are particularly worth noting here. (1) The demand that we accept many things is conceptual and not simply a sign of our weakness. Without a background of accepted beliefs, we would have neither guideposts nor touchstones for our thought. (2) These things that we accept are not first principles in the philosopher's sense, they are commonplaces. The bedrock of my thought is simply the thick sedimentary layer of the obvious. Naturally what is taken as a matter of course by one person need not be by another. Much will depend upon background and training. There are, however, many things that are accepted by everyone straight off, and doubt and inquiry will arise in only the most extraordinary circumstances. We all assume that we understand the language we are speaking, although pathological cases might arise that would cast even this into doubt. (3) Perhaps most importantly, we typically learn things indirectly as part of other activities:

476. Children do not learn that books exist, that armchairs exists, etc. etc., — they learn to fetch books, sit in armchairs, etc. etc.
Later questions about the existence of things do of course arise. "Is there such a thing as a unicorn?" and so on. But such a question

is possible only because as a rule no corresponding question presents itself.

In trying to decide whether unicorns ever existed, I might consult certain books. I do not, however, raise the prior question of whether books exist. All this points to a fundamental tenet of Wittgenstein's later philosophy: our participation in shared language games lies beyond justification; it is a brute fact of our nature:

> 475. I want to regard man here as an animal; as a primitive being to which one grants instinct but not ratiocination. As a creature in a primitive state. Any logic good enough for a primitive means of communication needs no apology from us. Language did not emerge from some kind of ratiocination.

I think that we can now see what Wittgenstein's later critique of scepticism comes to. The sceptic is pictured as a figure who constantly calls things into question, constantly asks for justification of even the most ordinary beliefs. If this is the sceptic's enterprise, then something can be said against him. The very questions he asks depend *for their sense* upon a background of commonly shared beliefs. But the sceptic's doubts have a totalizing character—he will raise the same kind of objections to any reason that is brought forward as evidence. But as the sceptic's doubts expand, their sense contracts and his wholly generalized doubts finally amount to nothing.

This, I think, is an interesting argument—a kind of transcendental refutation of vulgar scepticism—but how does it relate to classical scepticism as it was actually maintained? In the first place, it seems not to apply to classical scepticism at all, for the Pyrrhonians (at least) had no interest in challenging common beliefs that are modestly held. It is simply wrong then to say, as is sometimes suggested, that the sceptics arbitrarily impose impossibly high standards and then condemn common belief for falling short of them. Thompson Clark has it right when he remarks that the sceptic comes upon the scene "without an independent thought in his head concerning what knowledge requires."[10] He encounters philosophers who often disparage common belief and, anyway, claim an authority for their doctrines that transcends the brute acceptance of the plain man. The sceptic simply takes these philosophers at their word, meets them on their own ground, and then shows that they cannot stand up to *their own* pretentions. Classical scepticism was not a critique of common beliefs, for it recognized that, for the most part, it is not in our power to suspend them and, in any case, no useful purpose would be served by doing so. Classical scepticism was a critique of philosophizing and the anxieties it generates. In this latter respect, Wittgenstein captured the spirit of their enterprise when he said:

> The real discovery is the one that makes me capable of stopping doing philosophy when I want to. — The one that gives philosophy peace, so that it no longer is tormented by questions which bring *itself* in question. (*P.I.*, 133)

For Wittgenstein, philosophy becomes a therapeutic method where, as noticed earlier, philosophy as traditionally pursued is the disease to be cured. I think Wittgenstein's methods represent an important advance over the techniques of the ancient sceptics, for their criticisms tended to be stereotyped, wooden, and external. Wittgenstein's techniques proceed from a profound understanding of the internal character of philosophical reasoning. To use one of his favorite metaphors, to untie a philosophical knot one must repeat all the original motions — but in reverse order.

## Conclusion

At the beginning of this paper, I said that Wittgenstein is often credited with saying something important against scepticism. I think that this is true if by scepticism we mean an indiscriminate challenging of all belief, including common belief. But if scepticism is understood in its historical sense — in particular, in its Pyrrhonian form — then we might better say that Wittgenstein rediscovered scepticism, endowed it with insight and thus gave it its most powerful statement.

## NOTES

1. Again to simplify, all other propositions are constructed out of elementary propositions by using such operations as conjunction, disjunction, negation, and so on.

2. Here I am ignoring tautologies which, in Wittgenstein's technical sense, are propositions devoid of sense rather than pseudo-propositions that are nonsensical.

3. See Sextus Empiricus, *Outlines of Pyrrhonism*, trans. R. G. Bury (Cambridge, 1933), pp. 95 ff.

4. David Hume, *Treatise of Human Nature*, Selby-Bigge ed. (Oxford: Clarendon, 1888), p. 186. Hume maintains that sceptical arguments — though immune to rational refutation — are destroyed by their subtlety.

5. This is not quite right, for if we followed Epicurus in thinking that the Gods were simply finite aggregates of atoms, then question 1 would be meaningful. Wittgenstein would, however, reject both suggestions. See *TLP*, 6.4 ff.

6. The first example comes from Moore's "Proof of the External World," the second from his "Defence of Common Sense."

7. All citations are to the numbered entries in *On Certainty*, ed. by G. E. M. Anscombe and G. H. von Wright, trans. by Denis Paul and G. E. M. Anscombe (Oxford: Blackwell, 1969).

8. Of course, the very same form of words can express a genuine doubt in some other, nonphilosophical, context. I come out of anesthesia to see my lower arms covered with bandages. Here a doubt about the existence of my hands can be genuine.

9. Though most philosophers seem to think that Moore's knowledge claims are ineffective against the sceptic and the idealist, it may be hard to accept the idea that they are actually meaningless. Again, we must remember not to trade upon the fact that this very same form of words might be meaningful in some other context.

10. See Thompson Clark's important, though difficult, essay entitled "The Legacy of Scepticism," *Journal of Philosophy*, 70 (1973), 762.

# 15

# Thinking and Doing

I

In a brief, and distressingly incomplete, account of the practical syllogism, Aristotle traces out a connection between thought and action. He tells us that what happens seems parallel to the case of thinking and inferring about the immovable objects of science:

> There the end is the truth seen (for, when one conceives the two premisses, one at once conceives and comprehends the conclusion), but here the two premisses result in a conclusion which is an action — for example, one conceives that every man ought to walk, one is a man oneself: straightway one walks.

A bit later he says this:

> [T]he actualizing of desire is a substitute for inquiry or reflection. I want to drink, says appetite; this is a drink, says sense or imagination or mind: straightway I drink. In this way living creatures are impelled to move and to act, and desire is the last or immediate cause of movement, and desire arises after perception or after imagination and conception.[1]

Examined closely, these passages admit of two very different interpretations. The first I shall call the obvious interpretation; the second, the interesting interpretation. I shall not try to decide which interpretation best fits the text as a whole; I shall only ferret

"Thinking and Doing," in *Perception and Personal Identity*, Care and Grimm, eds., (Cleveland: Case Western Reserve Press, 1969), pp. 478–80. Reprinted by permission of the publisher.

out the interesting interpretation and then — setting Aristotle's text aside — explore it in its own right.

The obvious interpretation goes something like this: Aristotle pairs off various components of a theoretical syllogism with various psychological components. He then suggests that the action itself follows from these psychological components in much the same way that a conclusion follows from a set of premises. The parallel looks like this:

(A)   All $M$ is $P$.                    I want a drink.
      All $S$ is $M$.                    This is drink.
      _____                     _____
   ∴. All $S$ is $P$.                 ∴. Glug, glug, glug.

Somewhat dogmatically, I shall say that Aristotle's text is only minimally illuminating under the obvious interpretation. It does suggest that human actions are connected with thought and desire in a way that is not simply contingent. It does not, however, reveal anything about the structure of this noncontingent connection.

The interesting interpretation takes its cue from Aristotle's initial phrasing. There the analogue is not an argument, but instead a *process* of reasoning. We might spell out this process of thinking and inferring about the immovable objects of science in the following way:

(B)   (1) Comprehending that all $M$ is $P$, and that all $S$ is $M$,
          Mr. So & So reflected as follows:
      (2) All $M$ is $P$.
          All $S$ is $M$.
          _____
       ∴. All $S$ is $P$.
      and (3) straightway comprehended that all $S$ is $P$.

We now unfold the analogy by pairing off the act of drinking, not with the conclusion of the embedded argument, but instead with the "mental act" of comprehending the truth of this conclusion via argument.

The interesting interpretation is on a par with the obvious interpretation in being at least minimally illuminating: it too suggests that the connection between thought and action is somehow more than contingent. Beyond this, the interesting interpretation presents a more natural analogy: the mental act of comprehending is on a par with the physical act of drinking in a way that the proposition "All $S$ is $P$" is not on a par with any physical act. Finally, the interesting interpretation is interesting, for it traces out a very rich system of connections. Without worrying about Aristotle's true intentions, I propose to exploit the interesting interpretation for all it is worth. The result, I think, will be an outline for a theory of human action.

## II

Our task is to construct a pattern for thought passing into action that mirrors the schema for thinking and inferring about the immovable objects of science. Part of this pattern can be filled in with little difficulty:

> (C)  (1) Comprehending that $\phi$ is drink and . . . , Mr. So &
>        So reflected as follows:
>      (2) . . . . . . . . . . .
>          $\phi$ is drink.
>          ——————————————
>      ∴  . . . . . . . . . . . .
>      and (3) straightway he drank $\phi$.

We must now find a plausible way of filling the blanks.

Once again, Aristotle helps us along. He says this about the premises of action: "the premisses of action are of two kinds, of the good and of the possible."[2]

It is clear from his examples that by possibility Aristotle is thinking of the availability of an object of desire. ("This is drink," says sense or imagination or mind.) This in turn suggests that the major premise of the embedded argument is hypothetical with the minor premise satisfying its antecedent. The pattern now looks like this:

> (D)  (1) Comprehending that $\phi$ is drink and if $\phi$ is drink,
>         then . . . , Mr. So & So reflected as follows:

(2) If $\phi$ is drink, . . .
   $\phi$ is drink.
   _____
∴ . . . . . . . . . . . . .
(3) and straightway he drank $\phi$.

How can we fill in the remaining blanks in a plausible way? Aristotle tells us that the major premise of action is about the good (in some examples he uses an ought statement), and this, following current fashion, suggests that the premise has a prescriptive force. A sweeping way of tying the whole pattern together is to fill the blanks with a suitable imperative, thus generating the following completed schema:

(E) (1) Comprehending that $\phi$ is drink and accepting the prescription, if $\phi$ is drink, then drink it, Mr. So & So reflects as follows:
    (2) If $\phi$ is drink, then drink $\phi$.
        $\phi$ is drink.
        _____
    ∴ Drink $\phi$!
    (3) and straightway he drank $\phi$.

Here the embedded argument exhibits a valid prescriptive inference but, even more importantly, the third component now describes just that action that directly satisfies the prescriptive conclusion of the embedded argument. Thus we have a systematic connection between the commitments expressed in the first component and the actual event described in the third component via inferences contained in the middle component.

It will prove convenient to have a name for this pattern: I shall call it the Prescriptive Model for Human Action, since the use of prescriptive components is its distinctive feature. Before exploiting this model it is necessary to say some general things about the nature of prescriptions.

### III

As far as I can tell, philosophers have employed the notion of a prescription in two different ways: as the generic name for a class of speech acts, and as an abstract entity more or less on a par with propositions. In the former case, commands, requests, suggestions, etc. are thought of as different kinds of prescriptions and the task, then, is to sort them out. This is a useful activity, since there is a temptation to take one of these species of prescriptive discourse as paradigmatic for all the rest.[3] The idea of a prescription as an abstract entity is usually one of tacit assumption rather than explicit avowal. We notice, for example, that the very same thing can be prescribed in different speech acts. A general may order a man to go, a friend suggest it, and his wife request it; and for all the differences in these speech acts they have this much in common: they express the same prescription, that the man go. It thus becomes natural when studying prescriptive inferences to set aside all the pragmatic features pertaining to speech acts that formulate prescriptions and instead to concentrate upon the prescriptive content itself. In this way, prescriptions take on the role for practical discourse that has traditionally been assigned to propositions in the examination of theoretical discourse.

In this essay I shall use the notion of prescription in an abstract-entity fashion. When the occasion arises to speak about prescriptive speech acts, we can simply use the device of calling them prescriptive speech acts (i.e., speech acts that express prescriptions). I have no clear idea about the correct analysis of the relationship between prescriptive speech acts and the prescriptions they express; I have the same trouble here as I have trying to understand the relationship between an assertive speech act and the assertion it expresses.[4] Here I want to endow prescriptions with all the rights and privileges traditionally assigned to propositions. In particular, I want to speak about prescriptions in isolation from the speech acts that might express them.

Some further ideas about prescriptions are more important for our present inquiry. In the course of developing the prescriptive model, I have spoken to Mr. So & So *accepting* a given prescription. In the model we find two kinds of prescriptions: the hypothetical prescription "If $\phi$ is drink, then drink $\phi$," and the categorical prescription "Drink $\phi$!" I shall adopt the following principle governing the acceptance of a categorical prescription: a person who accepts a categorical prescription will straightway act in accordance with that prescription unless something interferes with the execution of his act.[5] Thus, when Mr. So & So accepts the categorical prescription "Drink $\phi$," he straightway drinks $\phi$ unless something interferes with his act. If something does interfere with his drinking $\phi$, we will then say that he *tried* to drink $\phi$.

It is important here to recognize the difference between *accepting* a categorical prescription and believing that a categorical prescription is *acceptable*. It is entirely possible for a person to believe that a prescription is justified, warranted, or what have you, and for all that not accept it. In different words, I want to insist upon the contrast between believing that one ought to do something and being committed to doing it. This difference can be brought out by contrasting the moral psychologies of Kant and Hare. For Hare, if there are no interfering factors, the mere fact that a person does not do something shows that on that occasion he did not believe he ought to do it. Kant's view is very different. We can imagine a world where people, by their nature, act in accordance with moral laws. For these beings, moral laws would have the status of *laws of nature*, and, in a manner of speaking, an ought would not emerge at all. For Kant, an ought emerges in our world precisely because we can acknowledge the legitimacy of a demand *without* thereby being conditioned to act in conformity with it. It is just this doctrine, I take it, that Hare wishes to deny, and here, at least, I am on the side of Kant rather than Hare.

In the model for human action we also speak about accepting a hypothetical prescription "If $\phi$ is drink, then drink $\phi$." A person could, of course, accept such a prescription but never drink. He is committed to drinking only those things that he *believes* to be drink, and it is conceivable that this condition may never be satisfied. The emphasis upon the word "believes" marks an obvious, but still important, point. It is tempting to say that a thirsty person will drink water if it is presented to him, but this is not correct. A thirsty person will not normally drink the presented water if he thinks it is baby oil or brine, and, conversely, he may drink baby oil or brine if he thinks, quite mistakenly, that it is water. It is not what the thing is, but what it is *taken to be*, that counts in the determination of action with respect to it.

## IV

Subject to all kinds of hedging, cheating, and taking back, I shall say that a statement formulates an act description if, and only if, the statement plays the role of the third component in the prescriptive model of human action. Of course, I do not mean that the statement must be prefaced by a recital of the items in the first two components, nor even that the person who makes the statement must have these two components before his mind. The prescriptive model is, after all, only a model, and its virtue is exhibited, not by showing how things really are, but through mirroring and making intelligible fundamental features of act descriptions.

One point that emerges immediately is that act descriptions can not be identified merely by a reference to features of the sentences that are used to express them. In particular, I do not think that we will get very far by trying to collect a group of verbs that we might call action verbs. As a matter of fact we describe the performances of the lucid agent and the madman using pretty much the same verbs, and over a wide range we use many of these verbs to describe events that occur in the course of nature. It is not the verb, nor even the sentence as a whole, that counts; it is the use of the sentence in an appropriate setting that makes the difference.

Granting all this, it is still true that there are sentences that are normally used to formulate act descriptions and other sentences that are not normally used in this way. In most contexts the sentence "John dropped the franchise" would be taken as an act description, simply because dropping a franchise is a fairly sophisticated legal performance. In contrast, the statement "John dropped his pen" is not usually taken as an act description. Unless we think that there is something special afoot, it does not cross our minds to inquire into his *reasons* for dropping the pen. "He didn't have any reasons; the pen just slipped from his hand when he was jostled."[6] On occasion, however, we wish to reverse (or at least modify) such presumptions. We can do this in a variety of ways, but for the most part we do not accomplish this through changing the verb. Our language does not have a full stock of special verbs ready at hand to deal with every special occasion. Instead, this is normally accomplished through the device of adverbial modification. The sentence "John dropped his pen" is converted into an explicit act

description simply by saying "John *intentionally* dropped his pen."
Conversely, the presumed act description "John dropped the franchise" is significantly modified when converted to "John dropped
the franchise through a mistake." In the former case we can inquire
into reasons where previously this seemed out of place; in the latter
case a whole range of questions about reasons is set off limits.

The situation is interestingly complicated, however. A human
performance can fail to be a human act in various ways and to
various degrees, and we have adverbs to mark these specific aberra-
tions. On the other side, we have a stock of adverbs that we use to
*counter* a presumption that a performance is not an act (or not
fully an act). It was Austin's brilliant idea that an examination of
such adverbs could cast light on the structure of human action. If I
may use two barbarisms in one sentence, through the study of
methods of actification and deactification our attention is drawn
to the various components of a human act. Austin's procedure
was, however, piecemeal—showing, perhaps, a warranted distrust
of architectonic. Here I am proceeding in the reverse fashion: if
the prescriptive model has any bearing upon the nature of human
action, it should provide a framework for sorting out and clarify-
ing the system of adverbs that are used to qualify human actions.
Next I shall try to show that it can perform this job.

## V

As I now see it, the adverb "intentionally" is simply the most general term for giving something the status of an act description, and
the adverb "unintentionally" is the most general term for doing the
opposite. Saying that something was done intentionally excludes,
in one sweep, a whole range of potential qualifications; if something is done intentionally, then it is not done unknowingly, unwit-
tingly, accidentally, mistakenly, inadvertently, and so on. Using
Jonathan Bennett's terminology, the word "intentionally" is an "ellipsis excluder."[7] Extending Bennett's terminology, I shall call the
word "unintentionally" an "ellipsis dummy." When I say that something was done unintentionally I indicate, without giving my special
details, that the performance in some way falls short of act-hood.[8]

Ranging under the ellipsis excluder "intentionally" and under the ellipsis dummy "unintentionally" there is a whole family of terms that gives more detailed information concerning the presented performance.

| Intentionally | Unintentionally |
|---|---|
| knowingly | unknowingly |
| voluntarily | involuntarily |
| willingly | unwillingly |
| purposely | inadvertently |
| deliberately | accidentally |
| | mistakenly |

The relationships between these terms are complicated: they do not always pair off neatly into contrasting couples, nor do the members of each group fit into an orderly genus species structure. About all that the members of the first group have in common is that they seem vaguely affirmative; members of the second group seem somehow vaguely negative. Due to the limits of space, I cannot consider all these terms, but a few illustrations will exhibit the general strategy.

What is involved in saying that Mr. So & So *knowingly* shot the Prime Minister? At the very least, this remark entails that at the time he knew it was the Prime Minister whom he was shooting. But does the entailment hold in the reverse direction; in other words, is the claim that someone did something knowingly *equivalent* to the claim that he knew (at the time) that he was doing it? It seems to me that the answer to this question is no, and a clue to the difference lies in the inarticulate notion that adverbs modify, qualify, or otherwise clarify the status of act descriptions they govern. Perhaps an example will bring this out. When Mr. So & So shot the Prime Minister, he might have known (by the way) that it was a man, wearing clothes, standing on the sidewalk before him, that he shot. Yet it seems completely wrong to say that he knowingly shot a man, wearing clothes, standing on the sidewalk before him, even though he knew all these things *about* the man he shot. None of these items of knowledge helps to clarify the character of the act in question, and for this reason, I suggest, they seem out of place as part of an adverbial construction.

My own suggestion is this: to say that someone knowingly $\phi$ed is to indicate that an item of knowledge entered into his practical reflection *in one way or another*. Suppose Mr. So & So shoots the Prime Minister because he believes that he is his wife's secret lover. The embedded practical reasoning might have the following form:

> (F)   If $x$ is my wife's secret lover, shoot $x$!
>       The Prime Minister is my wife's secret lover.
>       This man is the Prime Minister.
>       ──────────────────────────────────
> ∴     Shoot this man!

And straightway he (knowingly) shot the Prime Minister. Notice that in this example, the fact that the person was the Prime Minister was not relevant to Mr. So & So's *motives* in the shooting. We might try to bring this out by saying that he did not shoot the man *because* he was the Prime Minister, but, perhaps, *in spite of* this fact. In sum, then, the claim that someone knowingly $\phi$ed indicates that an item of knowledge entered (in some manner) into his practical reflections. The exact location of the item of knowledge in the practical reflection is not given by such a remark, but it is usually apparent in a concrete setting.

Staying with the same example, it may be clear that Mr. So & So knowingly shot the Prime Minister, but would we also say that he shot him *intentionally*? Here, I think, we are tempted to say two things at once, both yes and no. This much is clear: he intentionally shot a man he knew to be the Prime Minister, but this seems somehow different from the claim that he shot the Prime Minister intentionally. The difference lies in the fact that *we normally couch our act descriptions in a form that reflects the person's reasons for acting as he did*.[9] Thus if I say that John intentionally shot the Prime Minister, I will be suggesting that his reason (or at least part of his reason) for shooting him was that he was the Prime Minister. Of course, if the facts are clear, this suggestion will be canceled out, and it is always possible to cancel such a suggestion simply by saying all that needs to be said: "John knowingly shot the Prime Minister, not because he was the Prime Minister but because the Prime Minister was his wife's lover."

Suppose, however, that John shot the Prime Minister without realizing that he was the Prime Minister. Here I think we would say that he shot him unknowingly, that is to say, the knowledge that the person he shot was the Prime Minister did not enter into his practical reflection. This, of course, is very different from shooting him by mistake. Mistakes involve error (not just ignorance); in particular, they involve some sort of error pertaining to the descriptive content of the practical reasoning. Thus, I can shoot the janitor mistaking him for a thief, or shoot the Prime Minister on the mistaken assumption that he is my wife's lover. In the latter case I might mistakenly shoot the Prime Minister knowing full well that he is the Prime Minister.

Accidents, as Austin has noted, are different animals altogether. If I say that John shot the Prime Minister accidentally, I have then blocked *all* questions concerning his reasons for doing it. In fact, I have done more than this; I have indicated *why* such questions are out of place, but it is surprisingly difficult to specify any of this in detail. Anyway, it is important to notice why accidents differ from mistakes. If John shot the Prime Minister mistakenly, the fact that it was the Prime Minister whom he shot is not relevant to his reasons for shooting him, but he did act from other reasons, and these other reasons can be interrogated.[10]

Thus far this ramble through a child's garden of adverbs has been limited to those that are related to the model as a whole (intentionally, unintentionally, accidentally) and those that concern the descriptive aspects of the model (knowingly, unknowingly, mistakenly). Some other adverbs operate in the region of the prescriptive major. Here I can consider only two contrasting pairs: voluntary–involuntary and willingly–unwilling. The general idea is this: certain adverbs indicate the relationship between an agent and the prescriptions he accepts. If a person voluntarily $\phi$s, then he accepts the prescription to $\phi$ under no constraint or duress. If he willingly $\phi$s, then he accepts the prescription to $\phi$ with a glad heart. And so on. Needless to say, $\phi$ing unintentionally and $\phi$ing involuntarily are very different notions. If a hooligan sticks a gun in my ribs and tells me to hand over my money, when I do so it is not something that I do unintentionally; but it surely is something that I do involuntarily (and, *a fortiori*, unwillingly).

Finally, and very quickly, we can notice one adverb that ties into the inferential aspect of the prescriptive model. When we say that a person deliberately $\phi$ed (in the sense of $\phi$ing after deliberation) we are simply underscoring the fact that his action was a considered action, in other words, that the reflection marked by the second component took place pretty much explicitly. I have already said that the prescriptive model is not a script for inner dialogue, but for deliberate action it at least approximates this.[11]

## VI

Thus far I have been discussing adverbs that modify performances that have actually taken place. Next I want to talk about constructions concerning prospective or envisaged acts. For example, if we speak of what someone intends (or even intended) to do, we are not thereby committing ourselves to saying that it took place. In particular, I want to examine a set of verbs that *accept* (not simply form) infinitives, yielding constructions of the following kind:

| | |
|---|---|
| intend to $\phi$ | want to $\phi$ |
| hope to $\phi$ | have to $\phi$ |
| like to $\phi$ | need to $\phi$ |
| desire to $\phi$ | wish to $\phi$ |

Excluded from this list are those constructions that admit of an in-order-to expansion. Thus, "John loves to play golf" is in, but "John lives to play golf" is out; for while John may live in order to play golf, he does not love in order to play golf (unless, that is, he is a golf-playing gigolo). There are probably other constructions that should be excluded from the list, but there isn't time to go into any of this in detail. For want of a better name, I shall call this system of verbs "quasi-auxiliaries."

If we pursue the idea that these quasi-auxiliaries govern envisaged or prospective acts, we can see how the prescriptive model can be modified to take them into account. First, the third component is eliminated altogether—the man who intends to do something need not straightway do it, for the occasion may not be at hand. If we are to abandon the third component, we must throw a monkey wrench in the second component as well. The device for doing this could hardly be more simple: we merely put the descriptive minor in a tense that is future relative to the tense of the antecedent in the prescriptive major. For example, the claim that John intends to shoot the Prime Minister comes to this:

> John accepts the prescription "If the opportunity arises, then shoot the Prime Minister!" and he further believes that the opportunity *will* arise.

The past tense construction is, in a way, more interesting. "John intended to shoot the Prime Minister" comes to this:

> John accept*ed* the prescription "If the opportunity arises, then shoot the Prime Minister," at the same time believing that the opportunity *would* arise.

Because of the tense shift, the reasoning to a prescriptive conclusion does not go through:

> If the opportunity arises, then shoot the Prime Minister.
> The opportunity will arise.
> 
> ∴ nothing

On the other hand, the person who intends to do something looks forward to the time when the tenses will be aligned, and for this reason *the person who intends to do something believes that he will do it*. In the past tense, the person who intended to do something believed (at that time) that he would do it.

We can get a deeper insight into the character of intend-to constructions by contrasting them with want-to constructions. Provisionally, I shall say that a person wants to do something if and only if:

(1) He accepts a hypothetical prescription of the form "If the opportunity arises, then do *x*."
(2) Without, either:
   (a) having any settled belief that the opportunity will arise, or
   (b) taking into account every overriding demand.

The two qualifications mark two ways that wants differ from intentions. The first qualification brings out this difference: a person can want to do something without having any firm belief that he will do it, but, as we have seen, if he intends to do it, he does firmly believe that he will do it.

The second qualification is more interesting. A person may want to do something but still not do it when the occasion presents itself because he gives precedence to some other prescription. This is logically possible because wants involve a qualified commitment to a prescription, and this qualified commitment can remain in force *at the very same time* that we are not doing what we want to do. Intentions are different. A person who intends to do something believes that nothing overrides his commitment. Of course, he may be mistaken (or self-deceived) on both counts, but when he becomes aware of his mistakes he will *abandon* his intention in precisely a fashion that he need not abandon his wants or desires. This may sound like too strong a claim, but notice that both of the following remarks are aberrant:

> I intend to do it, but I won't do it because I now see that the opportunity will not arise.
> I intend to do it, but I won't do it because I have other more important things to do.

In order to restore sense to these remarks, we have to cast the verb in the past tense to leave open the possibility that the intention is no longer operative.[12]

If we move further away from the strong commitment involved in intentions, we come to wishes and even idle wishes. In an idle wish I accept a prescription in full knowledge that I will never act upon it. I may idly wish to insult the chancellor to his face, knowing full well that such doings are ruled out by demands of prudence. Or, I may idly wish to issue a papal encyclical, recognizing that my chances for the needed preferment are absolutely nil. The commitment of an idle wish is pretty thin, but still there is some commitment involved; what I idly wish to do is something I'd intend to do in some other possible world.

# VII

Before concluding, I shall say some general things about purposes and motives. One striking feature of the prescriptive model, as it now stands, is that it gives no account of purposes. In its present form, the middle component does not provide a way of reflecting the fact that we sometimes do one thing in order to accomplish something else (or, somewhat differently, that we do one thing *as a part* of doing something larger). To accommodate these notions we will have to expand the model to include instrumental (and mereological) premises. This is hardly a routine undertaking, and for my own part I am willing to wait until logicians have completed their labors before exploring matters further.

In saying that the prescriptive model as it now stands is seriously incomplete, I am not trying to disarm the reader with my candor. The incompleteness is serious. In particular, without a much richer account of the structure of practical reasoning, we cannot give an adequate account of the variable scope (or accordion character) of human actions. It is now a commonplace that the very same performance can be truly described by act descriptions differing in temporal stretch, differing in generality, or (seemingly) differing in just being different. My idea now is that different act descriptions are possible in virtue of the fact that the line of practical reasoning can be sliced by a description at different points. Crudely, we can imagine a segment of practical reflection having the following form:

$$(G) \quad \phi!$$
$$\text{In order to } \phi, \theta!$$
$$\therefore \quad \theta!$$

If our act description cuts the practical reasoning above the instrumental premise, we will then say that Mr. So & So $\phi$ed; if it cuts it below this premise, we will say that he $\theta$ed. Thus we can say that Brutus stabbed Caesar and also that he killed Caesar. We might also recognize the connection between these two claims through understanding their respective roles in the practical reasoning. In other words, we might realize that Brutus stabbed Caesar *in order* to kill him. It is, however, the relationship within the practical reasoning that counts here; with a sufficiently morbid imagination, we could think of a case where someone kills a person in order to stab him.

In considering motives, we first must see that motives and purposes are different. I may know, for example, that a person is climbing the trellis in order to dance on the roof, but I may be completely in the dark about his motives for dancing on the roof. Furthermore, we often talk about purposes where talk about motives seems out of place. When I discover that the man is climbing the trellis in order to dance on the roof, I do not ask about his motive for climbing the trellis. Talk about motives centers on what he is out to accomplish, not on the means he uses to bring it off. This suggests that motives concern the ultimate commitment (or commitments) that stand at the beginning of practical reflection. Thus a person's motive for dancing on the roof might be that he wants to show off. Thus he starts out from the prescriptive major "Show off!" Then, through a process of instrumental reflection, he settles upon what he sees to be the best way to accomplish this: he will dance on the roof.

Once more, an act description may cut this pattern of reflection at different points. In response to the question "What is he doing?" we might answer:

Dancing on the roof.
Making a display of himself.
Showing off.

Again, we can relate these claims in a manner that reflects their role in his practical reasoning: he is dancing on the roof *in order to* make a display of himself, and he is making a display of himself because he *wants to* show off. Of course, he might have some further reason for wanting to show off, and this would reveal that we have yet to penetrate his motives fully. Then again, his acceptance of the prescription "Show off!" might be the end of the line, and further talk about motives simply would be otiose.

Of course, when reasons (in the sense of a practical premise for action) give out, we may still press on and ask about the *causes* that led to the acceptance of the practical premises. A person might want to show off because of an inferiority complex, but it would be an odd context where a person would act in this way as the result of accepting the practical premise "Manifest the symptoms of a person with an inferiority complex!" The best example I can think of where a person might act under this practical premise is the case of a person *pretending* to have an inferiority complex. An inferiority complex involves the tendency to accept certain prescriptions in given circumstances, but "Manifest the symptoms of a person with an inferiority complex!" is not among them. A similar remark holds for terms describing character traits, but this is not the place to examine this in detail.

# VIII

The major weakness of the prescriptive model as it has thus far been developed is in the structure of the practical reasoning embedded as its middle component. It certainly must be expanded to include instrumental and mereological premises, and beyond this its simple linear form must be replaced by a branching structure that reflects the plurality of reasons that can bear upon a single action. Furthermore, I think that the acceptance of a categorical prescription straightway issues into action only when the action prescribed involves a skill or capacity possessed by the agent. Otherwise, the practical reflection continues until it terminates either (1) in a prescription that the person can straightway perform, or (2) in a prescription that the person thinks he will be able to perform some time in the future, or (3) in a simple blockage. In the first case we get an action; in the second, an intention; and in the third, a want or wish (which may perish in the face of the blockage).

In sum, then, a fully developed treatment of the middle component of the prescriptive model will reveal structures of argument that I have hardly touched upon. Nonetheless, even in its nascent form the prescriptive model has two general features that create a presumption in its favor. One fact about statements describing human actions is that they admit of questions concerning a person's *reasons* for doing what he has done, where reasons are somehow thought to be different from causes. The model accounts for this datum in an entirely natural way by relating it to the connection between a premise and a conclusion. Another fact about statements describing human actions is that they seem to be somehow directional or teleological. On the prescriptive model this feature is captured quite simply through the use of prescriptions, for prescriptions are paradigms of constructions with a forward-looking reference. So, however incomplete (or faulty) my account of this model might be, there is at least some reason to believe that the general approach is not entirely misguided.

## NOTES

1. Aristotle, *De Motu Animalium*, trans. A. S. Farquharson, in *The Works of Aristotle* (London, 1912), Vol. V, chap. 7.

2. *Ibid.*

3. For example, it would be hard to estimate the amount of harm done by the assumption that moral (and legal) prescriptions have the character of commands.

4. Problems about abstract entities are not avoided by the simple refusal to use the traditional terminology that suggests them. For example, talking about statements instead of propositions carries some advantage; it underscores the fact that what is expressed by a sentence is a function of the context in which it is used. But still, the statement made and the act of stating are very different things. A statement is something made *in* the act of stating; thus, statements are not really very different from the older notion of a proposition.

5. This will be modified in the concluding section of this essay.

6. Part of Freud's genius was to search for reasons (and find them) where others would never think to look. Freud, however, did not abandon the distinction between those things that people do and those things that happen to them; instead, he redrew the boundary for important theoretical reasons.

7. Jonathan Bennett, "'Real,'" in *Mind*, LXXV (1966), 504–507.

8. It should also be clear, on this account, why it is not always appropriate to say of an act that it is either intentional or unintentional. Still following Jonathan Bennett, using an ellipsis excluder has a *point* only when there is some presumption to be countered. Saying of an ordinary intentional action that it is intentional can sound strange and even be misleading.

9. And this accounts for the opacity of act descriptions. If our description is intended to reflect the speaker's reasons for acting as he did, then referring expressions with the same reference cannot be exchanged in a willy-nilly fashion. On the other hand, if the point of our remark is to identify who it is that John shot, then the reference can be transparent.

10. But even accidents are subject to criticism: "You should have been

more careful." But this involves a shift in levels; we do not criticize the person for $\phi$ing, but for comporting himself in such a manner that allowed the $\phi$ing to take place.

11. Austin has argued that an action can be done deliberately, but, for all that, not intentionally. Although I cannot go into this, his examples turn upon varying the scope of act descriptions.

12. In most cases, not doing what we want to do is a sign of strength of character; not doing what we intend to do is a sign of weakness of the will.

# Index

Abstract ideas: Berkeley on, 57–59, 67–68n. 47; Hume on, 54–55, 66n. 35
Agrippa: 218–19
Allegory of the Cave: 8, 11n. 6, 12, 18, 21–25
Anscombe, G. E. M.: 148n. 14
Aquinas, St. Thomas: Five Ways, 9, 26–44; (The Fifth Way, 29–31; The First Way, 39–40; The Fourth Way, 31–33; The Second Way, 33–39; The Third Way, 40–41); the problem of evil, 26–28
Ardal, Pall: 147–48n. 11
Aristotle: 9, 31, 32, 43–44n. 18, 48, 65n. 10; on the practical syllogism, 10–11, 232–34
Arithmetic: Berkeley on, 67–68n. 47
Arnauld, A.: 45
Associationalism, Hume's: 83–85, 90–93
Atomism: in Hume 72–76; in Wittgenstein 224
Austin, J. L.: 137, 139, 148n. 12, 239, 242, 250n. 11

Barrow, Isaac: 46–47, 62, 64n. 7
Bayle, Pierre: 45, 46, 48, 54, 64n. 1
Bednarowski, W.: 165n. 4
Belief, Hume's theory of: 121–22

Bennett, Jonathan: 239, 249n. 8
Berkeley, George, on: abstract ideas, 57–59, 67–68n. 47; arithmetic, 67–68n. 47; diagrams, 57–60, 67n. 45; infinite divisibility, 10, 46, 55–64; mathematics, 10; minimal sensibles (perceptuals, visibles etc.), 49, 56–57, 59, 61–62; signs, 57–60, 67–68n. 47
Bogen, James: 171–72
Boyle's Law: 109–12
Brouwer, L. E. J.: 176, 196

Cantor, G.: 174
Capaldi, Nicholas: 130n. 1
Causality, Hume on: 76–77, 86, 92, 93n. 5, 121–22
Causation: as constant conjunction, 102–3; direction of, 111–12; efficient, 33–39, 43n 9.; *per accidens*, 35–38; *per se*, 36–38; regularity interpretation of, 102, 108–109
Charity, principle of: 38–39; alethic principle of, 3, 7–8, 11n. 1; semantic principle of, 3
Clark, Thompson: 229
Clifford, W. K.: 130n. 2
Coleman, Dorothy: 95
Conditionals, contrary to fact (subjunctive): 107–8

Consistency: 5
Contingency, and necessity: 40–41
Conventionalism: 207
Copleston, F. C.: 26, 34–35
Cornford, Francis: 16
Cosmological Arguments: 33–44
Criterion, argument from: 115, 118
Cudworth, Ralph: 144
Cummins, Robert: 71, 80

Davidson, Donald: 11n. 1, 37,
    43n. 15
Degree, matters of: 131n. 11
DeMorgan, A.: 10, 149, 151–52,
    155, 162, 164n. 1, 167–68
Descartes, Rene (Cartesianism): 45,
    83, 85, 93, 143–46
Design, argument from: 30–31
Diagrams, Berkeley on: 57–61,
    67n. 45
Distribution (of terms): 150–53
Divided Line: 8, 11n. 6, 12, 17–22,
    25n. 3
Double existence, theories of: 85
Doubt: 114, 122, 130, 215, 225–26
Duggan, Timothy: 69n. 60

Epicurus: 48–49, 55, 65n. 16, 65–
    66n. 23, 231n. 5
Evil, problem of: 26–28
Excluded Middle, Law of: 196,
    199–204

Fallibilism: 129, 130n. 6
Fictions, Hume on: 85–86
Fit, direction of: 139–40
Fitch, Frederick B.: 198–99
Five Modes of Agrippa: 218–19
Five Ways of Aquinas: 9, 26–44
Flew, Antony: 95, 100, 101n. 3
Fogelin, Robert J.: 93–94n. 6
Forms of life: 209, 225

Forms, Plato's Theory of: 12–17,
    32
Frege, G.: 169, 183n. 1, 184n. 19,
    215, 216
Freud, Sigmund: 249
Furley, David J.: 65–66n. 23

Garrett, Don: 66n. 34, 82, 84,
    93nn. 3, 4
Garrigou-Lagrange, R.: 34
Geach, P. T.: 10, 150, 165n. 3
Geometry, Hume on: 52–54
Gilson, É.: 26, 34, 43n. 11
God, existence of: 9, 26–44
Good, the Form of the: 17, 21; and
    the Sun, 13–17

Halley, Dr. Edmund: 55
Hamiliton, Sir William: on quanti-
    fication of the predicate, 10,
    149–68; on the syllogism, 149,
    155, 157–62
Hare, R. M.: 237
Heath, Peter: 164n. 1
Hempel, C. G.: 66n. 27
Hobbes, Thomas: 143–46
Holism: 224
Huet, Pierre: 131n. 14
Hume (Humean philosophy): 5, 6–
    7, 11n. 5, 143–46, 210
Hume, on: abstract ideas, 54–55,
    65–66n. 23, 66n. 34; association-
    alism, 85, 90, 92; atomism, 72–
    76; causality, 76–77, 86, 93n. 5,
    121–22; fictions, 85–86; geome-
    try, 52–54; identity over time,
    93n. 5; infinite divisibility, 46,
    49–55; minimal sensibles, 49–52,
    65–66n. 23; miracles, 9, 95–101,
    128; the missing shade of blue,
    9–10, 70–80; modern philoso-
    phy, 87; natural religion, 123–

27; necessary connections, 76–77, 86; peritrope, 219; personal identity (over time), 76–78, 81–94; probability, 117–20; promising, 133–34; simple ideas, 70–79; simple impressions; 70–79; simultaneous causes and effects, 102–113; skepticism, 10, 114–31, 221, 231; skepticism concerning induction, 117, 128; skepticism concerning the external world, 129; skepticism with regard to reason, 85, 115, 117–22, 124, 128; skepticism with regard to the senses, 85, 117, 128; space, 76, 93*n*. 5; substance, 76–77, 86, (immaterial, 87–90; material, 93–94*n*. 6); the soul, 86–90; time, 76, 93*n*. 5; naturalism, 114, 116, 130
Hume's Fork: 51

Idealism: 223–26, 231*n*. 9
Ideas, simple: Hume on, 70–79
Identity (over time), Hume on: 93*n*. 5
Identity (self), Wittgenstein on: 10, 169–85
Identity of indiscernibles: 173–74
Impressions, simple, Hume on: 70–79
Infinite divisibility: Epicurus on, 48–49, 55, 65*n*. 16, 65–66*n*. 23; Bayle on, 64*n*. 3; Berkeley on, 10, 55–64; Hume on, 49–55; proofs of, 46–47, 60–62
Infinite Regress: 33–34, 37–39, 43*n*. 16, 44*n*. 22, 119
Infinity: 27, 201; Axiom of, 169
Interpretation: global principle of, 6–8; holistic principle of, 6; local principle of, 6–9

Intuitionism, and Wittgenstein: 196–213

Jones, W. T.: 131*n*. 11

Kant, Emmanual: 4, 5, 38, 82, 139, 237; on simultaneous causes and effects, 102–13
Kenny, A.: 26, 32, 34, 35–36, 40, 41–42, 42*n*. 5
Kremer, Richard: 69*n*. 60
Kretzmann, Norman: 64–65*n*. 9

Language-games: 207, 225–27, 229
Leibniz, G. W.: 4–5, 173–74, 176
Locke, John: 67*n*. 41
Luce, A. A.: 66–67*n*. 36
Lucretius: 48
Lying: 139, 143

Malcolm, Norman: 224
Milton, John: 129
Minimal Sensibles (perceptuals, visibles, etc.): Epicurus on, 49, 65–66*n*. 23; Hume on, 49–52, 65–66*n*. 23; Berkeley on, 49, 56–57, 59, 61–62
Miracles, Hume on: 9, 95–101, 128
Modern philosophy, Hume on: 87
Moore, G. E.: 223, 226–27, 231*n*. 6, *n*. 9
Mysticism: 221–22

Naturalism, Hume's: 114, 116, 130
Nazzam: 64*n*. 7
Necessary connections, Hume on: 76–77, 86
Necessity, and contingency: 40–41
Negative elementary propositions, Wittgenstein on: 10, 186–95
New, C. G.: 147–48*n*. 11
Nicole, P.: 45

Oscanyon, Frederick: 165n. 9

Paradigms: 197, 209–10
Peirce, C. S.: 227
Performatives (performative utterances): 137–40, 145, 148n. 12
Peritrope: 120, 219–21
Personal Identity, Hume on: 76–78, 81–94
Picture Theory (of meaning): 192–93, 217
Pike, Nelson: 131n. 12
Plato (Platonism): 59, 183, 197, 203–207
Plato: Allegory of the Cave, 8, 11n. 6, 12, 18, 21–25; Divided Line, 8, 11n. 6, 12, 17–22, 25n. 3; Theory of Forms, 12–13, 32
Pope, Alexander: 129
*Port Royal Logic*: 45, 46–47, 59, 68n. 48, 69n. 56
Positivism, Logical: 11n. 215
Practical syllogism: 10–11, 232–50; Aristotle on, 232–34
Prescriptions: 235–37
Prescriptive Model of Action: 235–49
Presentism, fallacy of: 4
Price, Richard, on promising: 10, 77, 132–48
Prichard, H. A.: 76, 78, 132–34, 137, 147
Probabilism: 129, 130n. 6
Probability, Hume on: 117–20, 131n. 9
Promising: Hume on, 133–34; Richard Price on, 10, 132–48; Prichard on, 132–34
Proofs: indirect, 46–47, 68n. 48, 202–204, 210; nonconstructive, 196, 201

Propositions: elementary, 170, 217, 224, 231n. 1; existence 169–71; general form of, 193–94; negative elementary, 186–95
Pyrrhonism: 217–18, 229–30

Quantifying the predicate, Hamilton on: 10, 149–68
Quine, W. V.: 172

Ramsey, F. P.: 171, 173–80, 183n. 7, 184n. 19, 196
Rapheal, D. Daiches: 148n. 17
Realism: 197, 203; representational, 85
Reductio ad Absurdum: *See indirect proof*
Reid, Thomas: 11n. 4, 77, 130n. 4
Religion, natural, Hume on: 123–27
Representational realism: 85
Robins, R. H.: 147
Ross, W. D.: 146
Rule, following a: 182–83
Russell, B.: 171–73, 186, 194, 195n. 5, 211

Scepticism: *See skepticism*
Schlick, Moritz: 177
Sextus Empiricus: 217, 221
Signs, Berkeley on: 57–60, 67–68n. 47
Simultaneity (of causes and effects): Hume on, 102–113; Kant on, 102–113
Skeptical doubts: 209
Skeptical solutions: 209, 213
Skepticism (kinds of): Academic, 116, 122, 130n. 6; general, 218, 220; mitigated/unmitigated, 116, 118, 120, 123, 127–30; moderate, 116, 130n. 6; normative, 115;

practicing, 116; prescriptive, 115–16, 120; Pyrrhonian, 116, 122–23, 127, 129–30, 217–18; theoretical, 115–16, 120, 122, 124, 126, 128

Skepticism (targets of): induction, 117, 128, 129; the external world, 129; reason, 115, 117–22, 124, 128, 129; the senses, 84–85, 117, 128

Smith, Norman Kemp: 114

Sorabji, Richard: 64*n*. 7, 64–65*n*. 9

Soul, Hume on: 86–90, 93*n*. 6

Space, Hume on: 76

Space, physical vs. pure: 54, 62–63

Stoicism: 125

Strawson, P. F.: 85

Stroud, Barry: 78–79, 84

Substance, Hume on: 76–77, 86, 87–90, 93–94*n*. 6

Syllogism: Hamilton's treatment of, 10, 149, 157–64; practical, 10–11, 232–50; theoretical, 233

Teleology: 29–30

Time, Hume on: 76

Translation, radical: 3–4

Utilitarianism (utility): 143–47

Verifiability Principle (verificationism): 11*n*. 3, 214–15

Voluntarism: 143–47

von Wright, G. H.: 196

Waismann, F.: 176

Warnock, G. J.: 140, 147–48*n*. 11

Weyle, Hermann: 176

Wittgenstein, Ludwig: 4, 11*n*. 2, 59

Wittgenstein and: intuitionism, 196–213; skepticism, 214–31; existence propositions, 169–71; identity (self), 10, 169–84; mathematical proof, 10, 67*n*. 46; negative elementary propositions, 10, 186–95

Zeno's Paradoxes: 49, 65*n*. 14